ELEMENTS OF LOGIC;

TOGETHER WITH AN

INTRODUCTORY VIEW

OF

PHILOSOPHY IN GENERAL,

AND A

PRELIMINARY VIEW OF THE REASON.

BY

HENRY P. TAPPAN.

NEW YORK:
D. APPLETON AND COMPANY,
346 & 348 BROADWAY.

M.DCCC.LVI.

Entered, according to Act of Congress, in the year 1855, by
D. APPLETON & COMPANY,
In the Clerk's Office of the District Court of the United States for the Southern District of New York.

PREFACE.

THE work here undertaken differs somewhat in its scope and design from systems of Logic which have hitherto been given to the world. The Aristotelian Logic is simply the method of deduction; and, as such, it is complete. Subsequent works, in so far as they have been strictly logical, have closely copied the great master, and have confined themselves to an exhibition of the deductive principles and processes. Now, the deductive method comprehends merely the laws which govern inferences or conclusions from premises previously established. These premises may, in their turn, be inferences from other premises, and so on, to a certain extent; and just so far this method is all sufficient. But it is evident that the evolution of premises and conclusions, and conclusions and premises, must have a limit. There must be premises which are not conclusions from other premises, but which arise in some other way. Now, a complete and adequate

Logic ought to exhibit this other way likewise: it ought to inform us how the most original premises arise, and upon what basis they rest.

Other methods, indeed, have been abroad in the world, but without being systematically propounded as parts of Logic. Thus, the Platonic philosophy really contains a Logical development of the most original forms of human thought, springing out of the intuitive faculty. And the *Novum Organum* of Bacon contains a logical exposition of the method of establishing first principles through the observation of phenomena.

Both Plato and Bacon have had many able disciples and expounders; and both are daily coming out into a broader and clearer light, not as opponents, but—to adopt the thought of Coleridge—as the opposite poles of one great and harmonious system.

The present attempt, therefore, is to make out the system of Logic under its several departments; and to present it not merely as a method of obtaining inferences from truths, but also as a method of establishing those first truths and general principles which must precede all deduction.

With all humility, I acknowledge my indebtedness to the great thinkers who have preceded me. I have of course read as well as thought; and my thinking and reading are naturally blended together. With this acknowledgment, may I be permitted to go on with my work, without stopping to note narrowly in my own mind, or to remark to my reader, when I am drawing from original, and when from other sources? I ought, perhaps, in justice to myself, to remark, that the entire plan of this work was struck out several years since, and different portions of it written before Professor Whewell's and Mr. Mills' elaborate and suggestive works had fallen under my eye.

That Logic really embraces all the parts which I have assigned to it, I think will fully appear in the sequel. It is that branch of philosophy which expounds the laws of the Reason as the faculty of truth and reality.

The view which I have taken of Logic, will justify the prolegomena. I give the Introduction to Philosophy in General, in order to point out the relative position and importance of Logic in a philosophical system. And I give the Preliminary View of the Reason, because, since this is the faculty which reasons, or *logicizes*, I deemed that such a view, if given both clearly and briefly, would be satisfactory in this place.

CONTENTS.

PART I.

INTRODUCTORY VIEW OF PHILOSOPHY IN GENERAL.

PAGE

SECTION I.—Definition of Philosophy. 15
II.—Distinction between the Phenomenal and the Metaphenomenal. 23
III.—Of the Reality of the Metaphenomenal. 27
IV.—The Objective and the Subjective. 32
V.—Reason and Sense. 39
VI.—Sensualism and Transcendentalism. 42
VII.—Ideas and Laws. 50
VIII.—Primary and Secondary Phenomena. 58
IX.—Antecedence in Time and in Necessary Existence. 60
X.—Ideas the last Authority of all Judgments or Knowledges. 64
XI.—Divisions of Philosophy. ....
I. Metaphysics. 70
Comprehending
Psychology. 71
Dynamics. 73
Anthropology. 74
Ontology. 75
II. Nomology; comprehending
The Morale. 80
Esthetics. .... *ib.*
Somatology. 82
Logic. 83

PAGE
SECT. XII.—Of the Relations between Philosophy and the Sciences and Arts 86
Geometry 89
Sciences of Discrete Quantity 91
Natural Science 92
Conditional and Unconditional Science 95
Art 99
XIII.—Reason, the Organ of Philosophy 103
XIV.—Criteria of a True Philosophy 108

PART II.

PRELIMINARY VIEW OF THE REASON.

SECTION I.—General Introductory Considerations respecting the Reason... 123
II.—Outline of the Ideas and Functions of the Reason 129
III.—Explication of Ideas 138
IV.—Explication of the Functions of the Reason 143
V.—Does Logic comprehend all the Functions of the Reason? 144

PART III.

LOGIC PROPER.

BOOK I.

PRIMORDIAL LOGIC.

SECTION I.—General Laws of the Evolution of Ideas 148
II. Metaphysical Ideas; comprehending
I. Subject and Objective Exteriority 155
II. Time and Space 156
III. The Infinite and the Finite 159
IV. Quantity .... *ib.*
V. Quality 165
VI. Relation 167
VII. Modality 172
III.—Nomological Ideas; comprehending
I. Law 177

PAGE
II. Matter and Spirit ... 178
III. Perfection ... *ib.*
IV. Right and Wrong ... 180
V. Freedom and Responsibility ... 182
VI. Personal Identity ... 183
VII. Immortality ... 184
VIII. The Beautiful, comprehending
Symmetry ... 187
Grace ... 188
Regularity, Uniformity, Variety ... *ib.*
Determinate Form ... 189
The Sublime ... 190
Melody ... 191
Harmony ... *ib.*
IX. The Useful ... 196
X. Centralization and Diffusion ... 198
XI. Affinity and Repulsion ... 199
XII. Life ... *ib.*
XIII. Polarity ... 200
XIV. Instinct ... 201
XV. Regularity, Uniformity, Variety, Symmetry, and Determinate Form ... 202
XVI. Identity, Difference, Resemblance ... 203
XVII. Design, Final Cause, Means and End ... 205
XVIII. Truth ... 207
XIX. The Philosophical Idea ... 209
XX. Intuition ... 210
XXI. Involution and Evolution ... 211
XXII. Analysis and Synthesis ... 213
IV.—Primary Sensuous Cognitions, or Cognitions of the Exterior Consciousness ... 219
V.—Primary Subjective Cognitions, or Cognitions of the Interior Consciousness ... 222
VI.—Axioms ... 224
Metaphysical Axioms ... 226
Nomological Axioms ... 228
VII.—Of the Characteristics of Axioms in general ... 235
VIII.—General Relations of Axioms ... 240
IX.—Definitions ... 243

BOOK II.

INDUCTIVE LOGIC.

PAGE
SECTION I.—Introduction 249
II.—Causes and Laws 252
III.—The Human Reason, as related to the Objective World 259
IV.—General View of Classification 262
V.—Principles determining the Induction of Phenomena in Classification 265
VI.—Distinction between a General Fact and an Absolute and Fixed Law 276
VII.—The Logic of General Facts 283
Principles of Elimination:
I. General Difference with Uniform Agreement in One Point 288
II. General Agreement with Uniform Difference in One Point 289
III. Elimination by Corresponding Quantities and Intensities 291
IV. Elimination of the Terms of a Sequence, in order to determine which is the Antecedent and which the Consequent 294
VIII.—Inductive Logic of Universal and Necessary Laws 303
IX.—The Logic of Art 315

BOOK III.

DEDUCTIVE LOGIC.

SECTION I.—Introduction 318
II.—Analysis of Propositions 320
III.—Of Propositions, as opposed to each other 325
IV.—Of the Conversion of Propositions 328
V.—Propositions constructed into Syllogisms 332
VI.—Of Moods and Figures 347
VII.—Of the Reduction of Syllogisms 351
VIII.—Of Modal, Hypothetical, and Disjunctive Propositions 354
IX.—Hypothetical Reasoning 357
X.—Of the Dilemma 362
XI.—Of the Sorites 365
XII.—Application of the Deductive Formula 368

PAGE

SEC. XIII.—Of Fallacies.
Fallacies of Deduction.... 377
Comprehending
I. Fallacies in the Formula.... 378
II. Fallacies in the Matter.... 380
1. Ambiguous Middle.... *ib.*
2. Fallacies relating to the Connection between the Matter of the Premises and that of the Conclusion. 383
Fallacies of Induction; comprehending
I. Fallacies of Observation.... 393
II. Fallacies in Determining General Facts.... 396
III. Fallacies in Inducting Laws.... 398
Fallacies in respect to Intuition.... 399

BOOK IV.

DOCTRINE OF EVIDENCE.

SECTION I.—Nature of Proof.... 403
II.—The different kinds of *à priori* and *à posteriori* Proof.... 408
III.—Of the Nature of the Relation between Antecedents and Consequents.... 413
IV.—Of Degrees of Evidence.... 416
V.—Of Testimony.... 430
VI.—Circumstantial Evidence.... 436
VII.—Argument from Progressive Approach.... 443
VIII.—Proving by Example.... 446
IX.—Reasoning from Experience.... 451
X.—Reasoning from Resemblance and Analogy.... 454
XI.—Demonstrative Proof.... 462
XII.—Calculation of Probabilities and Chances.... 463

PART I.

INTRODUCTORY VIEW OF PHILOSOPHY IN GENERAL.

PART I.

INTRODUCTORY VIEW OF PHILOSOPHY IN GENERAL.

SECTION I.

DEFINITION OF PHILOSOPHY.

THE term PHILOSOPHY in common usage has obtained an indefinite and often an improper application. When employed alone, and without relation to any specific subject, it is generally supposed to refer to natural science: and thus a Treatise, or Essay, or Lecture, on Philosophy, would be expected to embrace something relating to Mechanics, Astronomy, Chemistry, Electricity, or Magnetism.

Some undoubtedly would go beyond this; and regard the term in its higher applications, as expressing something in relation to the doctrines of the intellectual and moral powers: or they would simply identify it with *Metaphysics*, a term no less vague and obscure to common apprehension.

It is to be expected that the affirmation will at first appear to many paradoxical, that Mechanics, Astronomy, Chemistry, &c., are not branches of Philosophy: but in the end it will appear perfectly just. Philosophy indeed holds a close and most important relation to these sciences: they are grand results of philosophy; but they are not philosophy itself. And even Metaphysics, general and comprehensive as it is, does not comprehend all philosophy—it only forms one of its important divisions.

In defining philosophy, we may go on to say, that it is the *Scientia Scientiarum*—"the Science of Sciences; as its object is to explain the principles and causes of all things existing; and to supply the defects of inferior sciences, which do not demonstrate, or sufficiently explain their principles." * Or we may call it the "Science of the Universal and the Absolute." But this is not enough. It would be like defining Astronomy as the "Science of the Heavens." A definition may be just, and yet by reason of its dry, general, technical, and elaborate form of expression, may fall short of the true end of all definition, viz., to lead the intelligence to a clearer insight and a more perfect comprehension.

PHILOSOPHY is a word formed from the Greek *Φιλοσοφία*. It primarily expresses a mental affection—a love of knowledge or of wisdom.

It cannot be questioned that such an affection is inherent in the human mind. It appears in feeble infancy—it stimulates the activities of the busy prattling child—it forms the wakeful earnestness and joy of youth—it stirs nobly in manhood—it decays not with the decay of age. It is a moving spirit even in savage life, and shows man, when lowest, as still above the brute. This impulse TO KNOW, this restless CURIOSITY, is connected with the whole development of humanity in Science, Arts, Government, and Religion. Co-existent with this love of knowledge is the love of external action. Hence, the development of humanity appears not only in the cultivation of the intelligence and the consequent unfolding of the sciences; but also in the construction of implements and machinery, and

* Ed. Ency.

in the changes and improvements wrought upon the face of Nature. The eager love of knowledge, and the no less eager love of action—the impulse TO KNOW, and the impulse TO DO—these are elements spontaneously at work in human nature, and may be appropriately termed *philosophical* elements.

Let us conceive of that period when the Heavens and the Earth were finished, and man was created and placed in the Earth its inhabitant and lord. Then he had the same faculties which he now possesses ; and the Earth was under the government of the same physical laws which govern it now ; but his faculties were undeveloped, and science and art had not yet appeared ; and the Earth, whatever modifications it might be capable of, stood as it came from the hand of the Creator, in uncultivated beauty. But man, as he walks abroad upon the Earth, with all the endowments of intelligence and feeling, observes the Heavens and the Earth, exercises thought, generalises, and forms conclusions. What is working within him, impresses its form upon all outward things :—the forest is levelled, and cultivated fields appear ; the mountain and the valley feel the touch of his hand, and put on new appearances ; he opens a way across rivers, and covers the ocean with fleets ; where rivers are wanting, he creates them ; he digs into the crust of the Earth, and brings up minerals and appropriates them ; he calls into being a thousand useful arts ; he scatters over the face of the Earth convenient habitations, and crowds them together into cities. But not only does he change the face of the Earth, and put to his uses its various materials—he also establishes government, administers law, and awards justice : he speaks eloquence into being ; poetry born in his heart, is expressed in flowing numbers ; he perfects sound into music; he takes the chisel, and from the marble quarry spring up forms whose beauty is divine; and majestic temples, which seem born with them as their fit habitation; he takes the pencil, and dipping it in the colors of heaven, imitates every form of life, and advances beyond Nature herself: he affirms, reasons, and believes; draws out pure abstractions from his thought; advances into Nature, and searches out laws for her phenomena; and thus builds up systems of science: he invents a method of analysis, and, in the laboratory, compels Nature to reveal her more secret processes; and, not content with this world, the light of heaven, which has lighted him to his labors here, he seizes upon as his minister, and makes it reveal to him the worlds from whence it has travelled. Still more—from these finite forms, he ascends up to the INFINITE; he is a worshipper of GOD, and an expectant of immortality.

"Imagine a being who had been present at the earliest days of the universe, and of human life; who had seen the external surface of the Earth, as it came forth from the hands of Nature, and looked upon all the beauty of those ancient times; who had seen the beautiful forms which Nature presented, and heard the melodious sounds which she then uttered; in a word, a being who had been a spectator of the first exhibition of the primitive world, and who should return at the present day amidst the prodigies of our industry, our institutions, and our arts; would it not seem to him in his astonishment as if he no longer recognized the ancient dwelling-place of man; as if beings of a superior order had transferred their abode to the Earth and had metamorphosed it?" * Or contemplate an

* Introduction Générale à l'Histoire de la Philosophie, par M. Cousin, Lec. I.—Linberg's Translation.

epitome of the whole mighty development of mind in a single individual, appearing first on the shore of this world a feeble infant, and in less than a century assuming the character of a Newton, a Leibnitz, a Milton: and as an illustration of the changes made in the condition of the world by human invention and skill, take the history of Mechanics, of the Needle and the Telescope.

In contemplating these developments and changes, what enquiry springs up, yea, irresistibly springs up, in the mind? Do we not ask, *how* all this came to pass, and *why* the developments and changes came up under these particular forms? Do we not ask, why did man change the face of the Earth? Why did he create government? Why did he give birth to science and art? Where and how did the development of his mind begin; and how did it proceed? What are the laws of his thought, the ground of his knowledges and beliefs, the forms of his reasonings, and the methods of his investigations? What are the laws of his emotions and passions? What are the capacity and force, and what the laws of his will?

Enquiries like these evince the workings of the philosophic spirit; they are found under some form, in some degree, in every human mind. Few, indeed, take in that whole field of enquiry, which embraces the complete development of humanity; but whether in the child, or in the adult, in the savage, or in cultivated man, you perceive questionings after the origin and reason of things—after efficient and final causes—an earnest prying of the mind into something beyond mere visible and tangible forms, you there perceive the workings of the philosophic impulse —the *Φιλοσοφία*. This is the DAWN OF PHILOSOPHY. The impulse TO KNOW and TO DO, the elements of philosophy spontaneously at work in the mind, lead forth the developments and changes above mentioned. The enquiry after the causes and reasons of these developments and changes, after they have in any degree taken place, is the higher form of the *Φιλοσοφία,* and leads forth the mind to the construction of philosophy as a system. Under the first form, the mind appears intent upon its objects, thinking, feeling, doing, and making its inherent energies to appear in external effects. Under the second form, it turns back upon itself,—that is, makes itself its own object by an act of reflection, and finds out its own reach and limits, its own aims and laws.

Φιλοσοφία, from expressing the impulse TO KNOW and the consequent causal activity of man, and from expressing, after the development of humanity has taken place, the impulse to seek after the laws and principles which have governed this development, comes to express these laws and principles themselves. These laws and principles, like the simple desire of knowledge, act spontaneously in the development of humanity. They are in the highest sense philosophical elements of our being, inseparable from it, and energizing as a plastic power within, and as such distinguishable from philosophy as an expressed system without, laid down in books, or in the lectures of the schools. The first, of course, gives birth to the second, as thought gives birth to language.

In that early period of humanity to which we have adverted, it could not exist as a developed system: it was then in man as a light and a power, under which he thought and acted, but upon which he did not reflect: Thus the *idea of the useful,* led him to change the face of nature and to originate the ordinary arts: The *idea of justice,* led him to constitute government and law: The *idea of the beautiful,* led him to the creations of painting, sculpture, music, and poetry: The *inherent laws of his intelligence*, guided him in his reasonings; he believed, because he could not disbelieve, and faith appeared in him like a sublime and divine instinct: When he looked out upon the phenomena of the world, he assigned them causes, because he could not think of them without this relation: And from finite being, his mind necessarily rose up to the conception of the Infinite Being—he became a worshipper under the energy of a spontaneous and irresistible idea.

At length reflection began—when it began we know not, but its beginning was the birth of philosophy as a system developed and recognized. By the act of reflection, or self-consciousness, the mind turns back upon itself, and makes itself the object of its own contemplations. All the phenomena of the mind, are presented in the field of its consciousness;—the sensations which are caused by the external world—the affirmations of the reason—the volitions—must all alike appear there, in order to be known. There is an ordinary consciousness which belongs necessarily to every man; but reflection is a special and voluntary consciousness, and thence called a philosophic consciousness, which appears only when the mind becomes the object of its own observation by an act of self-determination.

Now in the exercise of this philosophic consciousness, the mind questions itself respecting the grounds of its knowledge and its faith—respecting the forms of its thinking, and the modes of its investigation—respecting the grounds of its decisions in arts, morals, government, and religion: it makes those very enquiries which we recognize in ourselves, when, reviewing the progressive development of humanity, we are struck with wonder and admiration at what man has accomplished, and at what man has himself become. The results of these enquiries form systematic philosophy.

Let us sum up here the preceding observations, so as to present a succinct definition.

1. Philosophy, from *Φιλοσοφία,* expresses the inherent desire of knowledge in the human mind; and as closely connected with this, the desire of action. Under the impulse of these desires man begins to acquire knowledge; and to exert his causality in appropriating the materials supplied him from the earth—in working in various arts, and in modifying the face of nature.

2. After a time he begins to reflect upon the development of his mind, the facts he has observed, and the works of his own power and skill: and now the *Φιλοσοφία,* or love of knowing, takes a new direction, and impels him to search out the causes, laws, and forms of the various development of his own being.

3. These causes, laws and forms really existed subjectively, inseparable from himself, before he began to make them the object of his thought and curious inquiry: and they, as the first principles of his being, and as governing its manifestations, are the substantial elements of philosophy.

4. These first principles of his being are known through reflection, or self-consciousness; and when stated methodically, under proper divisions, and with clear definitions and expositions, form Didactic Philosophy.

The term *Φιλοσοφία,* which at first expressed only the desire of knowledge, or love of truth spontaneously working in the human mind, is thus employed to express all the grand results of this high and glorious impulse.

SECTION II.

DISTINCTION BETWEEN THE PHENOMENAL AND THE METAPHENOMENAL.

CONSCIOUSNESS is the common field of all our mental activity. All our sensations, our perceptions, thinking, and reasoning, our imaginations and fancies, our emotions, passions, determinations, and volitions, alike appear, and are recognized here. These affections of our being are not the movements of an insensate mechanism : we know them in their going on, and we know ourselves as the SUBJECTS of them.

Now there is an important distinction to be drawn here. The distinction between the immediate objects of consciousness, and those objects which, although known, or at least supposed to be known, yet lie without the sphere of consciousness. The immediate objects of our consciousness are *phenomena*, and these only are *phenomena* ; while those objects which, by supposition, lie beyond immediate consciousness, are *metaphenomenal.*

What are the immediate objects of consciousness, or of what are we immediately conscious ? This is the first enquiry.

Let us begin with our sensations. The sensations are affections of our inner being, and unquestionably are the immediate objects of consciousness. But there are many perceptions and judgments which come up to view in connection with the sensations, which, together with their objects, are entirely distinct from the sensations. The bare sensations are those of color, of sound, of fragrance, of taste, of touch, of heat and cold, of titillation, and of pain and pleasure. In these are contained what are commonly called the secondary qualities of matter: but this designation cannot be made from the bare sensations. We have in the sensations mere internal experiences, or movements of our own inner being. We are not conscious of matter, distance, space, substance, or cause;—we are conscious of sensations only. We may be conscious of the action of other faculties of our being, affirming or perceiving the existence of body, distance, space, substance, and cause; but the bare sensations are no such affirmation, or perception. I think it must be plain to every mind that will reflect a little, that if we had only the sensations above mentioned, we should have no knowledge of an external world whatever.

The same conclusion must be drawn with respect to the primary qualities of matter. These are extension and resistance. But resistance to immediate consciousness is only an internal experience, and extension only a repetition of this experience. There is nothing in this experience to give us a knowledge of any thing external: time, space, substance, and cause, are not contained in a mere inward experience, a mere modification of our own being. In the primary qualities, therefore, we have no immediate consciousness of an external world. It thus appears, in general, that we have an immediate consciousness only of certain affections or modifications of our own being. What immediately appears to us, what we immediately know, are these affections. These are truly the *phenomenal*. If there be an external world,—if there be substance, space, time, and cause,—they are not phenomenal, or immediately recognized in the consciousness, nor do they come directly from the sensations.

Let us suppose, then, that we have faculties by which we can know an external world, and by which we can know substance, time, space, body, and cause, either through the sensations, or independently of them ; then, with respect to these faculties, the enquiry arises also, what are the immediate objects of consciousness ?

The faculties themselves are not the immediate objects ; nor are the objects perceived, and the truths affirmed, the immediate objects : simply the acts of these faculties are the immediate objects of consciousness. Thus in perceiving any external object, as a house or a tree, I am not immediately conscious of the house or the tree, but of sensations of color, and of the act of perceiving. The external object does not come into my consciousness, but only the sensations and perceptions, and these are simply movements of my own being. Indeed, my own being, as a substance endowed with faculties of feeling, knowing and willing, is not immediately presented to my consciousness : I am conscious only of certain phenomena, and of acts of judgment connecting the phenomena with external objects and internal faculties.

In processes of deep thinking and reasoning, the same holds true. In studying out some mathematical theorem, for example, the recondite mathematical relations,—the necessary and absolute truths are not immediate objects of consciousness ;—but the acts of attention, the acts of thinking and reasoning—the modifications of my own being in order to know and comprehend, and in knowing and comprehending. The mathematical relations, the necessary and absolute truths, do not come into consciousness as phenomena,—the acts and modifications of my own being are the phenomena, while the relations and truths are metaphenomenal.

Again, God is invisible : He is neither as a substance addressed to the senses, nor is he manifested to the consciousness as a modification of our interior being ; but still, if known at all, he must be known by these modifications : He is not the phenomena of consciousness, but known through them.

Here, then, we have the broad and clear distinction between the *phenomenal* and the *metaphenomenal.* Sensations, emotions and passions, acts of perceiving, judging, reasoning and imagining, acts of choice and volition—these, as the immediate objects of consciousness, are phenomenal ; but the causes of sensation, emotion, and passion, the objects and truths perceived, affirmed, or deduced, the objects of the imagination, of choice and volition—these, not being the immediate objects of consciousness, are metaphenomenal.

SECTION III.

OF THE REALITY OF THE METAPHENOMENAL.

The reality of the phenomenal is not questioned. That I have certain sensations, perceptions, emotions, passions, and volitions, this is immediate knowledge and consciousness: but whether the objects of these acts and experiences of my being have a real, positive, and independent existence, this may be and has been questioned, and even denied: The reality of the metaphenomenal has been questioned and denied.

It will be readily granted by all, that by the imagination we can create objects which are unreal; and that in our actual perceptions we are often mistaken, and seem to perceive what we afterwards discover to have no reality, or to be a very different object from what we thought it to be. But, beyond all this, it has been contended that there is no objective reality whatever;—that the tree and the house which I now see, and which everybody sees, has no existence out of, and independently of, the perception of which I and everybody are immediately conscious; and the same of all objects, whether external things, or internal truths.

It is undeniable that men generally believe in the reality of the metaphenomenal; nay, that only a few speculative philosophers, have ever denied it.

Now, the aim of philosophy is to explain the actual development of our being, of all that man has thought and done. Hence even the errors of man must be explained. If, therefore, men have erred in their belief in the reality of the metaphenomenal, it must be shown both that it cannot exist, and *how* men have come to entertain this universal but erroneous belief.

Those who believe in the reality of the metaphenomenal are indeed required, as philosophers, to show, how it is legitimately attained: but, on the other hand, those who deny this reality, in opposition to a common sentiment, are justly required to explain this common sentiment.

The denial of the metaphenomenal had its origin in a mode of explaining the attainment of it. Its reality was at first assumed as unquestionable; but the explanation given, finally developed the denial as a legitimate consequence.

The cardinal principle of this mode, was the assumption that the mind could perceive only by coming in contact with the object of perception, in accordance with a supposed axiom, *nihil agit, nisi cum, et ubi est, nothing can act except when and where it is.* This principle was suggested by an apparent law in physics, viz.: that one body can act upon another only by actual contact. The truth of this law is now disputed, and even the impossibility of an actual contact between the particles of bodies firmly believed. But if the law were unquestionable in respect to physics, on what legitimate grounds can it be taken as a law of equal appropriateness and validity in explaining the perceptions of the mind? That the mind can perceive only by coming in contact with the objects of perception, must be a mere assumption. Besides, by the physical analogy, the mind perceiving as well as the object perceived must be material.

Having assumed the law, however, the great aim now

naturally became to explain how the contact between mind and its objects takes place.

In the first place, it was plain that mind and the external material objects do not immediately come in contact. The mind perceives, therefore, not the material objects themselves, but certain representations of these objects, which were variously called *species*, *forms*, *images*, and *ideas*. But what are these representative forms? Various were the explications. The old Aristotelians held that they are made up of fine material particles which enter the different organs of sense, and form themselves into the required image in the brain, and that there the mind comes in contact with them.

After the age of Des Cartes, this theory was abandoned; and the image or idea was spoken of as an impression made upon the brain like that made upon wax by a seal. Here no material particles were received into the brain through the organs of sense; but, impressions being made upon the organs from without, images were shaped upon the brain corresponding to the external objects.

It is evident that the representative image once admitted, must become a fruitful subject of speculation. These speculations, however, all tended to one result—a result proclaimed in part by Berkley, and fully by Hume —namely, that above mentioned, the denial of the metaphenomenal.

If we know only the representative images affirmed to be in the mind, then we can have no legitimate knowledge of any thing out of the mind; for, as in all our attempts to approach exteriority, we are met merely by these images, they are all that we can possibly attain to. Hence, Berkley, on this principle, cannot be confuted, when he affirms, "The existence of a body out of a mind perceiving it, is not only impossible, and a contradiction in terms, but, were it possible, and even real, it were impossible that the mind should ever know it."—Hume is equally consistent in his sweeping affirmation: "Now, since nothing is ever present to the mind but perceptions, and since all ideas are derived from something antecedently present to the mind, it follows that 'tis impossible for us so much as to conceive or form an idea of any thing specifically different from ideas and impressions. Let us fix our attention out of ourselves as much as possible; let us chase our imaginations to the heavens, or to the utmost limits of the universe; we never really advance a step beyond ourselves, nor can we conceive any kind of existence but those perceptions which have appeared in that narrow compass. This is the universe of the imagination; nor have we any idea but what is there produced."

The denial of the metaphenomenal appeared under two forms:—First, that of Idealism. Here the facts of immediate consciousness were taken as the only universe, "the universe of the imagination." Secondly, that of Materialism. Here the representative images were merely considered as arising from material objects, and impinging upon material organs, and thence affecting the brain, or sensorium. What now is the soul which receives the next impression but a finer form of matter, and what are its sensations and ideas but a movement of the internal organism?

There is a class of philosophers, and Reid may be placed at their head, who endeavor to dissipate the dogmas of both Idealism and Materialism by the stern voice of Common Sense. Every man believes in the metaphenomenal—in objective reality and truth; therefore, it exists for every man. Here common sense pauses: but the philosophical impulse still urges to the enquiry, Is there not reality in opposition to Idealism and Materialism? Is there not reality independently of a mere subjective persuasion? The first are forms of a philosophy which, on its received principles, demonstrates conclusions in opposition to general belief. And is the general belief incapable of explaining itself by demonstrating the reality of its objects? Must it merely doggedly affirm itself in opposition to the philosophical diagrams paraded before it? And shall the united efforts of the human mind end in the birth of two great parties, both occupying absurd positions—the one affirming, "I prove, although I do not believe;" and the other, "I believe, although I cannot prove?" May we not prove and believe, and believe and prove?

It is now evident, I think, that the cardinal aim of philosophy must be to reach the metaphenomenal. If the existence of the metaphenomenal can be demonstrated, then the facts of consciousness, the phenomenal, are accounted for.

SECTION IV.

THE OBJECTIVE AND THE SUBJECTIVE.

In determining the actual development of our being, in its various relations, we find ourselves at once introduced to two forms of being: the SUBJECTIVE, and the OBJECTIVE. The subjective, under its simplest and most unique form, is myself; and the objective, under its most general form, comprehends whatever is not expressed in the term *me*, or *myself*. Again, the simple subjective, myself, becomes objective, when, in an act of self-consciousness, I make it the object of my thought. And again, the objective general, or whatever is not myself, must be subdivided into the purely objective and the subjective general. The purely objective is that which is not only not myself, but totally unlike myself—different in kind—having no properties in common. The subjective general is that which, embracing myself, is like myself—the same in kind—having properties in common: a distinction of personalities, of laws, causalities, and sympathies—but yet agreeing in being connected with personalities, in implying the presence of mind, and in being capable of being referred in kind to the finite and the infinite mind.

I will explain: I have developed to my own consciousness a thinking principle, a will or free causality, and various emotions and passions; and these, either as constituting or as being inseparable from my own personality, constitute the simple subjective. Now, I conceive of other personalities like my own, each being to itself the simple subjective ;—and of these distinct personalities I conceive of one as the Eternal and the Infinite, while all the others are finite of various degrees.

Now, all these personalities come under the denomination of the subjective general. They are all of one kind, and each one is capable, by an act of self-consciousness, of making itself the simple subjective, and of considering all else in relation to itself as objective ; and capable of even making itself an object to itself.

Besides these distinct personalities, which are directly like myself, and palpably of the same kind, there are other forms of the subjective, which, however, are ultimately resolvable into the former. The vegetable and animal life —the forces and laws of the material creation, chemical affinities—the informing power of animal and vegetable physiology, that power by which every animal and every plant is produced invariably after its own kind, from the vitalized seed ;—these forces, laws, affinities, and informing powers—these busy workers and co-workers—these wise and exact regulators of the whole natural world—what are they ? There is design and causality here which cannot be conceived of without mind : Whether the mind be in the material masses, formative and governing by direct influence and immediate presence ; or whether it have invisible, unconscious, and incomprehensible agents, makes not ; mind is here as the seat of power, and the fountain of law. If all that is personal belong to the subjective general, then also must these laws and forces belong to the subjective general likewise ; for, although they do not directly appear as personalities, because giving us no manifestation of self-conscious determination, still they cannot but be involved in some way in such personalities, since their explication and conception is impossible in any other way.

But what is then the pure objective, or that which can in no sense be subjective? Whatever is directly known by the senses, or by the muscular organism, is purely objective. I see and smell a flower—that is, I have certain sensations, which arise from the correlation between my senses and a certain substance lying in space and exterior to myself. Now, I say not that I could form the judgment here expressed, without subjective principles; but the exterior substance which I name a flower in expressing this judgment, I conceive of not as life, but as a product of life, and upheld by life; not as a formative power, a *forma formans*, but as a substance informed, a *forma formata*. Again, a ball is tossed towards me, and I catch it in my hands. In doing this, I have the sensation of hardness, or, in other words, I experience a muscular resistance. Now, here again, I do not say that I could have formed this judgment without subjective principles; but the ball, or body, I conceive of not as itself a resisting cause, or as a gravitating power, but as that in which such a cause and power are habitant; and while cause and power belong to the subjective, I cannot but assign the gross material phenomena to the purely objective. They are not me, nor like me: they are not life, or formative power: they are not a force or a law. "In the material sense of the word Nature, we mean by it the sum total of all things, as far as they are objects of our senses, and consequently of possible experience—the aggregate of phenomena." * All that is exterior to me, and phenomenal

* Coleridge.

to the outer senses, and which does not account for and explain itself—as, for example, effects require causes to explain them,—is purely objective.

But not only are all material phenomena purely objective; all phenomena of consciousness which are known merely as acts or movements of the thinking, willing, and sensitive faculties—that is, all which comes into the consciousness through the outer senses, and thence called sensations; and all which is presented in the activities of the internal faculties, the perceptions, reasonings and imaginations, the acts of memory and fancy, and the volitions, emotions, and passions, are objective likewise.

The distinction between the subjective general, therefore, and the pure objective, is co-extensive with the metaphenomenal and the phenomenal.—But in this point of view, it is a distinction in the kind or nature of the particulars compared. The metaphenomenal is subjective, because it is that upon which the development of our being ultimately rests: the phenomenal is objective, because it is that in which the development of our being appears actually taking place.

The development of the Intelligence must ultimately rest upon ideas, principles, or first truths. In the process of this development, appear its perceptions, reasonings, imaginations, and so on.

The development of the Will must ultimately rest upon the laws of the Reason. In the process of this development appear choices and volitions.

The development of the Sensitivity must ultimately rest upon the laws of the Reason, likewise. In the process of this development appear the various sensations, emotions, and passions. When the subjective is fully attained,—that is, when all principles are known, all laws obeyed, all fitting sensations, emotions, and passions brought out and regulated by reason, then the development of our being is complete. While this development is going on, the phenomenal, or the purely objective, is thrown out.

But, although the phenomenal is always and only objective, we have seen that the subjective can also become objective ; but this last distinction does not, like the former, arise from a difference in kind, but merely from a change of position or relation. Every intelligent personal subject can make all else objective to itself—nay, can make itself objective to itself, by an act of reflection.

To sum up the preceding distinctions, we have all possible forms of being embraced under the subjective and the objective, as follows :

1. The subjective simple, or *myself ;*

2. The subjective simple, taken as objective to myself ;

3. The objective general, or whatever is not myself ;

4. The objective general, divided into the subjective general and the pure objective ;—the first comprising whatever is metaphenomenal—the second whatever is phenomenal.

The distinctions made and explained above, give us the leading philosophical conception, and enable us clearly and succinctly to state the leading problems. The leading philosophical conception is that of explaining the development of my being. Now this development presents me,

First, the phenomenal, or what appears to my immediate consciousness. This consciousness I can divide into the *exterior*, or that which contains mere sensations ; and the *interior*, or that which contains the movements of my own faculties. Now, all these phenomena, whether of the exterior or interior consciousness, constitute the pure *objective*,* because they lie before the reflective power.

Secondly, I have the metaphenomenal, or that which lies beyond the phenomena: and this admits likewise of a twofold division. The metaphenomenal in the world without, which is to account for the sensations; and the metaphenomenal within, which is to account for the acts which take place upon the sensations. Now, the metaphenomenal without and within, constitutes the subjective † general, because it lies under and sustains the phenomenal as the ground of its possibility.

Hence we announce a main problem in philosophy, namely: To determine the validity and the forms of the subjective, and to show its relations to the objective.

Again, in the development of my being, the earliest conviction at which I arrive is the *Ego sum*, I AM. Now, starting with this conviction, I find that all which I know, I know not only in the field of my consciousness, but also in the determination and activity of my personality. I find thus, that I am a simple, unique subject, lying in some sort under all being whatever, determining the mode and extent of its cognizance, and even its reality.

Hence we announce another problem in philosophy, no less important than the preceding, namely: To determine objective reality; or the reality of the objective general,—of that which is not myself.

The first problem is disputed by the sensualists, or those who derive the materials of all cognition from experience. The second is disputed by the idealists, or those who, like Berkley and Hume, deny the possibility of knowing an external world.

* Ob and jaceo. † Sub and jaceo.

Once more: The subjective simple which attempts to reach the objective general, attempts also to reach itself. This it can do only by making itself an object to itself. Hence arises a new and unique form of knowledge through the power of reflection or self-consciousness; and thus we have the problem: To determine the faculties and laws of the simple subjective.

These three problems cover the whole field of Philosophy, as will be apparent when we come to consider its cardinal divisions.

SECTION V.

REASON AND SENSE.

In the present developed state of my faculties, I know myself as Body and Spirit. Spirit is the subjectivity within, which thinks, feels, and wills. The body, the material tabernacle of the spirit, is a part of the great system of external nature: it is the same, mechanically and chemically; and it lives and decays like all other living things. What is its relation to the spirit? It is the curious and wonderful mediator between matter and spirit. Through the nerves, distributed into five external senses, and through the muscular organism sometimes called the "sixth sense" and the sense of resistance, nature reaches the spirit. What is the product of this union? Sensations, and nothing more. No thought, no knowledge—simply an experience of sound, color, sapidness, fragrance, touch, and resistance. But the cognitive faculty within is not unfurnished. It is prepared to know the world, from whence the sensations arise; and it is prepared to know itself. Sensation conditionates the reason in two ways:—

First—In sensation, in common with all the subjective faculties, it wakes to self-conscious activity. It here begins to live its knowing and thoughtful life.

Secondly—Sensation furnishes materials of cognition;

or signs which the reason appropriates readily and familiarly, in reading the external world.

The lower faculty, as it were, sings a joyful matin song under the window of the reason ; then this glorious power awakes, and looking out, recognizes the reality, beauty, and laws of God's works, and the Great Maker himself; and then, turning back upon itself, sees there the image of the Divine wisdom and love. In knowing the world, the mind is developed, and all its faculties brought into exercise ; and as consciousness necessarily accompanies every internal movement, the mind is likewise revealed to itself.

The first knowledge of both spirit and nature is spontaneous. Afterwards, comes the period for philosophical reflection upon the one, and philosophical observation upon the other; and then, psychology and natural science are born.

As our faculties become unfolded in their relations with nature, important changes take place. The sensations and muscular resistance, which originally could directly of themselves give us no knowledge, are now transformed into apt and familiar signs of all external bodies, forms and qualities. The different shades of light and color, now associated with bodies, forms and qualities, readily represent them, and we seem to know every thing by the eye. It is now almost an universal sense. So also the different sounds received by the ear, enable us to distinguish persons, things, places, and distances. The same principle applies to all the senses. The reason has appropriated them all, and made them such quick and familiar servitors of knowledge, that we now seem to have an immediate perception of the outer world. On the other hand, Reason, having from the first activity of the sense which opened the play of the mental powers, entered upon its career and unfolded itself to itself, is now no longer dependent upon sensuous experience as occasions of intellection. It can now retire within itself, and think with closed senses. Memory and Imagination now wait upon it, to supply it with facts and images; and within its own depths it has opened fountains of pure, absolute, and necessary truth.

As the body is thus the mediator through which the outer world reaches the spirit, so also it is the mediator and instrumentality through which the spirit reaches the external world, and impresses itself upon it. One set of nerves obey nature, and give sensations to the spirit. Another set of nerves obey the spirit, and move the muscular organism. The tongue and the hand are the two great instruments by which the mind does its work without. The arts of industry and beauty—all the changes—all the improvements which the spirit hath made in the great field of nature, it hath made by the tongue and the hand.

What, then, is humanity, but spirit conditionated on the one hand in its incipient activity, and in its knowledge of an external world, by sensuous impressions? And conditionated on the other hand, in the exertion of its causality and plastic power, by an apt material instrumentality?

SECTION VI.

SENSUALISM AND TRANSCENDENTALISM.

WE now arrive at the point of departure of two great systems of philosophy. Taken under their modern developments, Locke may be said to represent the one, and Kant the other.

Sensualism, concentrating its thought in the sensuous conditions of knowledge, loses sight of the truth that they are merely conditions ; and goes on to expound them as the primary and radical elements of knowledge itself. Hence the utmost development of the human intelligence presents us only the combination and expansion of these elements. The reason is absolutely incapable of arriving at any truth whose generating or constitutive elements have not first entered the senses. The senses thus become the sources and measure of all knowledge.

Transcendentalism begins with sensation no less than sensualism. Kant opens his great work with the affirmation, "That all our knowledge begins with experience, does not admit of a doubt." But then transcendentalism does not make the sensations, the radical, generating and constitutive elements of knowledge ; but conditions, under which the cognitive faculty begins to act, and suggestions, upon which, by its own force, and according to its own ideas and laws, it forms cognitions.

The views which the two systems entertain respecting

the primordial state of the mind, differ widely. Locke represents the state of mind before sensation takes place by a sheet of white paper, and Hobbes by a slate, in which there is no idea or element of knowledge, but merely a susceptibility of being written upon. To this view all the adherents of this system conform.

Transcendentalism represents the mind as having the possibility, the scope, the law and the form of all knowledge within itself. Whatever the mind be, whatever its faculty of knowing, and with whatever elements it be primordially furnished, it is easily conceivable that in the act of knowing it brings this faculty and these elements to bear. Now, in order to determine the reach of the cognitive faculty, and whether the mind really have primordial elements of knowledge, we need only examine our actual knowledges. The sensations can easily be analyzed : and if they be the primary elements of knowledge, they will appear every where in the composition and deduction of thought : for every mere composition must preserve the original elements, and can show nothing absolutely new ; and every deduction must keep within the measure and kind of the starting points.

But if in our actual knowledges, there be found elements which, so far from belonging to the sense, appear in their nature and characteristics to transcend the utmost capacity of the sense, then these elements unquestionably lay claim to a higher origin. And if these elements, when disintegrated from our complex knowledges and held up before the reason, are readily recognized and reaffirmed by this faculty as necessary, universal and absolute, then may they legitimately be claimed as the product of this faculty alone.

Now the sensations are those of the eye, consisting of

light and color; of the ear, consisting of the various sounds; of smelling and tasting, consisting of odor and sapidness in their endless varieties; of touch, consisting of simple and uniform impressions upon the nerves wherever they are distributed; of muscular resistance, consisting of hardness and softness, smoothness and roughness; and, in the last place, the sensations of pleasure and pain, and of titillation.

But our actual knowledges bring to view substance, cause, time, space, truth, justice, and many other ideas of similar characteristics—ideas which no analysis of the mere sensations can ever unfold. And while these ideas can be brought under the observation of the senses, even now that they are known, no more than they could at the first be evolved out of them, to the reason itself they are intuitively true, universal, and necessary.

When we speak, therefore, of transcendental truth in the just philosophical sense, we speak of nothing doubtful, but of that which both in itself is most certainly known, and in its relations makes all other knowledge possible.

The application of the term *transcendental* is convenient and appropriate, because it is descriptive. It tells the simple fact, that the human mind, while it is susceptible of impressions from without by means of the organs of sense—impressions which conditionate its first development, and afford materials for an important department of its knowledge,—nevertheless contains within itself those elements of truth, those forms of knowledge, those first principles of all thought and reasoning, which transcend the reach of the senses. The lower faculty is connected with that corporeal organism, through which spirit communes with nature. It occupies the sphere appropriated to it, and does its work well. The higher faculty of the pure Reason has its sphere also ; and is just as capable in its sphere of announcing primordial truths, the forms of perception, and the laws of reasoning, as the sense in its sphere is of giving forth sensations.

From this it is evident that the metaphenomenal and subjective identify themselves with the transcendental.

Locke is a great and venerable name ; and no one may speak lightly of him. But an excessive veneration has led some who disclaim sensualism, to claim for his doctrines certain saving clauses in those passages where he speaks of Reflection as one of the sources of ideas.

There is no school of philosophy that might not be ambitious of retaining, as an authority, such a man as Locke ; and one cannot well conceive how any thing less than a supreme and honest love of truth could influence any one to dispense with his authority.

For my part, I can say from my heart that I admire and love Locke. His clear and penetrating intellect, his good sense and manly candour ; his strong English heart, his pure English style ; and his decided moral and religious principles, always quietly about him like the coat he wears, like the air he breathes, like the familiar tones of his common discourse, and the prevailing expression of his honest face,—altogether I admire and love him. And notwithstanding the errors of his system, I shall continue to read and admire and love him.

Locke refers all our knowledge to two sources, Sensation and Reflection. The latter, as he defines it,* is undoubtedly the interior consciousness,—it embraces the operations of the mental faculties : and the former is equivalent to the exterior consciousness. All that appears

* Book II., ch. 1, § 4.

to us, therefore, appears in the consciousness; and all which there appears, consists of the simple sensations, and the operations of the mind, and whatever is revealed in or by the operations of the mind. Now so far the Transcendentalist will go with Locke; so far there is no difference whatever. But when we come to consider the mental operations themselves, we find the great point of departure of the two systems. According to Locke, the mental faculties, when they go into action, not only begin conditionally and in point of time with sensation, but they also derive all the materials and elements upon which their activity is expended, from sensation, and the conscious experiences of the mental activity itself. The sensations, together with the acts of "perception, thinking, doubting, believing, reasoning, knowing, willing, and all the different actings of our own minds," are the first radical elements from which all possible knowledges are formed.

Now, the introduction here of the ideas of reflection or the interior consciousness, by no means changes the character of the system; for these, no less than the sensations, are merely phenomenal. The operations of the mind, as well as the sensations, are conditions of knowing the transcendental truths. Thus the succession of thought, as well as the succession of sensations, is a condition of knowing time. Indeed, the most important truths are revealed upon condition of the experiences of the interior consciousness. But recollect that the contents of sensation and reflection, while to the transcendentalist they are mere conditions of conceiving time, space, substance, power, and so on; to Locke and his school they are the simple ideas or elements out of which these, and all the most abstruse truths are compounded, or drawn.*

* Book II., ch. 12, § 1 and § 8.

The transcendentalist can say that sensation and reflection, or the exterior and interior consciousness, are the only sources of our knowledge ; understanding by this that all that we know we know either upon the experience of sensations, or in the acts of knowing, of which we are conscious ; but this is a very different thing from making the sensations and the acts of knowing the materials or elements out of which all that we know is compounded. I have already distinguished between the mere act of knowing and that which is known, calling the first the phenomenal, and the second the metaphenomenal ; and just as broadly as that distinction are the two systems to be distinguished. Sensualism merges every thing into the phenomenal : Transcendentalism transcends or passes beyond the phenomenal, and reaches the universal and necessary truth, the substantial and real being ;—that which is the rational ground of all phenomena, without which they could have had no existence, and without which, now that they exist, they cannot be explained and accounted for.

Men generally, and even most philosophers, in daily thought and occupation, are more with the phenomenal than the metaphenomenal, and thus from the familiarity of use, the phenomenal comes to be regarded as more unquestionable and certain than truths of pure reason. I think, however, that a little quiet thinking must dissipate this illusion from every mind. How do we reach the phenomenal, that is, our sensations and the operations of our mental faculties ? Is it not simply by a form of knowing, —namely, consciousness ? Now, if there be a form of knowing adapted to the metaphenomenal, why do we not know this as well as the phenomenal ? But there is such a form of knowing, namely, Intuition, or the direct perception and insight of Reason ; and we are conscious of the exercise of the function implied in this form—we are conscious of knowing by intuition. Is not the act of intuition, of which we are conscious, as valid as the sensation of which we are conscious? Nay, more, is not the truth, which we are conscious of knowing in the exercise of the intuitive function, as valid as the conscious act by which it is known? To immediate consciousness, as a form of knowing, we refer sensation and the operations of the mental faculties. To the intuition of reason, as another form of knowing, we refer the transcendental truths. This is the whole account of the matter. The sensualistic school will insist upon it that the objects of immediate consciousness alone are the elements of knowledge—while the transcendental school affirm that the fundamental elements are found beyond immediate consciousness.

But the principles on which transcendental truths are denied, involve the denial of all objective reality whatever, beyond immediate consciousness. It is not merely the ideas of pure reason, which lie beyond immediate consciousness; all the pure mathematics transcend it likewise. Nay, the entire outer world transcends it; for all must allow, that not the received objects of the external world are immediate objects of consciousness, but only the sensations supposed to arise from these objects. Indeed, in this very way were Berkley and Hume led to deny all objective reality, out of consciousness. It is plain that they deduced their doctrines legitimately from the system of Locke.

I conclude here by remarking, that the denial of the metaphenomenal as that which transcends immediate consciousness must involve the destruction of all philosophy. If we are shut up to mere phenomena, we can account for nothing. We have only to observe, classify, and name; to mark a ceaseless involution and evolution, where nothing absolutely begins, and nothing can be truly finished. Thus the whole field of human thought becomes a panorama of shadows.

SECTION VII.

IDEAS AND LAWS.

THE word "idea," according to the usage of Locke, expresses whatever we are immediately conscious of. The word "idea," according to the usage of Plato, expresses what we cannot be immediately conscious of. In the usage of Plato, however, "idea" does not express any thing transcendental of consciousness in the external world, but only the metaphenomenal, lying in the mind itself. And here we see at once the fallacy of all that Locke has said respecting innate ideas. Taking the word in his usage, that ideas cannot be innate, is a truism; for nothing is more evident, than that mere sensations and acts of the mind, that is, mere phenomena, cannot be innate—they exist only as they appear in the consciousness. His reasoning, therefore, does not reach the point in debate. On the other hand, "ideas," in the Platonic usage, cannot but be innate, since the word expresses those primordial laws of knowing, thinking and reasoning, and those necessary and absolute elementary truths which are inseparable from the mind itself.

In order to form a clear conception of ideas in the Platonic, or transcendental sense, let us recur to the distinction of the subjective and the objective. The *subjective simple*, or mind, is directly opposed to all supposed forms of being, lying out of mind, and comprised in the phenomena of sensation, and whatever in the exterior world is connected with their production. It is the opposition of the *spiritual subjective*, myself, and the *unspiritual objective*, exterior to myself. Now, the true Platonist or transcendentalist views every thing existing beside mind, as made by mind, after the laws of mind, and primarily for mind.

It is a kindly doctrine, and to be heartily received, that one design of the great Creator, in forming the countless tribes of animals, was to multiply the forms of enjoyment. Every sensitive creature hath its sphere of life, its bountiful provisions, and its term of happiness. But irrational creatures comprehend neither the world in which they subsist, nor the curious workmanship of their own organism. The world, in its wise designs, its exact order, and its beautiful forms, is not made for them. It is made for them only in respect to the gratification of their mere animal wants. But under all these higher points of view, it is obviously made for rational beings. Our physical constitution, indeed, finds its fitting provisions and accommodations in the world; but we are not confined to these. To us, the world is a vast and sublime exhibition of design, skill, causative and regulative force, harmonious relations, and beautiful forms.

We can conceive of a period when there was as yet no creation, and the Creator dwelt alone in the immensity of his being. Now we cannot but believe there was arrayed before his mind, every possible form of being, every possible constitution of a universe, every possible variety of life ; and there, also, lay the map of the worlds which were ordained actually to be. In his mind was all the science and art, according to which, the Universe was to be bodied forth : and there, too, was that creative energy, which had but to exert itself, and Creation would stand forth in all its glory and magnificence. Now the preconceived laws, forms and relations of the universe, as they lay in the Divine mind, are a part of the Divine ideas. Viewed in relation to the Eternal Reason, as giving the original thought and law, they are ideas simply. Viewed in relation to the Divine imagination, as giving forth definite forms and relations, they become ideals, models, or archetypes. Divine ideas, as the originating thoughts and archetypes of worlds, cannot be exhausted in the actual creation, for God is infinite. Again, there must be in the Divine mind thoughts and conceptions which do not take their embodiment in material forms. Such are those which relate to pure science and moral government. Whatever thus lies in the Divine mind, constitutes the Divine ideas.

Suppose the infinite mind to constitute another mind like itself. This mind, of course, must be finite; but inasmuch as it is mind, it must have the same ideas, according to its measure, which are found in the Divine original. These ideas, perhaps, could not be given in a fully developed state, that is, drawn out into all their consequences and applications, for this would appear to border upon the infinite; but given in their elementary state, to be unfolded by the active and free thought of the being thus gloriously constituted. Such a being may be conceived of, as existing without a body and organs of sense —a pure spirit; and although thus without sensation, and supposed even to have no knowledge of a real world, in its pure thoughts and imaginations it might have, not only mental activity, but emotions of beauty and grandeur exquisitely delightful. For such emotions even now are awakened in our minds, without calling in the aid of immediate sensation, when in dreams, and esthetical efforts of the imagination, we are entertained with forms of greatness and beauty beyond the power of mere sense to reveal. But now, suppose this being to be introduced to the actual creation,—would not the possibility of its knowing and comprehending it, arise from the correspondence between the outward reality and the ideas within? Would it not understand the real world, just so far as it had the preconceived law and archetype within? At least, to a being destitute of sensation, no other possible way could exist. Let us, then, make another supposition, namely:—That a being be constituted like the Divine mind; but instead of existing as a pure spirit, that it be connected with a material body, with organs of sense—this body itself forming a part of the system of things without; and that its relations to this body are such that it cannot become conscious of existence, nor begin the play of its powers until sensations are produced within, by corporeal impressions without. Shall the law of perception and the forms of knowledge now be changed, because sensuous conditions are demanded for their development? It is impossible and inconceivable. The originating power and law of thought must still remain in the spirit, to which they of necessity belong. This last new form of being, is new only in respect to the conditions of its beginning to act, and the mode and conditions of its communication with the external world; while the possibility, and the determinate form of its knowing, still lie in its inherent spiritual faculties, and its necessary and constitutive ideas. The universe represents the Divine thought; and now it cannot but represent the thought given likewise to this highly endowed creature, whom we recognize as man himself.

When man, therefore, was placed upon the smiling outspread earth, and beneath the bright starry heavens, he did not find himself a stranger and out of place. His mind and heart responded to the works of his Creator. His spirit drank in the living beauty of all things, because he was formed to know the beautiful. He saw the wise design of Creation, because he himself was endowed with a designing mind. He searched and found out the order of the heavens and the earth, and the great and all-regulating laws, because the principles of science, the foundations of law, were laid in his own intelligence. We have a striking illustration of this mutual adaptation and harmony in the science of mathematics. This science is drawn directly from the reason of man. By this science he is enabled to measure the planets. The Great and Divine Mathematician made the universe according to these lofty and exact principles. He then gave his creature the capacity to construct this pure and unerring science; and thus man has a ladder by which he can mount from earth to heaven.

If ideas of the reason are embodied in the external world, determining its forms, relations, and movements, what do they become when thus embodied? The answer is given in one word—LAWS. Force or power has its origin in the Divine causality; but that which appropriates, compounds, directs, and governs force, is Law, answering to the Divine idea. All ideas do not become laws, regulating Force in the exterior sphere of their manifestations. Some ideas give the law to perception, and determine our knowledges:—others give the law to the fine arts, and determine the forms of the beautiful: others, again, give the law to the free casuality or the responsible will, and determine moral rectitude. But these all go out into some form of law. Law and idea are thus the same. Viewed in respect to the reason, originating, conceiving, and projecting, we speak of the idea: viewed in respect to the sphere of determinate movement and action, we speak of the law.

Now, if the object of science be to ascertain the laws of the universe, we see how it depends upon, and must grow out of, philosophy.

There is a period in the development of mind in relation to external nature, when observation and thought first awake. It is a period of spontaneous communication between the soul and nature, springing up from the relation between the ideas within and their embodiment without. A voice from without calls to the soul within, and the soul joyfully answers back. In the very impressions made upon the sensitivity by nature, the occasion appears when the ideas are required, in order to know and comprehend. The reason is noticing carefully, and struggling to comprehend: in the very effort of earnest thought it perceives ideas, vaguely, perhaps, at first, and immediately carries them out to nature as a tentative law. The first efforts to assign laws to nature, and to expound her great system, may be crude and imperfect, wild and imaginative, because observation is limited, and reason only partially developed; but the process is the same in kind, at the dawn of science, and at its glorious noontide. It is the union of ideas and observation. This first period may be called the TIME OF AWAKENING.

The second period is the TIME OF PROPHECY. The mind now realizes in clear and decided reflection, what it wants. It proceeds, therefore, to make out the system of nature by mapping out the related bodies, their forms, magnitudes, and relations, and assigning them forces and laws. In this work the mind is prone to become intoxicated by its first glimpses of the grand mechanism of the world, and to imagine that the great discovery is completed: here, then, it pauses, and gives itself up to dogmatizing. In reality it has only arrived at a theory, or a tentative system of nature: it has made prophecies more or less clear, but nothing yet is established.

The third period is THE TIME OF ELABORATE OBSERVATION, EXPERIMENT, AND CALCULATION. Dissatisfied with preceding results, and yet taking advantage of them, the mind now sets itself at work afresh. It endeavors to think more profoundly, to reason more logically, and thus to escape from empty conjectures and fallacies. Now it aims to observe more extensively and accurately, at the same time reducing its observations to an exact and convenient classification: and not content with the facts of nature as they present themselves of their own accord, by ingeniously contrived experiments it forces out new and more curious facts from the hitherto silent and veiled bosom of nature. Now, too, it diligently cultivates pure science, that it may construct formulæ for the solution of the problems which come thronging in.

The fourth period is the TIME OF DETERMINATE SCIENCE. Now imaginary conceptions, and the ideas of merely possible systems, are set aside, and the true idea finds its corresponding law.

Thales belongs to the first period; Pythagoras and Ptolemy to the second; Copernicus, Kepler, and Tycho Brahe to the third; Newton and La Place to the fourth.

In the amazing advance which has been made in determinate science, and in perfecting methods of investigation, the four periods in respect to any new subject may be said to be passed through in one generation and in the lifetime of one philosopher.

Natural science will then only be completed when all the phenomena of nature shall be reduced under a universal causality, and assigned to fitting laws known in their conformity to ideas. Then the ideas and the laws will, as it were, stand face to face, and the phenomena be the intelligible words which pass between them.

The Mathematical, Moral, and Æsthetical Sciences are formed in the same way. The ideas of the reason project the forms and relations, and give the laws. The perfection of these sciences lies in their conformity to the absolute ideas.

SECTION VIII.

PRIMARY AND SECONDARY PHENOMENA.

WE shall begin with the exterior consciousness. The *primary phenomena* are the simple sensations. These are in themselves incapable of projecting themselves beyond the sphere of consciousness. But when the ideas are added to them, moulding and appropriating them by the laws of perception, then they become merged into positive judgments respecting bodies, in space with forms, qualities, distances, magnitudes, and movements. The sensations now habitually are not thought of as simple affections of the sensitivity ; but whenever they arise, the mind is busy in noticing the goings on of the world in space. Hence, when we speak of phenomena in this developed state of perception, we mean not the mere sensations, but the actual appearances and changes of bodies, of which the sensations have now become such apt and familiar signs that we lose sight of their original simplicity and bareness. Just as in language, when we hear the familiar and appropriate sounds, or see the familiar symbols, we seem at once to be present to the world of thought and imagination.

Now the phenomena transferred from the sensitivity, and characterized and classified as the phenomena of an outward world, constitute the *secondary phenomena* of the exterior consciousness.

A similar transformation takes place in the interior

consciousness. Here the *primary phenomena* are simple acts, or movements. But the ideas here also add themselves to the phenomena, and we come to know a subject —a personality, endowed with power, intelligence and freedom. The mere phenomena could not carry themselves back into spiritual reality, but of themselves would remain a bare flow of appearances through the field of the consciousness, without telling the fountain from whence they came, or whither they were tending. But in the very giving forth of the phenomena in the consciousness, the ideas make their appearance under the form of an intuitive perception and affirmation ; and then the mind knows itself as spirit endowed with reason, power and freedom, and perceives design and law in every movement. Thenceforward there are no more bare phenomena ; but it is the reason, knowing, designing, and commanding ; the will exerting causality ; the sensitivity alive with emotion and passion ; the glorious mind exerting itself in its proper sphere. The acts and affections of definite powers are the *secondary phenomena* of the interior consciousness.

The above distinction is an important one ; for men generally think of phenomena under their secondary form in the developed state of the mind : many, therefore, might fall into some confusion when the phenomenal is represented as lying wholly in the field of consciousness, under its primary presentation.

SECTION IX

ANTECEDENCE IN TIME, AND IN NECESSARY EXISTENCE.

THIS is what Cousin styles Chronological, and Logical Antecedence.

The first is the antecedence of the primary phenomena; the second, the antecedence of ideas.

To a mind not placed under sensuous conditions, the phenomena of the interior consciousness would alone claim antecedence in time. To man, who is mind under these conditions, the phenomena of the exterior, as well as of the interior consciousness, claim this antecedence. Did the phenomena alone exist, no question respecting necessary existence could arise; but in the actual manifestation of ideas within the sphere of thought, this question cannot be avoided.

The distinction here held up to view is very important, and really not difficult to comprehend. In the actual development of our being, the primary phenomena obviously must first appear in the order of time; for sensation is the first awakening of conscious existence, phenomena are the immediate objects of consciousness, and consciousness is the first form of knowledge. The knowledges to which we attain through the consciousness of phenomena, are presented under the form of judgments or affirmations made by the Reason. But these judgments, as acts of the Reason, are phenomena of the interior consciousness; as phenomena they must rest upon something antecedent; but this something antecedent is not sensation, for sensation stands only in the relation of a condition, and does not contain the elements of the judgments. Upon analysis, these elements are found to be ideas. Ideas, then, must have the antecedence of necessary existence. Mere sensation, in a particular form of being, may exist without involving antecedent ideas in the sphere of that being; but judgments or knowledges formed upon the basis of ideas, necessarily involve their prior existence; and as ideas can be traced to nothing higher, their antecedence must be that of necessary existence.

Sensations demand a previous necessary existence, only as all phenomena demand antecedent causality. But the phenomena of the interior consciousness, in addition to this, demand a constructive reason.

Sensations are known before cause is known; and yet as without an antecedent cause they could not have existed, so neither could they have been known under the causal relation, without the antecedent idea of cause. Affirmations of the reason appear, before the reason and its ideas come into the field of reflection; and yet, had not these had a necessary prior existence, the affirmations would not have been possible.

Experience is the conditionating starting point in the order of time. Ideas are the determining starting point in the order of rational judgments.

Experience marks the time when the knowledges begin. Ideas alone make the knowledges possible. Experience is the dial-hand which tells the hour of the mind's morning when it awakes to thought. Ideas necessitate the movement of the dial-hand itself.

Again: As the sensuous experiences of the exterior

consciousness conditionate the reason in the order of time in the development of those ideas by which it knows the external world; and as the experiences of the interior consciousness conditionate it in the order of time in the development of those ideas by which it knows the intellectual world: while, on the other hand, in the order of necessary prior existence, ideas determine all the knowledges arrived at: so, likewise, the particular judgments formed respecting objects in either world, conditionate the universal truths in the order of time; while these truths, in the order of necessary prior existence, determine the particular judgments. For example: in the external world the particular judgment that a given body is in space, precedes in time the universal judgment that every body must be in space; while the universal judgment comprehended in the ideas of space and substance, must have had a prior necessary existence in order to make the other possible. And in the interior and intellectual sphere, although the affirmation that all phenomena must be assigned to causality, would not have been formed until a particular instance of causality had appeared; still, in the order of necessary prior existence, the universal truth must have been embraced in the inherent idea of causality, or the particular judgment assigning a particular phenomenon to an appropriate cause, would have been impossible, as having no basis on which to make its appearance.

To sum up the whole in brief: In the development of our being, the phenomenal as to time precedes the metaphenomenal; in necessary existence, the latter precedes the former. The phenomenal is first known, but it could not be known at all in its actual state, unless the metaphenomenal had had a prior existence: and as the universal belongs only to the metaphenomenal, the universal and particular come into the same conditionating relations. The particular is first known, and yet it could not be known at all unless there had been a necessary prior existence of the universal. The phenomenal, are first *appearances* in time: the metaphenomenal, cause them by a necessary spontaneous power. The metaphenomenal existed out of the relation of time, and independently of it; when the phenomena were given in this relation, then the condition was supplied, under which, the metaphenomenal could be apprehended by an act of knowing standing in this relation also.

SECTION X.

IDEAS THE LAST AUTHORITY OF ALL JUDGMENTS OR KNOWLEDGES.

A JUDGMENT or knowledge is an affirmation of the reason. When expressed in language, it becomes a proposition; because, it then passes beyond the sphere of the individual consciousness, and is propounded to general thought.

Every proposition consists of a subject and predicate. The subject is that of which the affirmation is made. The predicate is that which is affirmed of the subject. The affirmation is either positive or negative; that is, an affirmation of agreement or disagreement.

Fixing the mind upon the question of agreement or disagreement, it is evident that there are only two ways in which it can be determined,—namely, by deduction or by intuition. If by deduction, then the subject and predicate are compared by means of a third or middle term, with which they both agree; or with which one disagrees, and the other agrees. This forms the syllogism, which will be analysed hereafter. But a question arises, respecting the agreement of the two terms with the third, respectively:—Is this known by deduction or by intuition? If by deduction, then we have had a previous comparison subsidiary to the one in hand. But, again, how was the agreement seen in this previous comparison,—by deduction, or by intuition? If by deduction, then there must have been a comparison still more remote. Thus, A agrees with B, because they respectively agree with C. But A agrees with C, because A and C respectively agree with X. And B agrees with C, because they respectively agree with Y. Again, B agrees with Y, because they respectively agree with Z ; and so on.

It is manifest that this series of retrogressive deductions cannot be continued *ad infinitum.* We must at last arrive at a point where the agreement is seen, without a middle term, by direct insight or intuition. We thus arrive at what is generally called a FIRST TRUTH,—a truth which neither admits of nor requires a demonstration. Such are the axioms of geometry. Here, then, is a resting-place of thought—here is an absolute authority. The axiom is authoritative, because it is drawn out of the pure reason, and permeated with its ideas. For, plainly, the axiom could not be formed, if the reason were not furnished with the ideas of relation, eqality, and identity. The reason, out of its own thought, and by its own authority, forms the axiom. A succession of comparisons thus conducts us upward to the idea as the last authority.

Let us next view the subject and predicate separately. The subject can be thought of without the predicate ; and the predicate without the subject ;—each being a distinct cognition. Now the question may be started, How do we come by each distinct cognition introduced into the comparison ? And here it may appear upon analysis, that each is the result of a previous comparison ; and still further, the terms which enter into this previous comparison, may themselves be drawn from a comparison lying still farther back. But, as in the former case, the series of comparisons must at length come to an end, and we must arrive at cognitions which are obtained without a comparison of foregoing cognitions. Take, for example, the proposition, Every body is in space. We have here the cognition of body, and that of space: Now, if it were granted that body is derived from a preceding comparison, it is plainly impossible that space could be thus derived. In space, then, we have a simple original cognition. The same must appear in tracing back every cognition. These first elements of thought, whatever they be, must be the foundations of all the subsequent cognitions. If, according to Locke, these first elements were merely the phenomena which form the immediate objects of consciousness, they undoubtedly would be the foundations of all the subsequent knowledges, as he has represented them.

According to the transcendental system, however, the original elements are ideas or simple intuitions of the pure reason, given upon sensuous conditions, but not formed out of them. The truth of the latter system appears upon the last analysis of our knowledges, since this analysis does not give us bare phenomena of the interior and exterior consciousness, but ideas, as the constitutive elements.

We may next view the subject and the predicate in their particular relation to each other. Here propositions take a two-fold designation. They are either *Analytical* or *Synthetical.*

First, the Analytical.* Here the subject contains the predicate; and, in the form of the proposition, the predicate is wound out of it. Nothing more is really said in the predicate than what is implied in the enunciation of the subject; but for the purpose of definition or explanation, that which is implied in the subject, is stated fully and clearly. For example: when we say, *Body is ex-*

* Αναλυω, to unwind or unravel.

tended, the predicate *extended* affirms nothing more than what is implied in *Body*, for body is inconceivable without extension. The immediate basis of every analytical proposition must, therefore, be the cognition expression in the subject. Then the question comes up next, What is the basis of the cognition itself? And here, as before, we are carried back to some original element lying in the reason, or in the sense, or in both. But as the sense cannot supply the constitutive elements of the cognition, but only its condition, we are inevitably led to assign the idea of reason as the last authority and basis of all propositions of this class.

Secondly, the Synthetical.* Here the subject does not contain the predicate, but the latter contains a distinct cognition, which is added to the former for the enlargement of the thought. For example: when we say, *every body gravitates, or has weight*, the predicate is not contained or necessarily implied in the subject, for body, as a resisting and extended substance, is a possible cognition before the knowledge of gravity is attained; and this gravity is a new cognition, attained and joined to the former, in some other way. Now, there are but two ways by which the new cognition can be attained, viz.: by observation, or by intuition. Hence arises the distinction of synthetical propositions into *à posteriori* and *à priori*.

That *every body gravitates* is a synthetical proposition *à posteriori*, because we gain the cognition contained in the predicate by observation, or sensuous experience projected into the outer world, and revealing the secondary phenomena. But even this predicate does not find its ultimate authority in the observation itself, since the obser-

* Συντίθημι, to put together.

vation could not have been moulded without the *à priori* cognitions of space, cause, and substance. The *à posteriori* only gives us the sensuous fact which appears first in a succession in the relation of time; while the *à priori* gives us the constitutive idea.

Synthetical propositions *à priori* are those whose predicates are attained by direct intuitions, and without the intervention of any sensuous experience. For example: *Every phenomenon must have a cause.* Here, not only is the predicate not *unwound* from the subject, but no observation of phenomena in any succession whatever can afford any suggestion or type of it. The phenomena reveal only phenomena to observation: but these being given, the reason supervenes and reveals the idea of cause by its own insight and authority. Hume, indeed, very consistently affirms that there is no cause demanded or really existent, because he admits no elements of thought beyond the phenomena themselves. But unless we adopt this bare statement—for philosophy it cannot be called—we must make the synthesis of *cause* in the above axiom, by intuition of reason alone—that is, either the predicate is nothing, and the proposition absurd, or the basis is an *à priori* principle.

It appears, then, from the preceding analysis of propositions, that whether we consider them in the comparison of the subject and predicate, of which they are composed, or in the deduction of the terms taken separately, or in the particular and interdependent relations of the two terms, we are inevitably in the last result led to the ideas of the reason as the last authority on which they rest. But inasmuch as every form of knowledge and belief, when expressed in language, takes the form of a proposition, it must follow that the ultimate basis of all knowledge and belief must be the ideas of the reason.

In making our last appeal to Reason, we are not wanting in reverence to the Great God our Maker. On the contrary, we are bowing before him with the profoundest homage : for the ideas revealed in our reason, are there implanted by Him—are his own voice within us. And when by holy prophets he sends us a special revelation beyond and above that which is given naturally in the constitution of our reason, we receive it, both because it claims to come from the Infinite Reason by attending signs and wonders addressed to the sense, and because it contains everywhere, in its great truths, provisions and duties, the resplendent marks by which we cannot but recognize its source. It is as if, seeing with a clear vision the whole pathway up to the vestibule of Heaven, when the gate of Heaven itself is opened upon us we know that we are witnessing no illusion, for although new visions burst upon us, we feel assured they are those to which such a pathway must lead us.

SECTION XI.

DIVISIONS OF PHILOSOPHY.

The pure objective depends upon the subjective—the phenomenal upon the metaphenomenal. Hence the latter, as sustaining and accounting for the former, becomes the material of philosophy.

Now, in the most general conceptions which we form of the subjective and metaphenomenal, we have,

First : Substance, endowed with faculties or functions, and causes or forces.

Secondly : Laws, or that which determines and regulates the manifestations and movements of the first.

Philosophy in relation to the first, in accordance with old usage, we shall call Metaphysics.*

The second,—if we may venture to frame a term—we shall call Nomology.†

I.—METAPHYSICS.

Metaphysics treats of that which, as actually existent and productive or creative, lies beyond the physical, or the merely phenomenal. I think, feel, and will : What is that which thinks, feels, and wills ? What is that which

* Μετα Φυσικη, i. e., beyond the physical.

† Νομος λογος, i. e., the doctrine of law.

lies beyond the mere phenomena of the thoughts, feelings, and volitions? Again: through my senses, and my muscular organism, I attain to an exterior world, whose forms I call material. What lies under or beyond these primary and secondary qualities, and these various forces? What accounts for these changes—these perpetual modifications? In the development of my being, I am presented with the *physical* or *phenomenal*; and the enquiry is, What is the *metaphysical* or the *metaphenomenal*, which is to account for my development in this direction?

The answer to these enquiries is given by PSYCHOLOGY, DYNAMICS, ANTHROPOLOGY, and ONTOLOGY. These may be considered as the divisions of metaphysics, and subdivisions of philosophy.

PSYCHOLOGY.

Psychology * is that part of metaphysics which accounts for all the phenomena of consciousness, in so far as they are modifications or manifestations of the subjective simple.

In Psychology, we have the whole being of man given in its inherent powers and faculties, and in its relations to God and the world. In Psychology, we effect the analysis of the reason, and arrive at its eternal and absolute ideas. In Psychology, therefore, we find the basis of Logic, Esthetics, Morals, Politics, and Religion, and of Science generally. That the above is strictly true, any one may realise to himself by reflecting upon the operations of his mind, when endeavoring to attain to any knowledge whatever, or when endeavoring to execute any thing, or when disciplining himself to any state or condition of the pas-

* Ψυχη λογος, the doctrine of the soul.

sions. All his thinking, purposing, and willing, and all his discipline of the passions, lie within his consciousness, and are inseparable from himself. Whatever he may attain to as really exterior to himself, becomes his, only by some modification of himself in relation to it.

What is the psychological method? It is to examine the facts of consciousness, and by these to arrive at the faculties and compass of our being. It is by facts of consciousness that we arrive at every thing; and yet there can be no facts of consciousness without bringing to view the *simple subjective*. My aim may be to arrive at something belonging to the subjective general, or at something belonging to the purely objective, but still, I, the simple subjective, am there permeating the whole—I am there thinking, imagining, remembering, comparing, generalizing, reasoning, determining, exerting causality, or putting forth emotions and desires: and whatever else I may arrive at, I do not arrive at it without a further development of my own faculties, without knowing something more about myself. Indeed, I do not only in this way perpetually see myself, however I may be engaged, but my own faculties assume to me the importance of measuring to me the universe: I can know only upon condition that I have the faculty of knowledge; and however abundant may be the objects of knowledge, the number and perfection of the cognitions must depend upon the capacity and vigor of the cognitive faculty.

But although Psychology, as embracing the science of our mental constitution and its faculties, embraces in some sort all science, since whatever is known, is known by these faculties, and since in every act of knowing, feeling, or doing, these faculties are brought to light,—still it is clearly distinguishable, as a particular branch of Philosophy. It is strictly the doctrine of the mind as a distinct entity—the doctrine of the simple subjective :—in fine, it is self-knowledge.

When through the phenomena of the mind we have arrived at a knowledge of the faculties of the mind, together with their characteristics, their distinction, their relations, and their unity, we have arrived at Psychology.

DYNAMICS.

Dynamic* Philosophy treats of the life and working powers of nature. On every side we see the forms of a universal life—in the myriads of the animal and the vegetable tribes. Everywhere, also, powers and energies are at work, in large masses and in small, as presented in the vast forms of astronomy, in the winds and tides, in magnetism and electricity ; and in the minute forms of chemical affinities. It is impossible for us to reflect upon the productive life of nature, and the forces at work in nature, without enquiring after their origin, their dependency, their centre. In this enquiry the mind is irresistibly led upward to the infinite and absolute life, and the infinite and absolute power. Dynamic philosophy ends its enquiry in God, who filleth all in all.

We have before us the distinction between the *phenomenal* or purely *objective*, and the *metaphenomenal* or *subjective.* We have also the subjective as embracing the energies of thought, will, and feeling, as found in myself, and in other beings like myself, both of the finite and infinite degree ;—and the energies, life, and forces at work in material masses, those masses which are extraneous to

* Δυναμις, energy or force.

me, and known to me by their correlations with the sensitivity as given through the five senses, and by muscular resistance.

Now it is plain from this, that Dynamics expresses in relation to this life and energy working in extraneous material masses, what psychology expresses in relation to the faculties working within the substance of the mind. Assuming here the distinction between material and immaterial substance, we may say of Psychology that it treats of the faculties or powers which produce or develope the phenomena given in connexion with immaterial substance; and of Dynamics, that it treats of the faculties or powers which produce or develope the phenomena given in connexion with material substance. In both we begin with the phenomenal, and arrive at the subjective as accounting for the phenomenal. We may sum up the whole by saying, that Psychology respects the subjective faculties of the mind; Dynamics respects the subjective powers of matter.

ANTHROPOLOGY.

Anthropology* takes up man in the union of his spiritual and simple subjective being, with a physical and animal life and organism.

View man in his mere animal nature and functions, and he appears different from all other animals. The spirit within, modifies, enlarges and ennobles the animal without—he is the most glorious and interesting of all animals.

This animal nature is also affected variously by the external world with which it is linked, and, indeed, of

* Ανθρωπος and Λογος, the doctrine of humanity.

which it forms a part: climate, natural scenery, food, and employment, all act upon it. It is thus modified at the same time by the spirit within, and by influences from without.

On the other hand, the animal thus closely communing with spirit, reacts upon the spiritual sphere. The most susceptible point of this reaction is the sensitivity, through which the emotions and passions become strikingly modified. In every theatre, therefore, of human passion —in social life, in government, in war, in commerce, in the arts of beauty, you may see the influcnces of the external nature. But inasmuch as man is a unity, this modifying action cannot be exerted upon his sensitivity, without reaching in some form and degree his entire being; so that his thinking and reasoning, his free activity, and even his moral character, gain a tone from the objects which surround him, and show the complexion of the sun which shines, and the atmosphere which breathes upon him.

Anthropology is thus a union of Psychology and that part of Dynamics which informs the science of physiology. Indeed, as actually cultivated, it is hardly a pure philosophy, but rather a mixture of philosophy, physiology and natural history. In its determining elements, however, it is strictly philosophical.

ONTOLOGY.

After having considered the life and forces belonging to the pure subjectivity of being, as distinguished from the phenomenal or the pure objective,—we come next to consider the SUBSTANCE of being. The idea of substance, like the ideas of time and space, of cause, and of right and wrong, is intuitively given in the reason.

Upon the observation of phenomena, we not only assign them *causes* and *laws*, we also assign them *substance.* Substance is therefore metaphenomenal, and belongs to subjectivity in general; and hence the consideration of substance forms a part of philosophical speculation.

Metaphysics, as relating to substance, is ONTOLOGY.*

To Ontology belong such questions as the following: —What is substance? Is substance distinguishable from its properties? Do substance and properties necessarily imply each other? Is the relation between substance and properties to be distinguished from the relation between cause and effect? What are the distinctions and relations of spiritual and material substance? Is the soul material? Is God in his substance identified with the world, or is he extra-mundane? What are the relations between infinite and finite substance? Is space substance or attribute? Is it to be referred to matter or spirit, or is it independent of both? Does the omnipresence of God suppose his essence of substance to be diffused through all space?

Questions of Ontology do, undoubtedly, exist in the human mind; and because they exist, they require an answer. No question of the mind is to be arbitrarily set aside. If its aim be an impossibility, it must be proved to be so, but as long as a hope of its solution remains, it must remain as a question. Now, a great many vain and idle questions have come up in Ontology, but it was philosophy itself that exposed them, and set them aside. On the other hand, many questions of the very last importance are presented here. Whether the soul be material or immaterial; whether God be identified with the world,

* Ουτος and Λογος, the doctrine of essential being.

or be extra-mundane, are not trifling questions, as the history of philosophy abundantly shows. If Ontology could arrive at nothing positive, its negative decisions would for ever give it an important place in philosophy.

We have distinguished the subjective and the objective; the latter the phenomenal, the secondary and dependent—that which consciousness directly recognizes, and which requires to be accounted for, by referring it to something antecedent: The former, the metaphenomenal, primary, independent,* not directly recognized by the consciousness, and which does not in like manner require to be accounted for.

The subjective general is that which accounts for the pure objective. This is their relation. Thus the will accounts for all choices and volitions; and is subjective in relation to them taken as the objective. Thus the sensitivity, in connexion with its external correlates, accounts for all the sensations; and is subjective to them taken as the objective. Thus the reason accounts for all acts of perception, knowing, and reasoning; and is subjective to them taken as objective. Thus the extraneous physical powers account for all the phenomena of matter; and are subjective to them taken as the objective.

In considering the relation of the subjective to the objective, we say generally as above, the former accounts for the latter. But the enquiry may still come up, How, or

* I do not mean here to exclude the fact, that both the powers of our own minds, and the extraneous physical powers, require and are dependent upon the First and the Infinite: I mean only the inherent and constituted sufficiency of these in relation to their proper phenomena.

under what forms, does the former account for the latter? Is it sufficient to say it accounts for the latter simply as the subjective? May not the subjective itself be presented under different relations to the objective? Unquestionably, there are two different relations which may be named and distinguished, viz. the relation of SUBSTANCE AND PROPERTIES, and the relation of CAUSE AND EFFECT. The subjective may be taken as either substance or cause; the objective may be taken as either property or effect. Cause is self-determined, creative, and contingent activity. Substance is fixed, and, relatively at least, necessary existence. Cause can be thought of as having potentiality to a variety of effects, without being connected with any particular effects as its necessary manifestations. Substance cannot be thought of without implying certain properties as its necessary and fixed manifestations. Effect begins to be after cause exists. Property is co-existent with substance from its beginning. Effect is related to cause contingently. Property is related to substance necessarily.

Again: Substance cannot be given without involving in some way the idea of cause. If it be finite substance, it is caused. If it be infinite substance, causality is conceived of as inseparable from its unity. Universally, immaterial substance or mind involves causality. Material substance, besides being itself caused, is the vehicle or medium of the manifestations of causality, either directly or indirectly: directly, if physical powers be taken as proper causality; indirectly, if they be taken as the properties of substance. On the former hypothesis, the Divine causality absorbs the supposed physical, and is all-pervading and omnipresent. On the latter hypothesis, the Divine causality is taken as having produced a certain form of substance, that is, material, different from the Divine substance, and constituted with these physical forces, as fixed and inseparable properties. On the former hypothesis, matter is represented as inert until permeated by activities; on the latter, it is inseparable from activities. For example: on the former, gravity is distinct from matter as a cause, and interfused by special constitution; on the latter, matter cannot be conceived of without gravity, nor gravity without matter. But not only does substance involve the idea of cause; cause also involves the idea of substance. Cause cannot be separated from mind, and mind cannot be conceived of without substance. This is true both of Will, directly recognized as such, and of physical powers, when taken as causes proper.

Taking the Subjective, then, as divided into Cause and Substance; and the Objective, as divided into Effects and Properties, the latter springing from the former, and being accounted for as existent, by being referred to the former, the enquiry arises, *How* do the latter spring from the former, or *what regulates* the action of cause, and the development of substance?

II.—NOMOLOGY.

This at once introduces us to the Doctrine of Law, or NOMOLOGY, which is the second grand division of philosophy. Nomology treats of the laws, according to which the subjective *ought* to cause effects and develope properties. It also explains the possible violations of these laws.

Nomology is divided into the MORALE; ESTHETICS; SOMATOLOGY; and LOGIC.

THE MORALE.

This comprises the laws which *ought* to govern the Will—the laws of *duty*, the laws which command what is *due*—what *ought* to be done in moral relations. If all causality is resolvable into Will,* then the MORALE is related to all creations, whether by the infinite cause, or by finite causes.

The laws of duty, however, must be distinguished from the rules of art. The first enjoin upon us what ought to be done in our moral relations, or in our relations to mind, embracing what is due to ourselves, to others, and to God. The second, point out *how* any rational, ingenious, useful, or esthetical design is to be effected.

ESTHETICS.

Esthetics † may be briefly defined the '*Philosophy of the Beautiful.*' As the *Morale* relates to the will, so this relates to the sensitivity. As the *Morale* determines what *ought* to be done in the moral relations; so this determines what *ought* to please, or what is really agreeable to the sensitivity in its unperverted and rightly developed condition.

There is in some sort an interchange between the Morale and Esthetics. Esthetics lays down the rules of the fine arts to the executive will. The Morale enjoins upon the sensitivity the proper moral emotions and desires.

Esthetics comprises the principles and laws of the beautiful, or of the agreeable, or of taste, (for all this variety of designation has obtained,) not only in relation

* Doctrine of the Will, p. 294.

† Αισθησις, perception or sensibility.

to the actual, but also in relation to the possible. That which *may be* is known, and the influence of its beauty felt, as well as that which *is*.

When man awakes to existence, his eye beholds the beautiful, the sublime, the graceful, the proportionate, the congruous; and his ear perceives melody and harmony, with the joy, the ecstasy of one recognizing the thoughts of his own spirit, the reflected forms of his own being. The splendors of the heavens above him—the scenery of the earth around him, are not strange to him; he knows them in himself, and he knows himself in them. But he cannot rest in these delightful contemplations. The fountains of his thought open and enlarge beyond the world which his senses have recognized. It would seem as if this world were presented him to call out the activities of a being, of which it cannot be the measure.

Hence, man creates: he creates in statuary, painting, music, architecture, gardening, poetry, and romance. He does not confine himself to imitations—he *creates*. His creations are not only of that which is possible in this world, but of that also which it requires a more perfect constitution, both physical and moral, to realize; and thus in his thought he knows other worlds. Salvator Rosa gives us nature as she is, with only finishing touches of the ideal; but Milton, in his "delicious Paradise," introduces us to a creation not indeed opposed to nature, but requiring nature under a more genial clime, in more glorious worlds.*

In poetry, and in the fine arts, generally, the ideal of the mind is indeed never perfectly expressed. The poet and the artist labor to make visible the thought upon

* Doctrine of the Will, pp. 130 and 131.

which they dwell in rapture; but they never satisfy their own earnest aspirations,—they have a vision which they cannot reveal to others; and they find that the world, as presented them, not only is not the measure of their being, but also that all the efforts of art cannot make its forms and materials even truly representative of that being; and the perfectly beautiful remains with them as a pure idea, of which they have only been enabled to give a dim reflection.

In Esthetics the human mind seeks to solve the mystery of the arts; it enquires after their origin, their laws, and their method; and seeks to comprehend their reach, and the grounds of their limitations.

This is that beautiful philosophy which leads us far back into the spirit of man, there to find the true Castalian spring, and there to converse with the "Sacred Nine" as living and real inspirations

SOMATOLOGY.

Somatology * holds a relation to Dynamics similar to that which the Morale, Esthetics, and Logic hold to Psychology; it comprises the necessary laws which govern the changes and motions of bodies, as the former do the necessary laws which govorn the mental activities.

It is difficult, however, in its present development, to represent Somatology as a branch of pure philosophy, and to distinguish it clearly from the Science of Nature. In the Morale, there are necessary and absolute laws of the good; in Esthetics, of the beautiful; in Logic, of intuition and ratiocination: but can we say with the same positive-

* Σωματα and λογος, the doctrine or law of bodies.

ness, that there are necessary and absolute laws for determining the relations and changes of bodies? The application of the pure mathematics in solving the problems which arise respecting bodies; the limitations which are fixed to the possible laws of forces now existing—for example, the necessity that the centripetal force should vary inversely as the square, and not inversely as the cube or any higher power of the distance; the fact that great minds, like Newton's, preconceived before they calculated —indeed, that all minds must preconceive before they calculate; and the necessary conception that, amid indefinite variety there still must exist fixed laws, go to show that absolute and necessary laws must somewhere exist in respect to bodies, and that of course Somatology must be a possible and real philosophy.

The difficulty in the way of determining with exactness this branch of philosophy, arises from the vast compass of nature, and the indefinite diversity admissible. It cannot be doubted, however, that Somatological ideas in the form of prophetic suggestions, direct the investigations of science. These ideas unite with phenomena in the inductive process through which science is determined. These were the preconceptions of Newton in determining the law of gravitation; and of Davy in inventing the safety-lamp.

LOGIC.

In the Greek, *Λογος* expresses the faculty of reason or intelligence. *Λογιζομαί* and *Συλλογιζομαι* are the verbs expressing the action of this faculty; the latter being particularly appropriated to express this action in drawing conclusions from premises, that is, syllogizing or proceeding according to the law and formula of the *Συλλογισ-*

μος, the Syllogism. *Λογικὴ* (τέχνη or επίστημη, understood), expresses the science and art of Reasoning, or Logic.

Λογικὴ, or Logic, has, indeed, been represented as a mere art, or at least limited to such forms of representation as to convey the impression of a mere art. It is plain, however, that under its highest acceptation, it must refer to philosophical principles; for if in relation to any part of our being we are stimulated by the *Φιλοσοφια* to enquire after the laws and the method of its action and development, we are thus stimulated in relation to the λογος, or reason.

The Reason is the faculty of knowledge in general. *Logic* expresses in relation to the *Reason*, what the *Morale* expresses in relation to the *Will*, and what *Esthetics* expresses in relation to the *Sensitivity*. Reason perceives and knows; seeks and arrives at truth. But what are the laws which regulate its perceptions? What are the methods which it pursues in seeking after truth? What are the ultimate grounds of its knowledges and beliefs? When we have answered these questions, we have Logic completed as a branch of philosophy.

Logic takes precedence of all the other branches of Nomology. The others are all dependent upon it. Laws, whether belonging to the morale, esthetics, or somatology, are all based upon ideas of the reason. But Logic determines the legitimate processes and characteristics of ideas themselves. Again, wherever the reason acts, there must be laws to determine and regulate its action. Logic, therefore, is co-extensive with these laws, for the province of logic is the laws of the reason. But as reason acts wherever there is intellection, it acts in every department of philosophy; and hence logic permeates the whole.

Logic permeates, but does not absorb the whole. Logic is present to give laws to thought, investigation, and ratiocination; but these laws are universal and irrespective of the particular subjects. Each subject, therefore, still retains its distinctive position, characteristics and aims. Psychology still aims to determine the faculties of the mind; Dynamics, the forces of nature; Anthropology, the union of man and nature; Ontology, the reality and distinctions of substance; the Morale, the laws of duty; Esthetics, the laws of the beautiful; Somatology, the laws of bodies. These do not sink into Logic; but as Reason is the universal organ of philosophical construction, Logic is everywhere present as the light and atmosphere of thought.

SECTION XII.

OF THE RELATIONS BETWEEN PHILOSOPHY, AND THE SCIENCES AND ARTS.

PHILOSOPHY and Science are often employed as identical terms. Philosophy, indeed, is science; and science, if not pure philosophy, is closely connected with it. The word science is strictly used in the sense of systematic knowledge in relation to a given and defined subject; and as in every such system, particular phenomena are accounted for and explained, the science puts on very much of the air of philosophy. But what, then, marks the distinction?

One obvious distinction is this, that philosophy is conversant simply with principles; while in a science, principles are applied to a particular subject. In the science of nature, for example, the philosophical ideas of cause and effect, of substance and properties, and general somatological laws, are applied to a particular class of phenomena.

The science begins with the phenomena, as the conditions of its development: and when the phenomena are reduced under common causes and laws, then the science is determined and fixed. But philosophy is taken, to account for the phenomena in the general. First: by affirming that there must be causes and laws: Secondly, by laying down in logic the principles of induction, investigation, and deduction: Thirdly, by conceiving somatological causes and laws, and applying them tentatively to the phenomena.

The subjective and the objective make up the sum of all knowledge, actual or possible. Philosophy finds its elements in the subjective, so that the determination of the subjective is the determination of philosophy. Science is conversant directly with the objective; but it proceeds by the aid of the subjective. Its aim is to distinguish and generalize the objective into particular spheres, under particular causes and laws.

We will suppose the subjective to have been determined—we will suppose the mind to know its own faculties, substance, and laws—and to know the external world in *its* substance, forces, and laws. In making this supposition, we do not mean to imply that the subjective is thus antecedently and primarily completed before science begins. On the contrary, the developments of philosophy, the constructions of science, and the inventions and workings of art, all go on together. But for distinctness of conception, and in order to show forth clearly the relations as well as the differences of the two, we may make this supposition. In making this supposition, I bring myself into possession of Psychology, Dynamics, Anthropology, Ontology, Esthetics, the Morale, Somatology, and Logic. I have named my reason, will, and affections—I have distinguished material and immaterial substance—I have conceived of the universal life in nature—of powers and forces—and of laws regulating their action. I have in the Morale distinguished the just, the benevolent, and the true; in Esthetics, I have conceived of the absolute laws of beauty, proportion, and sublimity; in Somatology, I have determined the necessary laws of bodies; and in relation to the Reason, I have laid down the formulas of a rigid logic.

Now, what is the passage from the purely subjective to the objective? We shall endeavor to give the answer.

Science is divided into the pure, exact, universal, and absolute, and the mixed, contingent, limited, and variable.

The first embraces the pure mathematics. The mathematical sciences are pure, because incapable of being formed out of sensible representations. They are exact, because never falling short of, and never transcending the principles and axioms on which they are based. They are universal, because never admitting of exceptions. They are absolute, because it is inconceivable that, in any relation, or by any power, they are capable of being changed.

Natural science, on the contrary, is mixed, because, although admitting, nay, demanding the application of the principles of exact and pure science, still it has such material properties, and properties so foreign to the pure science, as to prevent the strict application of these principles. Body is in space, and assumes forms in its conformations, and moves through lines in performing its revolutions, which, in the way of analogy, may be called geometrical; and these forms and lines may be taken as grounds of many important conclusions deduced by means of geometrical principles; but the mathematical astronomer knows full well, and takes care not to neglect the difference, between the pure and absolute geometry of his mind, and the rough sphericity of the planets, and the jagged lines of their orbits. If geometry were a philosophy, then its difference from, and its relations to, natural science, would form an intelligible illustration of the distinctions and relations of philosophy and science.

GEOMETRY.

Geometry, however, is a science, and our first aim is to distinguish it from philosophy, as well as to show its relations to philosophy. The philosophy upon which geometry is constructed, comprises ontology and logic. But ontology enters into it only so far as space is concerned. That space is not body, that it is infinite and necessary; the definitions of the point, of lines, surfaces, and solids, all belong to ontology in the determination of their absolute separation from substance, and their independent and unchangeable verity.

The point is a conception of absolute and indivisible unity. But although a unity, perfect and absolute, it cannot be called a quantity; it is, on the contrary, the absolute negation of all quantity; it is not length—it is not breadth—it is not thickness; but it is where quantity begins. We assume this point in space, by our thought, and then quantity is supposed to be formed in *one* direction; and the least departure from the point, in one direction, forms the line or simple extension. This line must of necessity be curved or straight. Then quantity is supposed to be formed in *two* directions; and the least departure from the point in two directions forms length and breadth, or surface. Surface, likewise, must of necessity be either plane or curved. Then, again, quantity is supposed to be formed in *three* directions; and the least departure from the point, in three directions, forms length, breadth, and thickness, or the solid. Solid, again, must of necessity be composed of plane or curved surfaces. Quantity, as thus conceived of, is exact quantity, because it has absolute limitations.

This conception of quantity is a pure ontological conception of the reason—not ontological positively as defining a particular substance, but negatively as defining a quantity absolutely independent of substance.

Having the pure quantity thus given, we may now begin to use it for the purpose of scientific construction. And now come in the other philosophical elements, viz.: —those belonging to Logic. There are, 1. The axioms—the conceptions of agreement and difference—of equality and inequality—of a whole and its parts—of measure and proportion. 2. The deductive formula.

As far as the conception of space, of the point, of the pure quantity, and of the logical elements goes, we have simply philosophy. But when we proceed to construct out of this pure quantity a variety of definite figures, and to consider their particular relations, and to apply to them the logical axioms and formula, for the purpose of eliciting particular conclusions in the form of regular propositions or theorems, we give birth to determinate science. It is true, indeed, that the conclusions of geometry are universal and absolute, and therefore it cannot be questioned that geometry is a most philosophical science; but, nevertheless, it is justly considered a science, inasmuch as antecedent principles are applied to a particular material or subject, which principles are true, wholly independently of the subject to which they are applied. All the axioms and the logical formula, are manifestly of this character; and the conceptions of a point, and of pure quantity beginning there, although more immediately connected with the geometrical constructions, are, nevertheless, independent and general:—A point—a line—a surface—a solid, may be thought of independently of all particular forms, relations, and propositions.

While thus the philosophy and the science are distinct,

the relation between the two is most intimate and important. The philosophy may exist without the development of the science; but the science cannot be formed without the philosophy. The philosophy does not require the science, either to account for it, or to make it more plain; but the science refers directly back to the philosophy as its only basis, and affording the only means of its explication.

SCIENCES OF DISCRETE QUANTITY.

Arithmetic and algebra, in like manner, have their philosophical basis. They do not begin with absolute unity in forming their quantities; the idea of unity as a philosophical idea, is antecedent to, and independent of, these quantities; but although their unit, always assumed and ever variable, cannot represent the absolute and invariable unit, still it has its origin as a conception of unity in the absolute and pure idea. Here, also, we have universal axioms, conceptions of abstract quantity, of equality, difference, measure and proportion, and logical formulæ. When we come to apply these antecedent and independent elements of thought, and primary conceptions, to the relations of a particular class of quantity—to *discrete* quantity, for the purpose of arriving at particular solutions and theorems, we construct a science; and, indeed, we may be almost said to invent an art—an art of representing quantities and relations, of giving deductions in detail, and of solving problems.

Here, again, the distinction between the philosophy and the science is clear, as well as the intimate and important relations between the two. It must be evident, also, that the same philosophical ideas and principles, give birth to distinct sciences, as in the case of geometry and arithmetic. The distinction of these sciences is grounded upon the distinction of their subject matter. The subject matter in both is quantity ; but in one it is *continued* quantity ; and in the other, *discrete* quantity ; or the one is quantity, beginning at an absolute limit, and increasing itself by extension in space ; the other is quantity beginning with any assumed unit, and increasing or diminishing itself indefinitely, by addition and division. In the one, we consider the relations of figures formed of lines and surfaces ; in the other, the relations of numbers, as abstract and universal quantities, capable of representing any real quantities whatever, on condition that these quantities be divisible into units. In respect of both, we have the same general ideas, axioms and logic.

NATURAL SCIENCE.

I shall take this as a general designation, embracing Mechanics, Astronomy, Magnetism, Hydrostatics, Physical Dynamics in general, Chemistry, and so on.

I do not intend to convey the idea, that every thing thus embraced under this designation, is strictly scientific ; there is much that is still theoretic. I comprise them all under this designation, because they refer to phenomena, which in their *psychological* relations are of one *kind.* All these phenomena, are *phenomena of sensation,* or of muscular resistance, which is closely connected with sensation. The quantities of geometry and arithmetic, and of the pure mathematics generally, have an existence wholly independently of the senses ; but all the forms, movements, and phenomena generally, of natural science, are made known in the consciousness by the correlations of external substance with the senses, or by a resistance to the muscular organism. By careful and repeated observations, that is, by addressing our senses to their correlative objects without,—by investigations and experiments,—we acquaint ourselves with the various sensuous phenomena, and their characteristics. These phenomena are next classified by resemblances and differences, and by common relations; and are attempted to be explained by the assignment of causes and laws. In making this assignment we may at first merely hypothesise the causes and laws: the system built up in this way is merely a theory, and not demonstrated science. A theory is taken up for the time being, with the understanding that it is subject either to be confirmed, or to be wholly set aside, accordingly as more extended experiments and observations shall enable us to decide. A science has for its basis, not mere hypothetical causes and laws, but causes and laws demonstrated and fixed.

Now, in constructing a natural science, we have recourse both to philosophy and to pure science.

1. We have recourse to philosophy. Ideas of time and space;—of substance and attributes;—of cause and effect;—of law;—of quantity, relation, measure, and proportion; ideas of distributed life and distributed causality; of central, and diffusive movement; distinctions of the subjective and the objective, and of personal and impersonal manifestations; the conception of generic wholes, and specific differences; ideas of unity, multiplicity, and totality; the relations and distinctions of the finite and the infinite; a knowledge of logical formulæ; a knowledge of mind, as the seat of all power, wisdom, design, and government—all work together in the scientific construction. It is impossible to step forth into this wide field of natural phenomena, without having *metaphysical* and *nomologi-*

cal questions crowded into the mind ; and every attempt, whether to build up a theory or a science, is made upon the basis, and in the light of philosophy. These first ideas, principles, and distinctions, are presumed by every one ;—the mind elaborates science under their spontaneous influence, even where they are not defined and comprehended in known, philosophical systems.

2. We have recourse to pure science, or the mathematics. The mathematics are the science of pure quantity —of simple extension from the absolute point ; and of abstract number. But physical bodies take upon themselves forms analogous to geometrical forms ; and move in lines analogous to geometrical lines : their distances, magnitudes, densities, temperatures, attractions, velocities, times, &c., are capable, also, of being represented comparatively by numbers. It is evident, therefore, that mathematical principles may be employed in the determination of physical relations and laws. But still, should conclusions drawn on mathematical principles respecting bodies, assume the perfect geometrical form of bodies, or regard them as pure and exact quantities, there would, of necessity, be error in the conclusions. The mathematics are conversant with pure space and abstract number; but body has properties entirely foreign and peculiar. Hence, in the determination of physical science, there is not an absolute, but a conditional application of mathematical principles. It is thus that the *mixed* mathematics are produced.

It thus appears, in natural science, that the *material* of the construction is that part of the objective, embracing the sensuous phenomena ; that the *ultimate grounds* of the construction lie in pure subjectivity or philosophy ; that the preparations for the construction are experiment, observation, and classification; and that the immediate organon of the construction is the mathematics. Deductive and inductive logic are, indeed, employed in the construction, but not as an immediate organon; they are a part of the all-penetrating and governing philosophy—the deductive logic pervading the mathematics throughout, and the inductive appearing in the determination of every general principle from particular observations.

Let us now sum up the preceding observations. PHILOSOPHY is the knowledge of the subjective, the absolute, the primary, and the universal;—SCIENCE is the knowledge of the objective within particular spheres, under philosophical conceptions, and with laws determined in relation to particular phenomena. Philosophy is complete without phenomena: Science must be constructed out of phenomena. Philosophy comprehends: Science is comprehended.

CONDITIONAL AND UNCONDITIONAL SCIENCE.

Geometry can have no relation to phenomena of the exterior consciousness—it cannot be constructed out of these phenomena. But to the phenomena of the interior consciousness it is related—it is constructed out of these phenomena. We have seen that after the formulæ of logic, the idea of space, and the conceptions of a point, and of quantity, in one, two, and three directions are given, as the necessary and the absolute;—the mind proceeds to construct certain definite figures in space, and to consider their relations in the light of the principles already developed; and so, also, with respect to discrete quantities, it proceeds to the formation of signs and symbols as representatives of these quantities and their general relations; and proposes to itself various problems for solution. This particular and definite action of the intelligence presents us the phenomenal of the interior consciousness.

The principles and conceptions above referred to, are independent, primary, and necessary; and the action of the intelligence in comprehending them as knowledges, is accounted for only in the fact that they are essential and inseparable elements of thought. The intelligence cannot think without logic: it cannot form cognitions upon sensation, without space—and the very idea of space involves the point absolute, and extension in three directions; number—as the one—the many—the total—is no less a necessary element. The intelligence within its actual relations and conditions cannot go into action without them. But it is not necessary that it should go on to form the triangle, the circle, the sphere, the polyhedron, and problems in discrete quantity; when it does so, it presents phenomena to the interior consciousness which demand to be accounted for by something antecedent; and when the antecedent principles are appealed to, these phenomena become a material out of which exact and pure sciences are constructed.

Reflection will show the analogy between this case and that of natural science, in its relation to the exterior consciousness. Cause and effect, substance and attributes, space, law, designing and governing mind—we cannot suppress the ideas of these amid the phenomena of nature, the intelligence cannot form its simplest cognitions independently of them. Neither could the objects of our cognitions be supposed to exist without these. But these primary ideas and principles can be supposed to exist without our particular cognitions and their objects. Now, our cognitions of the external world, by our sensations, are the phenomena* which, by philosophical principles, and the organon of the mathematics, we form into natural science. In the same way, by philosophical principles, and by logic in particular, do we form pure and exact science from our cognitions of these forms of space, and numerical problems. The science in both cases lies in the determination of particular laws governing particular relations.

In the case of the pure and exact science, the law is absolute and unalterable: but this arises from the nature of the object of the cognition :—forms in space, generated from the absolute point, and abstract numbers, are ojects given in the pure reason, and are, therefore, as absolute and unchangeable as the reason itself: but bodies in space are objects given in sensation, and because contingent, are capable of indefinite changes. While, however, the present constitution of bodies remains, the laws demonstrated of their particular relations must remain. In the one case, the law determined is universal in the particular relations of the quantities, unconditionally, because the quantities themselves are absolute: in the other case, the law determined, in the particular relations of the quantities, is universal, conditionally, because the quantities themselves are contingent.

This, obviously, lays a ground for a distinction of the sciences.

I.—UNCONDITIONAL AND ABSOLUTE SCIENCE.

This embraces, as we have seen, the pure mathematics.

* The secondary phenomena: vide Sec. VIII.

To this may be added the science of ethics, or the determination of particular laws for the particular relations which moral and responsible beings stand in to God, to each other, and to inferior beings. As these relations are immutable, so the science formed by the application of general philosophical principles to the phenomena appearing in them, must be immutable likewise.

The science of the civil law, or jurisprudence, is also to be ranked among unconditional sciences, because, based upon immutable moral relations. The distinction between ethics and jurisprudence is simply this; Ethics is the science of right and wrong, in its application to the relations of moral beings universally; jurisprudence, in its application to these relations as they appear under a particular government, in a particular state. The laws of ethics belong to man as man; the laws of jurisprudence belong to man as the citizen of an organized commonwealth. In the constitution of government, man cannot lose his inherent nature, and, consequently, cannot be lawfully compelled to violate any principle of necessary rectitude; but, still, in the constitution of government, he, as a moral being, comes into peculiar and marked relations. It is, indeed, true, that in the utmost scope of ethics, jurisprudence would be comprehended within its definition. The usage which has distinguished the two sciences, has not separated or opposed the cardinal principles.

II.—CONDITIONAL SCIENCE.

This exists on condition that the relations of the phenomena remain unchanged. All the natural or physical sciences are of this description. The great laws of Astronomy, for example, accurately determined as they are, and forming a stupendous and glorious body of science, are, nevertheless, science, only while the constitution of the universe remains as it is. Let the relations of the phenomena be changed, and the present science is destroyed. Now, it is plainly conceivable that changes might take place, to an indefinite extent. We can set no bounds to Omnipotence in modifying the forms of physical being and the constitution of planetary systems. The distinctions of right and wrong, the nature of truth, justice, and benevolence, can be changed no more than God himself can be changed; but our thought does not attach the same immutability and necessity to natural forces and laws.

ART.

We have defined Philosophy—we have defined Science—and shown the relation of the former to the latter; but it remains to define Art, and to show the relation which the first two hold to it.

Art, in common usage, is confined to express the exertion of human causality for the modification of bodies according to principles and rules.

The most enlarged idea of art is given in the work of creation itself, by the Almighty and Allwise Creator. The creation everywhere exhibits design, law, and skill. We may, therefore, without any figure of speech, call God the first and Great Artist and Mechanician. He created, arranged, and finished, according to principles and rules which his own exhaustless intelligence supplied. The variety, the number, the nice and elaborate perfection, the beauty, benignity, and glory of his works, exceed not only our actual knowledge, but the utmost flight of our imagination. From the glimpses which astronomy furnishes of the extent and the continual advance of creation, we are irresistibly led to the conviction, that the mind will find new objects to observe and admire, throughout its immortality.

Human art is comparatively a feeble, yet a beautiful copy of the Divine. God formed the substances together with their properties, upon which human skill is exercised. He fixed the laws under which this skill must accomplish its ends. We imitate the beauty of nature, or improve upon it, only by observing these properties and laws. If we attempt to do violence to them, we are not long waiting for a rebuke of our folly, and a demonstration of our weakness. But if we fall in with the suggestions of nature, and work according to the principles and rules on which she has been constituted, then the arts of utility and beauty will appear, rich and manifold, and the human will become both a co-worker with the Divine, and an instrument of completing its projections.

Now, in analyzing human art, we are led to perceive its connexion with both philosophy and science.

1. With philosophy. This appears in the *ideas* under which it works. There is, in the mechanical or useful arts, generally, the idea of utility itself—the idea of improving upon the actual forms and arrangements of nature, and of adapting them more perfectly to our wants, actual or fanciful. This idea is the forecasting thought, and the propelling energy of the reason itself, and hence is an element of pure philosophy.

In the fine arts appear the ideas of proportion, grace, symmetry, congruity, and harmony—forming the complex idea of beauty. This idea leading to all improvements upon the beauty of the existing forms of nature, as in landscape gardening, for example; and to the creation of new forms of beauty, as in statuary, architecture, painting, music, and poetry, has its origin also in the pure reason, and is, therefore, a philosophic element.

2. With science. Science being the determination of the laws governing the relations of phenomena, as they spring forth in succession from causality, the artist, when he undertakes a work, either of imitation or creation, is bound, in the use of materials, and in the arrangement of parts, to observe these laws. He not only works under the inspiration of pure ideas, or, in other words, the conception of the *ideal*, but working in the field of nature, he works in obedience to her material constitution—her fixed properties and laws. In architecture, he works under ideas of proportion, congruity, grace, and dignity; but, at the same time, he must regard the properties of his materials, and pay the utmost respect to mechanical laws. In musical composition, he is, indeed, led on by the ideas of melody and harmony; but in producing and arranging the sounds which form the material of the art, he cannot dispense with physical laws. Similar illustrations may be given in relation to the other fine arts.

That the mechanician, and the inventor of arts of utility, base their operations upon scientific laws, requires no illustrations.

Rules of Art are explicit specifications, expressed clearly in language, and by diagrams, and numbers, with respect to form, measure, proportion, combination, and adjustment. They lay down in simple terms *how* the causality must execute a given work. They direct the application of physical skill.

An individual may be a crude philosopher, and raw and uninstructed in science; but still, he may, by long practice, acquire the skill of obeying rules of art. The philosophy and the science implied in the rules, and from which the rules were deduced, he is incompetent to explain, and does not even comprehend; but skilfully and readily adjusting his physical instrumentality under the simple directions of the rules, he rears the stately temple, or fashions and arranges the curious machinery of the watch. Such men are mere *copyists* or *mechanics.*

SECTION XIII.

REASON, THE ORGAN OF PHILOSOPHY.

PHILOSOPHY is the knowledge of mind and nature in their faculties, forces, substances, and laws; and the knowledge of truth conceived of as independent of all being.

Science is the knowledge of phenomena, as accounted for, reduced under, and regulated by, these faculties, forces, substances, and laws. Art is reproduction, imitation, and creation, by human causality and skill, under the light and authority of philosophy and science.

Phenomena, or the purely objective, are the immediate experiences or objects of consciousness; and are either experiences of the action of pure reason, and simple choice and volition, or of sensations depending upon correlative objects without.

The metaphenomenal, or the subjective general, are the realities of being and truth, which do not form the immediate experiences of consciousness, but are known mediately through these experiences.

Philosophy relates to our whole being: but in constructing philosophy as a system, our whole being does not form the organ of this construction. Philosophy is not a creation of the will: nor is it an outflow of the emotions and passions. There is but one faculty which can claim to be the organ of philosophy, and that is the REASON.

The Reason is the faculty of all perception, whether by immediate intuition, or by mediate representation or deduction; whether of the interior or the exterior consciousness; whether of the past, the present, or the future; whether of the actual or the possible, or of the probable or the impossible; whether of phenomena, or of being and truth; whether of cause or law. All perception and all knowledge belong to this one faculty.

Now that the Reason should perceive the movements or phenomena of the other faculties, and assign them their laws in the *Esthetics* and the *Morale;* and that it should perceive all forms of being and truth taken as objective to itself, [illegible] to present no difficulties. But how does the reason, while perceiving all else, perceive likewise its own acts or phenomena; and while giving out the laws of the other faculties, give out, likewise, its own laws, thereby constructing Logic?

The difficulty here presented, it will be perceived, consists in the fact that the reason must perceive its own phenomena, while, in order to develope phenomena itself, it is engaged in perceiving something objective to itself; it must give out the laws which regulate its own movements, while, in order to develope these laws, it is engaged in determining laws for some other faculty, or in some similar exercise upon that which lies without its own immediate subjectivity. How can I observe my own perceptions and thoughts, and the laws which regulate my perception and thinking, when the acts of perceiving and thinking imply that the reason is intent upon objects? And if the reason be supposed to withdraw itself from objects for the purpose of examining itself, then, again, how can the reason examine itself without calling itself into action by fixing itself upon objects—which is a recurrence of the same difficulty?

The difficulty is to be answered by simply appealing to the fact—the fact of consciousness. In the very act of thinking or perceiving, and when I am drawing conclusions, or forming cognitions, I am conscious of these acts. The reason has this twofold capacity of knowing phenomena, and being, and truth, external to its own subjectivity; and of knowing, at the same time, its own acts and its own subjectivity in these acts. This is spontaneous and necessary self-knowledge.

The deduction of the laws of its own operations, and the construction of logic, can be effected only by *reflection* or philosophical consciousness.

The reason, when it perceives, thinks, or ratiocinates, does so under the consciousness of its own acts, and under convictions of the reality and truth of its operations. Its development begins and goes on to an indefinite extent spontaneously, before it pauses to look back upon its course, in order to trace out the laws of its own movement. In this way, not only had cognitions of an outward world been formed, and many admirable principles in morals, law, and government, been determined, but even geometry itself had been carried to a high degree of perfection, before logical investigation had become ripe. It is, therefore, not merely by attending to our thinking and reasoning in their going on, that we arrive at the laws of logic. In the actual developments of the reason appearing in works of science and art, and in all the institutions of society, there are, as it were, diagrams and charts which the reason can inspect for the purpose of ascertaining its own laws. But, then, even in inspecting these, it renews in the consciousness the original processes; and does not really intermit the exercise of its remarkable function, of knowing the laws of its own movements, while these movements are actually going on in reference to that which is objective to itself. These diagrams and charts are of the utmost importance, because they render reflection more easy, by presenting the work of investigation and deduction as already completed. Under these circumstances, the renewal in the consciousness of the original processes is effected with no great effort, and thus the reason is enabled to bend its strength to acts of reflection and philosophical insight. The difference may easily be conceived of, by supposing Euclid to have engaged in determining the abstract and universal laws of deduction during his first efforts at geometrical construction; or to have completed his geometrical construction under the spontaneity of the reason, and then to have reflected upon the operations of his reason in this construction, for the purpose of eliciting universal laws of deduction.

Taking the reason, then, as the organ of philosophy, how are we to decide when we have attained a genuine philosophy? This question, undoubtedly, is of the highest importance, for a great many spurious philosophies have appeared. In these *prolegomena* to my main purpose, I have no opportunity to enter into minute elucidations; I am only indicating thoughts. It would be no ordinary undertaking, by itself, to determine the *criteria* of a true philosophy:—What, then, can be accomplished in a few pages!—But as an artist, where he is not in a condition to give a finished work, can still, by a few lines and touches, give an intelligible and striking outline, so at least as to attract contemplation, to stir up thought, and to make the beholder desire a perfect picture, or rather to go and examine the original,—be it a quiet scene of hills and plains and flowing rivers, or of wild rocks and woods and cataracts, or the noble ruins of an old and mysterious temple; so here, a few hints and rough-hewn thoughts thrown out may serve a good end, by leading ingenious readers to put forth their thoughts afresh, and perhaps to correct their past conclusions.

SECTION XIV.

THE CRITERIA OF A TRUE PHILOSOPHY.

All that is secondary to philosophy, and dependent upon it, of course requires no other ground. Philosophy accounts for and explains every thing beside itself—it is the final authority.

Hence, there is an empirical way of testing a philosophy. There are a multitude of knowledges abroad among men, generally received and believed—nay, received and believed so confidently, that he who should question their reality, would be regarded as destitute of common sense, and unfit for the duties and responsibilities of society. A philosophy which appears to uphold these favorite convictions—to be the ultimate and unquestionable ground of them, is taken as a well-attested philosophy.

Now, I would not utterly reject these empirical criteria. They have their use, an eminently practical use, and one adapted to the people at large. There are, for example, certain convictions of a moral and religious nature, which widely pervade the human mind, and are the very life of the common social system. Men are tenacious of these, and that for the best of reasons, viz., the close connexion in which they stand to all that is most dear and valuable. It is just and worthy in human nature to cling to any philosophy which clearly appears to sustain high and invaluable beliefs.

But, while making these admissions, we must still insist upon other criteria, lying farther back, and which, indeed, are implied in those which we have above adverted to; and that for two plain reasons: First, The empirical criteria can have no legitimate authority in themselves. This is evident, since the secondary knowledges are assumed to establish that, without which they could have no reality. The secondary knowledges by hypothesis require an ultimate basis—they are not self-evident, they are not necessarily true; but their ultimate basis consists of philosophical principles, and the very principles which they are employed to establish. Now, we may not prove an antecedent by a consequent, and that, too, when it is granted that this consequent requires for its own basis the very antecedent which it is taken to prove.

And if it be admitted that those irrepressible and firm spontaneous convictions to which we have alluded, are an authority and basis in themselves, it will be found upon an accurate analysis that the spontaneous convictions do not arise from the phenomenal and secondary, but from the absolute and primary, which penetrates and sustains the phenomenal and the secondary. For example: One man is observed giving another man a purse of money, and the observer has an irrepressible and firm conviction that the act is right. By why has he this conviction? Because, by supposition, he knows that it is given in benevolence, or in payment of a just debt. Now, the payment of a debt cannot be taken to prove the principle of justice, nor the giving of money to prove the principle of benevolence; but the principle of justice commands the payment of the debt, and the principle of benevolence, the relief of the needy. From observing the benign influences of certain acts, I may commend that philosophy which elevates them into immutable moral principles; but then these benign effects require the existence of such principles in order to account for their manifestation. By inducting phenomena we may arrive at a principle, but the principle arrived at must have had a pre-existence in order to render the phenomena possible. It must not be forgotten that philosophy is incorporated with our proper being; and enlightens, guides, and determines us even when we do not recognize it by reflection, and are too unlearned to name it as formally laid down in systems.

To one untaught in systematic philosophy, a very natural prejudice would spring up in favour of some philosophy named to him, if he were informed that it lay at the bottom of his warmest and noblest feelings and beliefs; but it is perfectly plain that this philosophy, if, in reality, lying at the bottom of these mental phenomena of the individual in question, would really be that which gave rise to these phenomena. This *individual* may be *satisfied* with it, from its supposed connexion with his beliefs and sentiments; but it could never be legitimately determined by such *criteria*. We must determine independently of the individual, whether his beliefs have a true basis; that is, whether they are philosophical or unphilosophical: hence the proper criteria must be independent of the phenomenal of the individual mind.

Secondly, The empirical criteria cannot be legitimate in determining the truth of a philosophy, because, in themselves they do not, in the first place, sufficiently provide against the introduction of error; and in the second place, it is a matter of history that errors have actually been introduced in this way.

In the first place, they do not in themselves sufficiently provide against the introduction of error. Opinions and beliefs may be connected in the human mind with many other particulars besides an innate philosophy. They may be connected with prejudices of nation, family, and sect; with pride, ambition, favorite pursuits and pleasures. If an innate philosophy always governed our opinions and beliefs, then they would always rise above, and be independent of, these other connexions. But so far from this being the case, these other connexions do often exclusively determine them, and in spite of the innate philosophy. It is plain, therefore, that if actual opinions and beliefs are to settle our philosophy, it will not only have an ultimate basis beyond itself, which is absurd in the very enunciation, but this ultimate basis also, will be just as various, mutable, conflicting, and impure, as human passions themselves. It is impossible, then, in this way, to settle what is a *true* philosophy.

But, in the second place, it is a matter of history, that errors have been introduced in this way. The instances of Galileo and Abelard, may be taken as types of a multitude that might be sought out and adduced. Both were severely persecuted for resisting philosophies which had their origin in the prejudices of a learned unthinkingness; and in the pride and ambition of a corrupt hierarchy. The current opinions demanded different philosophies from those broached and expounded by these great apostles of freedom of investigation and thought.

Every man holds certain opinions in common with his nation, his family, his political party, or his religious sect. Are these opinions all based upon sound philosophy? No one would contend for such an absurdity. These opinions conflict with each other; they cannot, therefore, all be true. But if the mere strength of an opinion, and the zeal in advancing it, are to be taken as among the sure criteria of philosophy, then we shall establish a multitude of philosophies at war with each other, and all upon an equally secure basis. Philosophy is a word of such awful and momentous import and authority, that both he who advocates old opinions, and he who attempts to introduce new ones; both the venerator of unchanging institutions, and the reformer and revolutionist; both orthodoxy and heresy; both bigotry and liberalism, will be ambitious of its titles, and of marching under its banners.

From this Babel-like confusion of tongues—from this light rendered murky by the dust and steam of furious conflicts, we must retire to a calm and elevated region, where quiet thought has its home; and where the "light" is "dry" and pure.*

In introducing the criteria of a true philosophy, I will name one thing—not, perhaps, really ranking among the criteria strictly defined, but yet, the invariable attendant of such a philosophy:—It is the quality which characterizes the spirit of the philosophy. Philosophy is truth, nothing but truth, and truth immutable, arrayed in the glory and majesty of her own eternity. Now, that philosophy, which has developed itself in a mind which loves, fears, and adores truth, with a filial spirit; which takes up its cross and follows truth with an entire devotion; which counts all things else, whether they be the prejudices of family, sect, or nation—or old titles of honor won in the service of powerful and honored creeds and dogmas of the church or of the schools,—but loss, for the excellency of the knowledge of truth—counting truth all gain, and confiding in her with heartiness, fearing no evils—willing to endure all trials, and joyfully and certainly ex-

* "Lumen siccum."—Bacon.

pecting a satisfactory and peaceful end,—that philosophy recommends itself at once to respectful and earnest attention, and gives promises which cannot well deceive us. For as God hath made the mind for the apprehension of truth, and hath set forth before it a world of glorious truths for it to apprehend, so we cannot but hope, nay, feel a strong confidence, that an ingenuous spirit, looking out after the marks of truth, humbly, purely, and freely, as the eye, tired of the darkness, looks out for the morning light, will, according to the harmonious constitution given it, find her resplendent presence, and be accepted as her oracle, to make known her laws.

It is worthy of remark, also, that a preparation of mind is necessary, as well for the study of philosophical principles announced, as for undertaking an announcement of them. A genuine philosophical spirit is the pre-requisite of good learners, as well as of good teachers. The want of this, indeed, has been the great obstacle to the inculcation of truth in all ages of the world.

There always have been men of ingenuous and honest minds, and designed by Heaven to be the lights of their age, whose teachings, if the multitude had listened to, there would have been a wide diffusion of wholesome knowledge and pure morality. Thus would the philosophy and ethics of Socrates, as an example among the heathen, and the sublime revelations of prophets and apostles among the chosen people, have revolutionized society, by destroying old, stagnant errors, and bringing in rational and heavenly truths. But it hath ever been the folly of men, that although having eyes to see, and ears to hear, and understandings to perceive, they have chosen old traditions, and familiar errors, before new instructions, simply because these instructions demand at the first an honest confession of ignorance, or impose new labors, or are opposed to dearly cherished prejudices and passions. Bacon, in his great work, has exposed these enemies of new investigations, and revolutionizing truths, where they lie in the human heart. The "Idols of the Tribe," or those prejudices which belong to infirm human nature generally; the "Idols of the Den," or individual prejudices—the idiosyncracies of the man; the "Idols of the Market-place," or the prejudices connected with set forms of speech in the announcement of opinions and dogmas—where venerable phrases are mistaken for grave truths; the "Idols of the Theatre," or prejudices connected with wild and startling, but idle theories. When these "Idols" are worshipped by the philosopher, he can make no new discoveries, unless by accident, and then he will be prone to distort them. When they prevail among the people,—that is, the reading people, those who are seeking for information in different ways, and with different degrees of interest,—solid and rational truths can gain friends but slowly, and are liable to be silenced by the authority of public opinion, the rebukes of the church, or even by the force of civil law.

It holds true in philosophy, as well as in religion, that the sower may go forth to sow, and sow none but good seed, and yet if the hearers be impracticable, the labor will be in vain, and the precious seed will be lost; and it is only in the good and honest heart that truth finds a proper soil, in whose rich depth she sends forth her roots, and springs up an immortal fruit.

In proceeding to the direct enquiries respecting the criteria of a true philosophy, we cannot well avoid adopting as a leading thought, the subject of the preceding section, "Reason the Organ of Philosophy." If reason construct philosophy, she must be immediately conversant with these criteria; and as she is the faculty of all knowledges, she must be the last authority in determining them.

But where shall these criteria be sought for? We have shown that they cannot be empirical. Experience may be the condition of their development—may suggest them; but they, in themselves, must be subjective. Philosophy is subjective and metaphenomenal. The criteria of a true philosophy must be subjective and metaphenomenal likewise. It is evident, therefore, the criteria must be sought for in the pure Reason itself.

I will begin with Logic as an illustration. Logic gives the laws of all ratiocination. But how do I know when I have, in this respect, attained a true philosophy? I do not go to the common, concrete reasonings of men on various subjects. They may confidently believe their current conclusions—they may deem them of the utmost importance: but the aim of Logic being to test the legitimacy of these conclusions, it cannot go to them as criteria. What, then, is my only remaining resource? Why, to go to the Reason itself, and ask it whether these principles can be otherwise than true—whether their falsity is conceivable, or possible? The Reason gives the answer, from its perfect insight or intuition; and beyond this, there can be no appeal. Is there any other way of determining the truth of the "*dictum de omni et nullo?*" Whatever be the philosophical conception—whether substance, cause, proportion, harmony, space, or time;—whatever be the philosophical law—whether of Esthetics or the Morale, or belonging to Logic,—its reality and truth can evidently be settled only by an appeal to the Reason. What the Reason intuitively perceives, and undoubtingly affirms, must be reality and truth. The only legitimate way of arriving at philosophy, is to question the Reason: and so, likewise, the only true method of testing any system claiming to be philosophy, is to bring it in its parts, its relations, and in its constituted wholeness, under the review of the Reason, as the faculty of intuition—of original insight.

I may remark here, that we are claiming in the determination of philosophy, no more than what the mathematician claims in the determination of his science. How shall we test the definitions and axioms of Geometry—except by a direct appeal to the intuition of Reason? Nay, in every step of the long chains of reasoning drawn out from these definitions and axioms, the exact relations and dependencies defy the possibility of error, by submitting themselves to the intuition of Reason.

There is such a thing, then, as appealing directly to Reason, and receiving a reply of more authority than the hearing of our ears, or the seeing of our eyes; since what is generally received as the most exact and unquestionable of all the sciences, continually holds it up to our view. If it belong to the mathematics, much more must it belong to philosophy, which furnishes the ultimate grounds even of this science.

Philosophy, when taken up according to a true method, becomes rigid, exact, authoritative. It is only when wandering from this method, that vague and mutable theories and fancies, which belong neither to heaven nor earth, but which seem grotesquely to partake of both, become philosophies, falsely so called. Indeed, so rife has this tribe of vain and fanciful theorists ever been, that we might adduce in illustration of the emptiness which may belong to a current opinion, the very general opinion, that philosophy is but an ever-changing mysticism, which every new adept may mould to his peculiar fancies.

There have been two classes of men, called philosophers, in all ages. The one, very numerous, and composed of these vain theorists. The other, generally embracing the few, and plainly distinguishable from the former, first, by elevating philosophy from a mere deduction from experience, or a mere expedient created to *answer an end*, to the dignity and permanency of a system formed out of the primary and intuitive perceptions of pure Reason; and, secondly, by the identity of the system itself, exhibiting clearly that the same conception of philosophy, and the same method, was transmitted from age to age, if not in books, yet in the elemental working of the human mind itself; and showing the true philosopher to be a most natural and genuine, although a rare manifestation of humanity.

The criteria are all embraced in the fact of the Reason's authoritative affirmation. They are capable, however, of receiving a specific enunciation.

I. A philosophical truth, in its very nature, is incapable of being defined and demonstrated by any thing going before. The aim of philosophy is, as the ultimate ground of knowledge, to define, demonstrate, and account for that which in its nature is incapable of standing alone, and requires something antecedent to define, demonstrate, and account for it. There must be such primary truths, for if there were not, there would be an infinite *retrogressus* of thought in the labor of defining and proving; there would be no ultimate ground for the repose of enquiry.

II. A philosophical truth must be perfectly clear, and attended with no doubtfulness. It is incapable of being defined and demonstrated, both because it is primitive, and because there really is nothing clearer than itself by which to define and demonstrate it. For example, the idea of space is incapable of being defined and bemonstrated, not only because there is nothing before it, which comprehends it, and therefore adequate to defining it, but also because it is in itself eminently clear and certain. That space exists, I affirm with the utmost confidence. If I attempt to represent space by body, or to attain to its utmost stretch by the multiplication or enlargement of bodies, my mind soon becomes confused; but this confusion arises, not from any obscurity inherent in the idea of space, but from the absurd attempt to represent that under the phenomena of the senses, which is not attained by sensation, and is indeed antecedent to, and independent of, all phenomena.

III. A philosophical truth is a pure intuition of the Reason. It must be seen without doubtfulness—it must be affirmed with a positiveness which admits of no rational questioning in the mind in which it developes itself. But these characteristics belong only to intuitive truth.

IV. Philosophical truths being in a high and peculiar sense, elements of thought, cannot remain unproductive where thought is going on. Hence, a philosophical truth must make its appearance somewhere in the development of humanity. If we seek for it, we shall find it. This cannot well be confounded with the empirical criteria, against which objections have already been urged. These criteria suppose us to begin with phenomena as the basis of the philosophical construction. Here, on the contrary, we begin with the truth as an affirmation of the Reason, and seek for its manifestations. This criterion is especially useful to those who seize a truth because it fills the mind with a sort of inexpressible delight, and kindles it into a lofty enthusiasm, without calmly bringing it under the eye of the Reason. It will serve to dissipate this enthusiasm and delight, and to bring about a sober-mindedness, to call upon such, to search for the manifestations of the supposed truth in the actual phenomena of consciousness.

V. Philosophy cannot legitimately present itself under the form of isolated truths. Reason is one ; and hence it developes its truths woven into a system, and constituting UNITY. That construction, therefore, cannot be received as legitimate, which does not exhibit the most perfect agreement with itself. It will be faulty if its parts appear confused, so that there is manifest difficulty in determining whether any system is aimed to be constituted ; or if the parts being clearly brought out and arranged, they fail to work together, and are incoherent.

VI. Philosophy accounts for all phenomena ; it accounts even for error. Not that the error is the birth of the Reason, for this is manifestly absurd ; but that, Philosophy is adequate to giving an explanation of the grounds, the possibilities, the causes, and the modes of error. A true philosophy, therefore, as a system, will account for the universe as a system. Of course, the reason alone can judge whether the one accounts for the other. We are thus brought back to its simple authority.

The criteria above given must speak for themselves. I believe a careful reflection will lead to their approval in the mind of every genuine and candid philosopher. If all who have engaged in the work of philosophical construction, had governed themselves by these criteria, there would have been little difference among them ; and the world, long ere this, would have witnessed philosophy taking her stand as the *Scientia Scientiarum*, and possessing at least all the clearness and exactness which are claimed by many sciences dependent upon her. But when men are determined to preserve their "Idols" at all events; they are prepared either to discard philosophy altogether, or to make her the mere *tire-woman* of their prejudices and accidental and floating opinions. A theory in physics, a dogma in speculation, a creed in religion, a name or a degree in a mutable world, are permitted to give the leading thought; and hence they seek not for philosophy herself, but only to *philosophise* ingeniously and speciously, in order to satisfy the forms of truth while they preserve the body of error. They are willing to impose upon themselves,—why, then, should they scruple to impose upon others?

PART II.

PRELIMINARY VIEW OF THE REASON.

PART II.

PRELIMINARY VIEW OF THE REASON.

SECTION I.

GENERAL INTRODUCTORY CONSIDERATIONS RESPECTING THE REASON.

THE Reason can be comprehended only by a being endowed with reason. That which knows all things else, must know itself likewise. The very idea of objective knowledge implies self-knowledge.

The faculty of knowledge can be known only through acts of knowing in the consciousness. What are these acts? The answer is easy, for there is nothing more familiar to consciousness. You *know* this book, this chair, this table; you *know* this mathematical demonstration; you *know* this law of nature—the gravitation of bodies; you *know* this rule of morals—love thy neighbor as thyself; you *know* what happened yesterday—that the sun rose and set; you *know* what will happen to-morrow—that the sun will rise and set; you *know* the ideal beauty of a statue or a landscape; you *know* axioms, first principles, and generalizations; you *know* space and eternity. If you ask, What is it *to know?* I reply, Look within yourself—you read there directly what it is. What other answer can you desire—what other answer can you obtain?

If you ask, What is the Reason? I reply, it is that which knows—the *knowing substance*, if you please; or, it is yourself, as far as you are a knowing being. In all this, it is evident that we do not advance beyond the *fact of knowing*, and the conception of the faculty of knowledge in general.

But what, then, is the aim of psychological investigations with respect to the Reason? Does not the whole enquiry end in the simplicity and obviousness of the fact of knowing?

It is, indeed, true, that whenever, and in whatever relations, the Reason is exercised, there is a perpetual recurrence of this fact: a perception is a knowledge; an axiom is a knowledge; a demonstration is a series of knowledges; and all the relations of the parts in the making up of the whole ratiocination, are knowledges. But there must arise, upon the general fact of knowing, many enquiries respecting the various forms, the conditions, the limits, the relations, the characteristics, and the certainty of knowledge; the knowledge of the actual, as distinguished from the knowledge of the possible; the relative determination of knowledge by the inherent powers and forms of the reason, and by the objects of knowledge themselves; knowledge, primitive and intuitive, and knowledge secondary and deductive. All these and the like enquiries must be related to the psychology of the Reason.

The Reason may be regarded in certain points of view, as the cardinal faculty of the mind. It is by knowledge and in knowledge that we live and move and have our being. That I am—that there is any being whatever—and all the interests, relations, aims, and laws of being, can be possible determinations, only on the supposition that this faculty exists.

Hence men generally are prone, in representing mind, to speak of it simply as an intelligence. Let Reason be supposed to be extinct, and all other faculties are virtually extinct likewise. Emotions and passions are dependent upon perceptions for their existence. The Will, although a cause, and self-determined, could not go into action without objects and aims of action.* But the Reason, on the contrary, can be supposed to exist without emotions, passions, and volitions. Intelligence, like a pure "dry light," is conceivable without consequential emotions and volitions; but emotions and volitions, without intelligence, are inconceivable.

The Reason, in its full development, presents us various forms or offices, which by some philosophers are represented as distinct mental faculties. Consciousness, sensation, perception, judgment, abstraction, conception, attention, imagination, fancy, and memory, have all been analysed as distinct faculties. In the actual constitution of the mind, some of these faculties, so called, show largely, when analysed, the action of the Will. This is true particularly of attention, abstraction, and fancy. But as far as they express intelligence, I take them to be all comprehended in the Reason. These are not properly intellectual faculties; but the intellectual faculty, under its different modes, and in its different relations. This I shall presently exhibit. In the outset, let us accustom ourselves to look upon the Reason as one. It indeed

* Doctrine of the Will, p. 138.

exercises various offices; it perceives, it judges, it draws conclusions, it imagines, fancies, and remembers; but it is still the same faculty—it is, in all these, the one and indivisible Reason.

The Reason, as the faculty of knowledge, must have a peculiar constitution—it must be constituted for its office —it must be constituted *to know.* But it cannot know, unlees there are objects of knowledge—unless there is something to be known: and that which is to be known, must likewise have its peculiar constitution and properties. Now, if, on the one hand, the Reason does not make its objects in the very act of knowing them; so likewise, on the other hand, the objects do not make the Reason in the very act of being known. The Reason and its objects may exist in relation to each other, but they exist also independently of each other. I speak now of finite Reason.

In the Divine and Infinite Reason, all possible forms of being and truth must have pre-existed in conception or idea, before any actual development or creation appeared in time or space:—And whatever actual existence or development there ever has been, must be consequential to the forecast, as well as to the causality, of the Divine mind. But in the constituted and finite Reason, there is no dependence of its objects for their existence, upon itself. Every form of truth, every form of being beside myself, would have a perfect existence, although I did not exist. And so, also, although there were no objects for my reason, still, as a real intelligence, it would have its fixed and perfect constitution. Its development would, indeed, be impossible, but it would nevertheless be there, ready to be developed whenever the required conditions should be supplied. This may be illustrated by the analogy of a grain of wheat, or the seed of any plant. Let it be laid up in a granary, and there can be no germination; but let it have soil, light, heat, and moisture, and there springs up "first the blade, and then the full ear." But the seed had its own life and peculiar forms before it was introduced into the circumstances and conditions of germination. The soil, heat, light, and moisture communicated no life, or distinctive forms:—the seed, if wheat, was perfect wheat in and of itself; if some other seed, it was of its kind, perfect in and of itself. The soil, light, heat, and moisture, only supplied the circumstances and conditions of its germination, growth, and fruit-bearing. So the Reason; it is perfect in and of itself—it has its own life, energy, and distinctive forms inherent, inseparable, and independently of all exterior circumstances and conditions. The presentation of objects through sensation, is like soil to the seed; books, conversation, examples, the regular discipline of schools, are like light, heat, and moisture: these are requisite to its germination, growth, development, perfection, and fruit-bearing; but all that comes forth of it, comes forth of its own forms, capacities, and richness, as the Reason.

Now, it is very interesting and instructive to think of the principle of life and the distinctive forms of seeds; and by the aid of the microscope to look within its storehouse of wonders—its preparations for endless propagation and increase! Surely, he who thus thinks and examines, knows more of nature, attains to more truth, than he who merely plants and eats, without seeking any thing further.

But of how much higher moment, to comprehend, if possible, the forms of our own intelligence!

Is it possible to attain to this—can I know the inherent

forms—the fixed and independent constitution of the Reason? Can I find out with what preparations—with what pre-constituted and adapted capacities, the mind begins to know?

The earliest development of Reason must be spontaneous, like the germination of a seed sown in the soil. There can be no self-direction and forecast before knowledge begins. But after Reason has gone out to an indefinite extent among its objects, after it has germinated, sprung up, and increased toward perfection, unlike the plant, it has the power of reflection, or of looking back upon the process of its development, and of separating—at least so far as to establish enquiries—between its inherent and pre-constituted forms and capacities, and the circumstances under which they make their appearance. It has the power of doing in relation to itself, what it does in relation to the plant. Nay, may not its self-knowledge be presumed to be more perfect, since it knows the plant by *observation*, while it knows itself in the interior and most intimate *consciousness?*

The inherent and original forms and functions of the Reason, can indeed be known only on condition of experience; but when known, they are seen to have an *à priori* existence. They are not known *à priori*, understanding by this that they are known independent of experience;—they are known through experience, but as in their nature prior to it, or the experience would not itself have been possible.

SECTION II.

OUTLINE OF THE IDEAS AND FUNCTIONS OF THE REASON.

THE pre-constituted forms or elements under which the Reason forms cognitions, and assigns laws, are called Ideas.

The capacities of the Reason to know in different modes and relations, we shall call its Functions.

Ideas and Functions make up the constitution of the Reason.

IDEAS.

The ideas may be classified in two ways—

First: We may classify them as Ideas which determine our cognitions, and Ideas which determine our activity. Under the first head would be comprised the Ideas of time and space, the finite and infinite, of cause and substance, of quantity and quality, necessity and contingence, and the categories of purely cognitive ideas in general.

Under the second head would be comprised—

The Idea of Utility,—that which gives birth to human industry and all its achievements.

The Idea of Right and Wrong,—that which gives birth to Ethics, Law, and Religion.

The Idea of Beauty,—that which gives birth to the Fine Arts.

The Philosophical Idea,—that which leads man to attempt the explanation of his own development.

This classification, however, does not preserve its particulars entirely distinct, for the last class determine cognitions as well as activities.

We may therefore adopt a second method of classification according to the philosophical divisions given in Part I., Sec. XI. We shall then have,

I. METAPHYSICAL IDEAS. II. NOMOLOGICAL IDEAS.

The first determine our conceptions in Psychology, Dynamics, Anthropology, and Ontology. The second determine laws in the Morale, Esthetics, Somatology, and Logic.

In this classification we accept all Ideas as cognitive in their character; while the last division embraces those only which have the additional remarkable characteristic of becoming laws in the world of objective reality.*

FUNCTIONS.

I. INTUITION, or the function of primary and immediate knowledge. Ideas, Axioms, and First Truths in general, are the objects of this function.

II. SENSUOUS PERCEPTION, or the function of forming cognitions upon sensations or the phenomena of the exterior consciousness.

III. ABSTRACTION AND GENERALIZATION. It is by this function that the Reason, taking up the secondary phenomena, first views particular qualities separately, and then makes them the basis of extensive classifications. The quality is *abstracted*, and then *generalized* as a com-

* Vide Part I., Sec. VII.

mon sign ; and its name becomes the name of the class. Thus are formed genera and species. To this function we are indebted for a clear and distinct knowledge of things, and the formation of a ready and convenient language.

IV. JUDGMENT, or the function of perceiving the agreement or disagreement between two cognitions, united as the subject and predicate of a proposition.

V. INVENTION, or the function of finding out and applying principles and rules for the demonstration of theorems, the solution of problems, and the construction of machines ; and of making experiments for the determination of Science. The imagination acts conjointly with this, by calling up in the mind the images of diagrams, and of models or archetypes of the outward construction.

VI. MEDIATE PERCEPTION, or the function of inferring or deducing conclusions through a mediate cognition, as formally exhibited in the syllogism.

VII. INDUCTION, or the function of examining and arranging the secondary phenomena, so as to determine their causes and laws, and thus to construct scientific systems.

VIII. MEMORY, or the perpetuity of knowledge. The Reason which knows, retains its knowledges. A faculty of knowledge without this power would scarcely deserve the name.

Perhaps memory is too identical with the simplest notion we can form of Reason, to be called a function ; it is rather an inseparable characteristic.

RECOLLECTION is more properly a function. The act of recollection is based upon memory. Its aim is to bring a permanent knowledge within the field of consciousness. The energy of the will in directing and holding the attention, is involved in this act.

Whatever we learn, we learn in certain relations, commonly termed *association of ideas.* Hence, when our past perceptions re-appear, they appear in their original relations, or in relations nearly akin to them. Recollection implies a dim foreshadowing of the knowledge to be recalled in some of these relations ; upon this foreshadowing, the cognitive faculty is steadily fixed, until the whole comes forth in distinct form and fullness.

ATTENTION, which some have set down as an intellectual faculty, is really the energy of the Will exerted over the Reason in its several functions.

IX. IMAGINATION. Under its first and simplest presentation, this is the function of knowing objects which have form, or sensible qualities generally, when the actual sensations no longer exist. Thus in every act of memory, and in every conception of the distant, where the objects were originally known through the senses, the imagination revives the forms and sensible qualities.

Again, the Imagination appears as a mediatory function between the world of Ideas, and the world of the Senses. The Imagination forms upon the Ideas, Ideals or Archetypes, according to which the outward constructions are fashioned and related. Even in respect to the Divine Mind, we cannot but conceive of this function as forecasting and foreseeing the Universe before the creative act took place. The finite artist and mechanician—man, produces his works in the same way.

This appears in the Fine Arts, where the ideal conceptions of beauty and grandeur constitute the models or archetypes of the forms which spring up under the chisel, and upon the canvass, or which speak in poetry. This appears in the inventions of the useful arts, and in scientific discovery; for unquestionably, the imagination forms archetypes of mechanical construction and scientific systems. The Idea is not always strictly followed, and hence the Imagination degenerates into a fickle and wayward Fancy. But, nevertheless, where the Idea does become productive of scientific and mechanical results, this function must be employed.

Nor is the imagination excluded from the sphere of moral conceptions. Whenever man in his various relations and duties becomes the subject of thought, not only is the Idea of right and wrong the determining power of thought; but the ideals of character, also, under the different varieties of moral greatness and beauty, present themselves in the imagination as standards with which to compare the actual, or archetypes to direct the creations of genius.

The highest form of the imagination is the creative. Here the pure Idea generates an Ideal, which, surpassing the beauty of any natural form, inspires the artist to attempt a work of corresponding perfection. Whatever is created, is created according to the Idea. The Imagination is the creative function of the same faculty—the Reason,—which gives forth the Idea.

The Imagination is thus the representative, the mediatory; and the creative function.

Let none be startled or offended, when it is said, that man produces more beautiful proportions and forms than nature. Nature and man are both servants of the Infinite Mind of Beauty and Wisdom. The first works according to fixed and necessary laws, without choice or consciousness; the second works according to the same laws, but with choice and consciousness: the one shadows forth the Divine attributes as the effect related to the cause; the other is the very image of the Divine. Why should not God, therefore, empower the thoughtful hand of man to bring to light certain forms of beauty, which he has not committed to the insensate mechanism of nature? Has not the Idea of the Useful stimulated industry to make nature more commodious and bountiful? And why may not the Idea of the Beautiful inspire Art to make nature more beautiful?

"God has not limited man's knowledge to that which *is;* but has enabled him to perceive that which *may be;* and when he proceeds to modify God's work, he is not a trespasser and a violator, but a more noble instrumental power, by which God gives his creation a higher finish and a more perfect use." *

FANCY is arbitrary imagination, or imagination not governed by the pure Ideas of truth and beauty. It presents us, therefore, not Ideals, but humorous and grotesque images, created by intentional violations of esthetical laws, and incongruous and disproportioned combinations. Beauty and truth have defined and perfect archetypes, and therefore in given kinds, a limited variety; but fanciful creations can have no assignable limit, inasmuch as their very being consists in sporting with all law and rule. †

X. CONSCIOUSNESS, is that function of the Reason by which it immediately knows phenomena. ‡

Consciousness has an exterior and an interior direction. In the former direction, it knows the phenomena of sensation; in the latter, the phenomena of the mental activities beyond sensation. In the exterior and interior consciousness, we have all phenomena whatever, for we have comprehended here all the possible activities of our being.

If we enquire, Whence do the phenomena of conscious-

* Doctrine of the Will, p. 130.

† Ibid, pp. 133, 134. ‡ Vide Part I., Sec. II.

ness arise? the only rational answer that can be obtained is, that they arise conjointly from the simple subjective, and the objective general,—that is, when these form a unition in knowing, feeling, and willing. There can be no act of knowing,—that is, no phenomenon of knowing, unless there be both a faculty of knowledge, and an object to be known, either in the world of pure Reason or of the Sense,—at least, an object which shall be the foundation of the cognitions of the knowing faculty: even dreams, and the wildest imaginings, have some relation to objective reality. There can be no sensations, unless there be both a sensitive faculty and real correlative objects; and the same with respect to emotions and passions. There can be no volitions unless there be both a will or cause, and objects and ends of causation.*

From this unition of the subjective and the objective—unition, but not contact—the phenomenal appears, and is immediately known by the Reason in its function of consciousness; and then follow all the other functions in their due place and order.

SELF-KNOWLEDGE, the affirmation *Ego sum*, I AM, in antithesis to the objective general—the *not myself*—is often represented as a form of consciousness, and thence called *self-consciousness.* This, perhaps, is more justly comprehended in the intuitive function, since the self is not phenomenal, and therefore cannot be immediately recognized by consciousness. It is true, however, that the antithetical affirmation stated above, is the most primitive of all affirmations:—in the very unition of the simple subjective with the objective, by which a first phenomenon is given, the Reason knows the two terms, and makes the

* Doctrine of the Will, p. 138.

affirmation ; and with the consciousness of all subsequent phenomena, the affirmation is continually renewed. There is, therefore, a valid ground for representing self-knowledge as a form of consciousness ; and if properly explained and distinguished, the representation is striking, inasmuch as it expresses the intimate union of mind with itself when it awakes to the knowledge of its own being.*

REFLECTION, is a subsequent form of consciousness. While the common consciousness is a spontaneous and necessary recognition of phenomena, and a necessary self-knowledge, reflection is special and voluntary. In reflection, my immediate aim is to know myself; and it generally implies a proposing to one's self some particular analysis of the mind. In order to affect this analysis, we first reproduce a state of consciousness, or renew former experiences, by bringing into view the correlative objects : and then, in this state of reproduced consciousness, or renewed experiences, we awaken the reason to acts of close attention and thought. This state of mind is exceedingly complex : for the mind must at the same time keep before it, the correlative objects which are to awaken the required phenomena, and bend itself to the work of examining the phenomena in their subjective relations. But, still, let it be remembered that it is complex only as all thought and investigation are complex. In investigating the objective world, we do really produce within ourselves certain experiences or phenomena of consciousness, by means of the senses, and while these exist, we apply to them the Reason, in order to determine the forms and laws of nature.

Spontaneous consciousness embraces our necessary and

* Doctrine of the Will, pp. 1, 2, 3.

natural experiences of the senses, and the mental acts which necessarily and naturally arise in connexion with them.

Reflection, or philosophical consciousness, embraces the experiences produced intentionally in reference to some knowledges to be attained of the subjective or the objective.

SECTION III.

EXPLICATION OF IDEAS.

In the "Introductory View of Philosophy in General," much has been said respecting Ideas, and I cannot but hope some explication of them given in the natural unfolding of the line of thought there attempted. In bringing up this subject in this place directly, my aim is, if possible, in a clear and simple way to give an answer to what has always been regarded and treated as a very difficult question, viz.: What are Ideas? The difficulty which exists, arises chiefly, I think, from the primordial and predeterminative character of Ideas. Here all analogies must be exceedingly distant and imperfect, since Ideas precede every form of cognition. Thus, when it is said that Ideas are the moulds of the understanding, and sensations the materials cast in them and taking form, we have, perhaps, the most striking analogy that can be found; but, nevertheless, how vague the resemblance between the plastic power of material moulds upon material substances, and the action of the first elements of thought in determining cognitions upon phenomenal conditions!

We have spoken of several Ideas incidentally in the preceding pages, such as Time, Space, Substance, Cause, Beauty, Right, and Wrong. Now, the Idea of Time is not Time, the Idea of Space is not Space, the Idea of Substance is not Substance, and so also of the others. Nor, again, are the acts of knowing these Ideas, the Ideas themselves. That is, the Ideas are neither the realities from which they are named, nor the acts in which the realities are known. Time and space are realities; substance, as essential being, is a reality; cause is a reality; the distinction between right and wrong is a reality; infinity and spirit are realities. They *are*, even although I do not know them. But *how* do I know them? The mere experience of sensations does not give them. The Reason knows them by its own force or capacity. The Reason begins to act only when the sensations are experienced; but it knows not only, by consciousness, the sensations; it knows, by intuition, these necessary realities likewise. But what is the force or capacity of the Reason to know the metaphenomenal truths? We say, the Reason has in its own constitution as the faculty of knowledge, ideas of time, space, substance, cause, beauty, right and wrong, and so on; meaning by this, that the faculty of knowledge is preconstituted to know these objective necessary realities; and that, that within itself which capacitates or adapts it to know each of them, is called the Idea of this reality.

The word Idea itself contains no mystery or magical power. It is a word introduced by one of the greatest philosophers who ever thought, and using, perhaps, the most perfect language in which thought was ever expressed. We cannot find a better word for our purpose; and there is, therefore, no good reason for diverting it from its original use, or substituting any other in its place.

We have in the preceding Section divided Ideas into the Metaphysical and the Nomological. The first express the inherent capacity of the Reason to know the Reality of Being; the second, its inherent capacity to know the

Reality of Law. Mere phenomena, apprehended by consciousness, do not give either. These phenomena, as we have seen, arise from objective reality without, and subjective reality within. But what is the relation between the pure Reason, with its Ideas prepared to know Reality, and the phenomena known by consciousness which form the conditions under which the knowledge of Reality begins? Recollect Reality is of two kinds: the Reality of first and necessary truths and principles, relating both to being and law; and the Reality of actual being, having specific constitution and qualities, and reduced under determinate law. Now, under the constitution of humanity, it is not intended that mind should attain to the Reality of truths, principles, and laws, separately from the Reality of actual being. As man is himself reason and sense*—a union of the two Realities above named,—it seems to be designed that both shall be developed in his cognition, consentaneously, and at the same time. The first and second Realities are related to each other in so much as the first is embodied in the second; and man himself being the type of this union, he knows the two in their union. When he first awakes to consciousness, sensations or phenomena of the exterior consciousness first meet him, because thought in humanity is connected with physical life, and this life reveals itself in sensation. These sensations arise from the action of exterior causes upon his sensuous organism—the world without thus makes its approach to the Reason within. Here, then, is the occasion for cognition. If the mind had no cognitive power of its own,—a power expressed by the word Ideas,—if it were a mere passive recipient, then there would be a mere conscious-

* Part I., Sec. V.

ness of sensations, and nothing more : but now these sensations are like telegraphic signals given from the outer world, and the Reason has within itself the key or alphabet wherewith to read them. The Reason can know the world without, because it can know the great truths and laws—the first form of Reality—which are embodied in the world without—the second form of Reality. The first knowledges thus embrace, as we have said, the two forms of Reality consentaneously. The second could not be known at all without the first—it would not be logically possible. The first would not be known without the second, because, in the constitution of humanity, mind is imprisoned in its tabernacle, until the windows of the senses be opened, and the signals of life and being come rushing in.

Let me recur in this place to a thought thrown out in my Introductory View, Section VII. The Great Creator, before he formed the worlds, must have had the Ideas of all truth and law, and all forms of being—He knew, and then created. He foreknew all possible being, because he had the Ideas of all possible being. Man, the finite mind, knows after creation has taken place, and after he has received in his sensitivity, motions from that creation ; but that he knows at all, arises from a Reason made in the likeness of the Divine, and having pre-constituted capacities or Ideas adapted to primordial, universal, and necessary truths—the very truths in which the outer world, indeed the whole world of created being, "lives, moves, and has its being."

That man knows himself, is explained in the same way. He has the Idea of subjective, as well as of objective reality : And as the motions given in his sensitivity from without, and known by consciousness, give the call to the Reason furnished with its Ideas, to look without; so the action of the mind itself gives the call to look within also.

The two forms of Reality, which at first are concrete and complicated, are afterwards submitted to Reflection, and by Reflection distinguished.

It may, indeed, require a high effort of thought to comprehend Ideas; but let this effort be made, and in the whole range of philosophy there is nothing so clear and interesting. Ideas are the elements of thought, the elements of philosophy, because the elements of Reason itself. A Reason without Ideas is an impossible conception. Ideas are the cardinal psychological explication of the Reason

SECTION IV.

EXPLICATION OF THE FUNCTIONS OF THE REASON.

THE Reason, constituted with Ideas, goes into action. Its great office is to know. But the objects of its knowledge are not all of the same kind, do not stand in the same relations, nor under the same conditions. Some of these objects are truths absolute and necessary ; some are phenomena variable and contingent ; some are immediately, while others are mediately perceived ; some precede, while others are gathered from observation ; some are actual, while others are only possible ; some are in time present, others in time past, and others again in time future ; some, in space, are contiguous to the senses, while others are distant. Hence arises the necessity of considering the Reason under different functions. In its constitutive Ideas, it is not only adapted to every variety of knowledge ; it has, also, the power of searching out its objects under every variety of condition and relation. It can know phenomena and truths, and the relations between them ; it can know immediately and mediately ; it can know in various relations of time and space ; it can form pure cognitions, and cognitions upon sensuous conditions ; it can go out to the actual, and conceive of the possible. It has all these different functions. Its functions manifestly express the variety and scope of its activity.

SECTION V.

DOES LOGIC COMPREHEND ALL THE FUNCTIONS OF THE REASON?

Logic has been defined in the general as comprising the laws which determine and govern the activities of the Reason.* Unless this definition receive limitations, Logic evidently must reach to every function. Limitations, however, exist, and the reason for them is palpable.

In one respect Logic, plainly, has general relations, viz.: in so far as it determines the most original laws of thought and cognition.†

But when we enter the domain of particular functions, we find much that legitimately comes under other divisions of philosophy.

Logic comprises those laws of the Reason which determine the processes by which it reaches the two forms of Reality—the Reality of Truth and of Actual Being. This is its separate, unique, and peculiar domain.

But memory does not describe a process by which new truths are arrived at; it expresses simply the power of the cognitive faculty to retain old truths, or truths already gained. Hence it cannot belong to Logic. Recollection is memory permeated by the will, imagination, and fancy. It evidently can belong to Logic no more than simple memory. It sometimes even becomes a mere art.

* Page 83. † Page 84.

Imagination also gives origin neither to ideas, and truths, nor to facts of reality. It is a mediatory, representative, and creative function; forming ideals upon ideas, reviving the images of objects when the objects no longer address the sense, and combining forms of unreal beauty. Neither, therefore, does Logic comprise the laws of this function.

It would, indeed, be possible to give Logic a designation so general as to make it embrace all the functions. In this case Esthetics would cease as a separate branch of Nomology. But the distinction between Logic, as limited above, and Esthetics, is clear, natural, and convenient. They both, indeed, relate to forms of knowing; but the one determines the laws of knowing the real; while the other determines the laws of mere imitation of the real, and of knowing and projecting the possible.

Imagination, therefore, must be assigned to the nomological determinations of Esthetics.

Memory, considered as an inherent property of the Reason, belongs to psychology simply. The whole doctrine of the association of Ideas, which figures so largely in treating of this function, amounts to this:—Whatever is known, is known, not in an isolated way, but in various relations; these relations themselves making up a part of the objective reality. When, therefore, past perceptions are renewed in the consciousness, whether they be objects of the sense or pure truths, they must of necessity appear in their appropriate relations. Relations and parts of thought are often presented accidentally, or suggested by images of the imagination and fancy; and when so presented, they are, of course, apprehended by the cognitive faculty, and the whole train of thought carried through, or dismissed in its unfinished state, at pleasure.

Recollection, as a voluntary process, is, indeed, based upon the memory. When, however, its object is pure truth, there is often in reality a renewal of the process of investigation or ratiocination, by which it was originally arrived at. In this case, it is difficult to determine how far the recollection arises from memory, or from the pure reasoning power. There is a passage in Dugald Stewart, which illustrates this remark. "Sir Isaac Newton, as we are told by Dr. Pemberton, was often at a loss, when the conversation turned on his own discoveries. It is probable that they made but a slight impression on his mind, and that a consciousness of his inventive powers prevented him from taking much pains to treasure them up in his memory."

In Newton's mind the original proofs were renewed with little aid from memory. And Stewart farther remarks, that generally, while men of little inventive power trust to memory for the recollection of truths, men distinguished for this power are prone to rely upon it. What, therefore, often appears to others as memory, is in reality reasoning, and consequently comes under the laws of Logic.

The other functions, for the most part, come under the determinations of Logic, inasmuch as they contain processes by which the two forms of Reality are attained.

It is not necessary, however, to give Logic the multifarious divisions of these functions. The functions often co-work together; and there are a few general conceptions of the ends of Logic which happily embrace them all.

Logic comprises the laws which determine the processes of arriving at Reality—the Reality of Truth and of Actual Being.

First, therefore, we must consider the laws of the most

original cognitions, both through pure intuition, and through sensuous phenomena.

Secondly. The laws which govern the observation and classification of secondary phenomena ; and that inductive process by which general principles are obtained.

Thirdly. The laws of deduction, or inference.

Fourthly. The laws of evidence, and the method of proof.

This is the outline which, in the next Part, we shall attempt to fill up.

PART III.

LOGIC PROPER.

BOOK I.

PRIMORDIAL LOGIC.

SECTION I.

GENERAL LAWS OF THE EVOLUTION OF IDEAS.

In the *prolegomena* comprised in the two preceding Parts, many things were necessarily anticipated in an incidental way. As, however, they were merely preparatory to my main purpose, I may not mar the development contemplated in this Part, through an apprehension of appearing sometimes to repeat what had already been announced. Wherever this does happen, it will be found that a more formal and scientific announcement is attempted.

On the subject of Ideas, also, it is somewhat difficult to mark with precision what strictly belongs to Psychology, and what to Logic. Ideas, regarded as the determining powers of cognition, do certainly belong to the first; and I have so endeavoured to treat of them in the explication given in the preceding Part. In this Part, besides giving the general laws of their determination, I shall weave in much respecting the mode and conditions of their development, together with their characteristics, which may appear more justly to belong to psychological disquisition.

At one time, I had well nigh concluded to bring this all into the 'Preliminary View'; but farther reflection has induced me to believe that I shall make a more simple and satisfactory presentation of the subject, and, on the whole, more philosophic, by comprising all these particulars under Primordial Logic. Lest any should object to this course, I thought it best to say thus much to shew that the same thoughts had occurred to my own mind, and that the difficulties had not been passed over without consideration.

I. Humanity being the union of body and spirit,—the life of thought, and the physical life of the full-formed and constituted being, in the present sphere, begin, go on, and end together. Hence, even before birth, as Locke affirms,* there may be incipient thought, because, there is incipient sensation.

But although thought begins with sensation, sensation is not the determinative power of thought. This power lies in the Ideas of the Reason.

II. The first action of the Reason is spontaneous, and unattended by reflection. Mind in humanity being finite and dependent, hath not its starting point in itself. The main-spring is energised by an invisible and infinite power. But when it has reached a certain development, different in different individuals, reflection begins, and it now traces back the path through which it has run its course.

III. By reflection, it analyses the knowledges actually attained, together with the simple sensations. By this analysis it does not find the determining powers and forms, nor even all the materials of thought in sensation: but it finds certain conceptions which, when separated from the

* Book II., ch. 9, § 5.

sensations, are intuitively apprehended as universal, necessary, and absolute.

IV. These conceptions must have been given in the dawn of cognition, as well as during the whole line of cognition, since cognition is impossible without them; and yet they were not given before sensation, because, in the first place, as above stated, the life of thought, and physical life showing itself in sensation, begin together; and in the second place, the sensations are signals from the outward world of reality, that the time and occasion of thought have arrived, and that the field of thought stands invitingly open.

V. Hence arises the distinction of antecedence in time, and in necessary existence, or chronological and logical antecedence.* The sensations are first in time; but these absolute cognitions are first in necessary existence. But although we speak of an antecedence in time as something that we can conceive of, it is so slight, that consciousness cannot appreciate it, for no sooner does the sensation appear, than the absolute element is mingled with it.

VI. The first cognitions, or judgments, which take their expression in propositions, are not to be confounded with Ideas. The Ideas are the determinative power of cognition, which exists independently of all cognition. When the phenomenal conditions of thought are supplied, then the Ideas manifest themselves through the different functions. They manifest themselves through consciousness in the cognition of *subject* and *object;* through the imagination in the cognition of ideals; through sensuous perception in the cognition of exterior substances, causes,

* Part I., Sec. IX.

and laws. That is, the Ideas determine to particular cognitions of an objective reality, to which the universal is related—and in this way determine to the cognition of the universal itself. For example, sensations of resistance, of colour, and form, are given; upon this, the ideas of substance, cause, and space, determine to the cognition of a particular body, with its primary and secondary qualities; and in determining to this *particular* cognition by the function of sensuous perception, they determine at the same time by the function of intuition, to the universal and necessary cognitions of space, substance, and cause, as comprised within the first and highest form of reality.

VII. In the evolution of the Ideas we have thus four particulars: First, the phenomena of consciousness, as conditions in time, and effects of objective reality thrown within the sphere of the subjective simple; Secondly, the cognition of particular objective realities; Thirdly, the absolute and universal cognitions of the intuitive function determined by the Ideas; and, Fourthly, the Ideas themselves. The Ideas are first of all in the antecedence of necessary existence. The cognition of the universal in like manner is the antecedent of the cognition of the particular. But in the antecedence of time, the reverse order takes place. Reflection, analysing our actual cognitions first, separates the metaphenomenal from the phenomenal in the particular; Secondly, it separates the universal from the particular; and Thirdly, it evolves the Ideas as the necessary grounds and antecedents in the Reason itself, of every form of cognition.

SECTION II.

METAPHYSICAL IDEAS.

I.—SUBJECT, AND OBJECTIVE EXTERIORITY.

THE phenomena of the exterior and the interior consciousness are the antecedents in time. Among the phenomena of the interior consciousness there is one class which have the remarkable characteristics of self-determination and freedom, showing themselves in the acts of attention, or acts appropriating the cognitive faculty. All the phenomena of the interior consciousness appear, therefore, either directly,—as in simple volitions,—or indirectly, as in cognitions directed by volition, with these remarkable characteristics.

On the other hand, the phenomena of the exterior consciousness manifest themselves independently of this inward, self-determining activity. They *appear in me*, but are in no sense *produced by me*. Upon these phenomena, the Reason is determined by the Ideas of Subject and Object to cognize the particular subject myself, and an exterior something not myself. From this particular cognition, as the initiative, it cognizes the universal distinction of the interior subject and the exterior object.

Reflection now analysing the mental process, it becomes evident that the Ideas of Subject and Object must have had an antecedent necessary existence, or the several cognitions could not have appeared; since the bare phenomena, whether of the interior or exterior consciousness, present us, in themselves, not realities, but appearances only, as the name intimates. The two classes of phenomena mentioned above, with their different characteristics, are the conditions on which the cognitions take place, but the Idea can alone be the power which determines the form of the cognition.

II.—TIME AND SPACE.

That part of our knowledge which is obtained through, or by means of the senses and muscular resistance, is connected with the Ideas of TIME and SPACE. All the phenomena of body are given in space. All succession of phenomena is given in time. It is impossible for us to conceive of body without space. It is impossible for us to conceive of succession without time. In order, therefore, to know body, I must have the idea of space: and in order to know succession, I must have the idea of time.

The ideas of time and space are simple and primary; —they can be resolved into nothing antecedent—they are directly intelligible; they neither require, nor can receive any definition. Their characteristics are obvious. They are necessary, that is, they cannot be supposed not to be, or not to have been; they are infinite; and they admit of no representation that can be addressed to the senses.

It is impossible that they should have their origin in sensation. Neither the secondary nor the primary qualities of bodies bear any resemblance to them. This book which I hold in my hand, and the hand itself, are *in* space; but clearly they are not space. Form and solidity must be connected with space, and cannot be thought of without space, but they have nothing in common with space, and nothing analogous to space. Body, conceived of under any modifications, and under any enlargement, is still *in* space, and totally distinct from space. The characteristics of body are contingency, form, and limitation—the very opposite of those of space.

Time, if representable at all under forms addressed to the senses, must be representable by a succession of phenomena or events. But here we find the same opposition of cardinal characteristics. Time, taken as simple duration—the sense in which I here employ it, is necessary, without form, and unlimited—as simple duration it is eternity. Any succession that may be given is contingent —that is, it may be supposed not to be, or not to have been; it is limited—it must have had a beginning, and may have an assigned termination; and lastly, it may be represented in space, by the revolutions of the planets and a dial-plate. Succession must be *in* time, but is plainly totally distinct from time.

As the cognitions of time and space cannot have their origin in sensation, their origin must be assigned to the pure Reason itself.

How do these cognitions arise in the Reason? Are they innate? The just reply is, that the Reason has no innate or inherent power of forming or developing those ideas, when the proper conditions are supplied. The conception, or act of intelligence, cannot be said to exist before it appears in the consciousness. But the Reason, undoubtedly, in the potentiality of its substance, contains these ideas as constitutive forms of thought: and with these forms is prepared to give out true knowledges or judgments, whenever the sensations shall be supplied which form the occasions of its action. Sensations and muscular resistance are conditional to the development of these ideas; but the pure Reason is the origin of them.

Hence we affirm, that time and space are to be set down as original and inherent forms of the Reason;—meaning by this, that it is of the essential and necessary nature of the Reason, to think and form cognitions under these ideas; so that whenever certain conditions and occasions come up, the Reason moulds, as it were, into an exact knowledge, the sensations which otherwise were fleeting. If we were to suppose the Reason incapable of developing the ideas of time and space, what would become of all our notions of the forms, magnitudes, motions, and velocities of bodies? What would become of the notion of body itself? Time and space seem two very simple ideas—and so they are: but how vast and momentous their relations and bearings!

When, however, we represent these ideas as inherent forms of the Reason, we do not mean to affirm that time and space have no existence independently of the Reason: this would be contradictory to the Reason itself; for in the development of these ideas, the Reason assigns time and space an independent existence. Time and space are necessary, absolute, and infinite, and are conceived of as existing, although there were no mind to recognize them, and to contain their ideas as forms of its thinking and knowing. Time and space are independent realities, which do not impress themselves upon the Reason through the sense; but the ideas of which, Reason potentially contains within itself as the knowing power, and brings out into consciousness, whenever sensations or any phenomena appear there, whose causes hold to them an actual relation.

III.—THE INFINITE AND THE FINITE.

The very judgment which the mind passes upon any object of thought,—*it is finite*,—implies a conception of the infinite: for how could it affirm,—*it is finite*,—unless it knew the infinite? If it be said that the finite is a positive idea, and the infinite only negative of it; with equal propriety, to say the least, we may call the infinite the positive, and the finite the negative idea.

Does not the mind have a distinct and positive cognition when it affirms of any thing, it is infinite? Take space for example: when the mind affirms that space is infinite, does it not mean something more than that its limits cannot be assigned? Truly we say, space can have no limits,—it is necessarily and absolutely infinite.

When we can assign certain limits to an object, we say simply it is finite; when we conceive that there must be limits, while still we are unable to assign them, we call it the indefinite; but when no limit is conceivable or admissible, we say, it is infinite.

Plainly, no phenomena, whether primary or secondary, present us the infinite; it can be a cognition of pure Reason alone. Phenomena, indeed, are the conditions, but nothing more, since no multiplication of the finite can realize the infinite. Now, when through reflection we come to account for this judgment of the mind, we are inevitably led to assign the Idea of the Infinite, in the Reason, as the determinative power and only sufficient ground.

IV.—QUANTITY.

Our knowledges are connected, also, with the idea of QUANTITY. Quantity comprehends UNITY, MULTIPLICITY, and TOTALITY, or, ONE, MANY, and ALL.

Unity is the foundation of every form of quantity. *Many* is unity repeated indefinitely. *All* is the total sum of unities.

What is the idea of unity? Absolute unity is absolute indivisibility.

In nature, there is no absolute unity in the sense of absolute indivisibility—matter is continuously divisible. In numbers, there is no absolute unity in this sense;—every assumed unit is continuously divisible. But in matter, any body, any mass, or any organized system, may be taken as a unity relatively to any supposed or real multiplication of such body, mass, or system: and in numbers, any sum may be taken as unity relatively to any larger sum of which it is a fractional part. Here, every unity is made up of parts, and is itself but a part of some other unity. In matter, and in numbers, we have only parts and wholes; and no absolute unity. In geometry, we have the indivisible point, but this is not really quantity, but the negation of a particular kind of quantity—that is, extension. It is where extension begins.* A line is, indeed, often represented as composed of an infinite number of points; but the point in this case is really a degree of extension indefinitely and immeasurably small; and not a point which has neither length, breadth, nor thickness. A negation of all extension cannot be multiplied so as to compose a line.

Infinite number is a contradictory idea; for number precludes the idea of infinity, as well as the idea of absolute unity. Number may be continuously increased and diminished: but it can never reach the infinite.

When infinity and unity are united in the same idea,

* Part I., page 78.

we have *absolute totality.* Thus time ana space have unity, in that they are incapable of division into integral parts, or parts going to make them up: They are likewise infinite, and therefore are absolute totalities. God is the One, and Infinite being, and therefore an absolute totality.

There are successions in time, but they are not time. There are bodies in space, but they are not space. Figures having extension may be imagined as drawn in space, but they are no integral portions of space, for space cannot be divided into any number of such figures as shall measure the whole of space. An indefinite variety and number of beings may be comprehended within the being of God as their cause; but they are not God, nor a part of God: any possible multiplication of finite beings would not make up infinite being.

Pantheism is contradicted by our very senses, in connection with our Reason; for this which we see, we can divide, and multiply, and measure; and, therefore, if it were a part of God, God would be capable of division, multiplication, and measurement.

In our own minds we have absolute unity again. But we have here only finite unity. Consequently, we have not absolute totality. There can be but one absolute totality of being, that is, God. But what is this finite unity which I affirm of myself—and how do I know it? I am one in the idea which I cannot but have of my spritual substance, and its inherent and inseparable attributes. In my consciousness I find that *I* think, *I* feel, *I* choose, and *I* will.

In the first place, it is plain that this *I*, or myself, is not capable of physical division—it cannot be distributed into parts separated in space. Again: it cannot be logically divided, that is, distributed into genera and species. It is possible that its phenomena may admit of such a distribution; but the spiritual substance itself cannot be conceived of under any such distribution.

Neither can mind be numerically divided. It cannot be identified with any abstract number; and since it cannot be resolved into physical parts, nor into mere extension, it cannot be represented by the relations and conditions of abstract numbers. Numerical multiplication and division do not apply to it.

We may, indeed, have a *numerical multiplicity* of minds, and a *numerical totality* of minds; but this has no bearing upon the question of the substance of the mind itself.

A metaphysical division is equally out of the question, for such a division is, in itself, impossible. A metaphysical division would imply either a division of the spiritual substance itself, or a division of the attributes from the substance: but the first would reduce the mind to the conditions of body, and remove it from metaphysical consideration; and the last is metaphysically impossible, for substance and attribute mutually and necessarily imply each other, and cannot be conceived of as divided.

It is to be remarked here, that time and space, and God, being totalities, as well as unities, do not admit of the idea of multiplicity. It is, therefore, only in ourselves that we gain the idea of perfect unity, and yet admitting, also, the idea of multiplicity, and of totality without absoluteness.

Absolute unity, and multiplicity and totality based upon it, and absolute totality, plainly, cannot be gained from the senses. These give the continuously divisible and multiplicable.

Upon the experience of my own personality, in my thinking, feeling, and doing, I affirm that I am one, that I am neither a sum of parts which are separable units, nor is it possible for me to become a sum of parts. A collection of beings like myself will constitute multiplicity; a complete collection will constitute totality: and upon this judgment respecting myself, arises the judgment of an absolute unity and totality—A ONE AND ALL.

The origin of the cognition of absolute unity and totality must, therefore, unquestionably be referred to the pure Reason, as constituted with the determinative Idea.

But what is the origin of that unity which appears in *one* and *many* of a *kind*, where the particular representing unity is itself divisible; and of that unity which appears in abstract numbers?

The relative and the limited must have its origin in the absolute and unconditional. It is impossible that the latter should have its origin in the former.

But by the senses, in the order of time, the relative and limited are first given: and thus divisible and limited unity, in material objects, is first given. But were the mind unfurnished with the idea, or the potentiality of the absolute conception, of unity, the impressions of the senses could not lead even to the limited cognition: and thus the absolute idea becomes the logical antecedent of the limited cognition. This is a general exposition; the following is the particular: Through the impressions received by the senses, I awake to the conciousness of my existence—these impressions are the conditions and antecedents in time, of knowing, willing, and feeling. In knowing myself, I have the knowledge of a particular, finite, but absolute unity—and this idea of unity, realized in myelf, is the immediate logical antecedent of the limited, imperfect and relative, numerical and physical unity. But, on the other hand, the logical antecedent of the idea of the particular unity, myself, is the absolute and infinite unity, the ONE AND ALL.

Now, when we affirm that the idea of Quantity is a form of the Reason, we mean that the finite Reason is so constituted, that when it comes to know itself, it knows itself as an absolute and finite unity, because it has the power of conceiving of an absolute and infinite unity ; it is prepared to judge of itself as a unity and finite, in the potentiality of judging of a unity infinite as well as absolute. The infinite comprehends the finite ; the finite cannot be augmented to the infinite. And so, likewise, when the phenomena of sense are given, it is prepared, in this antecedent conception of unity, to form cognitions of material and numerical unity. The material unity is concrete ; the numerical unity is abstract.

The conception of the divisibility of material unity arises upon the experience that that which is assumed as a unity, because standing alone in space, is separable into parts, each standing alone in space ; and as the assumed material unity occupies and measures a portion of space ; and as the space occupied, taken as simple extension, is capable of constant division in an endless approximation towards the point absolute, so, likewise, the material unity is conceived of under the same conditions. Continuous divisibility is a struggling of the intellect after absolute unity : and continuous multiplication is a struggling after absolute totality. Numerical division and multiplication bear to the material the relation of the abstract to the concrete.

V.—QUALITY.

Our intelligential activity developes also the idea of QUALITY. The quality of propositions is the affirmation or negation contained in them :—the *nature* or *kind*, that is, the *quality*, of a given proposition, is, that it affirms or denies the predicate of the subject. But a proposition only expresses or represents a judgment : and hence, quality belongs to the judgment itself. Now, all judgments must be either simple or comparative. A simple judgment is the mere affirmation or denial of the existence of an object ; a comparative judgment is the affirmation or denial of agreement, relation, or connexion, between two simple judgments ; the one being the subject, and the other the predicate. Comparative judgments do thus evidently depend upon simple judgments : the simple are primitive, or the first outgoings of the Intelligence ; the comparative are secondary and dependent. In the simple, primitive judgment, the decision of the mind respects the reality or the negation of the object of thought ; and so in the secondary judgment, the reality or negation of the agreement of the two objects of thought compared. It will thus follow, that under QUALITY, as the general category, are embraced the particular categories of *Reality* and *Negation*. In addition to these, a third particular category must arise, which is in some sort a combination of the two, and that is *Limitation*. Every reality of the sensible world has its limitations. It is a reality, but only within a certain limit, and at this limit, negation takes the place of reality. It is plain, that without negation, this limit could not be conceived, as, without reality, it could not be demanded.

Now, let it be remembered, that the reality conceived

of by the intelligence is not the mere reality of the phenomena of consciousness, by which the world without, as well as my own actual existence, are given ;—It is the reality of objects lying beyond the phenomena, and existing independently of them. If the intelligence were a mere blank before sensation began ; and if its whole capacity and office were described as a mere receptivity of sensations ; then there never could be in the intelligence any thought of objective reality. Sensations are purely subjective affections : external causality and substance are not contained in them ; the reality of any being or thing is not contained in them ; not even is the reality of subjective existence contained in them ; for the mere sensations do not contain the subject ;—the sensations of seeing, hearing, and smelling, for example, no more contain the I, or myself, than they contain any external object : and even the sense of resistance, as it is but an internal experience, does not contain either subjective or objective reality.

It is true, that without sensations, the thought of reality would not arise in the consciousness, as, indeed, no thought whatever would arise—no knowledge—no experience. The sensations are conditional to the judgment of reality. But, then, whence comes the judgment of reality, whether objective or subjective? There is but one answer that can be given. It is an *à priori* judgment of the Reason, or a judgment determined by an Idea.

Now, when we speak of Quality as an Idea of the Reason, we mean that the Reason is so constituted, that when sensations are given, it on its part gives out the judgments of reality, negation, and limitation—it does not, analytically, draw them out from the sensations, but, synthetically, affirms them upon the sensations. The judgment of reality is its own, added to the experience of sensations.

The mind is a receptivity of the sensations only; its own inherent form of thought affirms the existence of a real subject and a real object.

The judgment of reality appears first, chronologically, in the particular and limited subject and object; but the Reason, as the faculty of the universal, extends the judgment to universality, and affirms that all sensations must be connected with subject and object—nay, that all phenomena of consciousness whatever must be thus connected. The judgment of reality extends to all our thinking, feeling, and volition.

Again: the Reason, as the faculty of the absolute, upon the particular and limited reality, conceives of the absolute and unlimited reality, or the infinite.

VI.—RELATION.

Relation is another category under which our knowledges appear. If relation were nothing more than juxtaposition, it would still follow that *à priori* judgments would be necessary, in order thus to comprehend objects; —for time and space, which are *à priori* judgments, would be necessary. But relation is not mere juxtaposition. Juxtaposition in space and time is, indeed, all the relation which experience of the senses affords—immediate contiguity of objects, and immediate contiguity of changes, forming succession. But when we reflect upon the objects of knowledge, we conceive of them as having interior relations, which are not representable under the forms of time and space. These relations are three:—

I. Substance and Accidents, or Properties. 2. Cause and Effect. 3. Action and reaction, or reciprocity between the Agent and the Patient.

I. External objects are related to the human sensitivity in the production or development of sensations ; and are related to each other in the production or development of changes in form, appearance, and properties ; all these last being judged of again through the new sensations produced. The subject, also, is related to the consciousness in the development of many internal phenomena within its field of view—as the phenomena of thinking, feeling, and willing ; besides those phenomena which are marked as changes in external objects from thc agency of the subject, such as the muscular movements, and their extended sequents. Now, while nothing is immediately presented to the consciousness but the juxtaposition of the phenomena, there is an *à priori* synthetical judgment respecting the interior relation ; and the object and the subject, in respect of the changes connected with them, are affirmed to be Substance and Cause. Thus the external objects, in their connexion with the human sensitivity, develope sensations which are commonly known as the result of properties in these subjects ; form and solidity receiving the designation of primary properties, because, without them, the objects cannot be conceived ; and heat and cold, sweetness and sourness, fragrance, and so on, receiving the designation of secondary properties, because, without these, the objects can be conceived, namely, by means of the primary properties alone.

Substance and property are thus necessary to the conception of the objects, and mutually imply each other.

So, also, with respect to the subject and its thoughts, volitions, and emotions—we cannot avoid taking the subject as substance, and as such developing its properties.

It is unquestionable, on the one hand, that unless the bare phenomena of consciousness were given, the idea of substance and property could not make its appearance; but, then, on the other hand, it is equally unquestionable, that this idea is not obtained by analysis of the phenomena—sensations, emotions, thoughts, volitions. These do not contain substance; but here, again, the synthetic judgment, *à priori* of the Reason, affirms the relation.

II. CAUSE cannot be developed from bare phenomena. Phenomena are not cause, nor do they contain cause; but the Reason demands to account for their existence; and in doing this, gives again a synthetic *à priori* judgment.

Those phenomena which connect themselves directly with the properties of substance, as well as those which are the immediate sequents of causality, must be referred to cause; because all finite substance must be referred to cause—cause absolute and infinite. It is impossible, therefore, to exercise thought without the judgment of the relation of cause and effect.

The Idea of cause could not be developed, except upon condition of phenomena. The phenomena form the antecedents in time. But neither could the phenomena lead to knowledges unless the Reason, in its own inherent capacity, contained the Idea of Cause—as the idea of originating power.

The idea of causality is first given specifically in the affirmation of the causality of the Will in every individual: and then generalized by the Reason, as the faculty of the Universal, into the axiom which connects cause with every phenomenon whatever, past, present, or to come.

But the individual will, as a finite cause, presupposes an infinite: I could not say of myself, I am a cause and finite, unless I had already the idea of cause, and of cause infinite. The antecedent condition, in the order of time, being supplied, the true logical order of the development must, therefore, be as follows: The Reason contains the Idea of Cause, and, as the faculty of the absolute and the infinite, forms the pure *à priori* cognition of an absolute and infinite cause; and this is the basis on which I affirm of myself, I am cause finite; and the basis on which I make any affirmation of causality whatever. As there is infinite and absolute cause, so, likewise, there must be infinite and absolute substance. Cause and substance are inseparable.

III. The third particular is that of action and reaction, or the reciprocity existing between two substances with respect to any change which takes place in one or both, from their correlation. Thus, when one body impinges upon another, as when a ball is thrown against a wall and rebounds, there is, plainly, an action of the ball upon the wall, and a reaction of the wall upon the ball; and it is in consequence of this reciprocity that the effect takes place. When fire is applied to a combustible substance, there is both an action of the fire upon the substance, and a reciprocal action of the elementary particles of the substance, as they enter into new combinations and increase the action of the fire, until its visible manifestations cease in the entire consumption. In all chemical changes and combinations, this reciprocity is exhibited. In the correlation of the human sensitivity with external objects, it appears again. Indeed, in all the developments of substance and property, and of cause and effect, this reciprocity comes into view.

The conception of this relation is, that in the system of reality and being, substances and properties conditionate the development of substances and properties; and causes and effects conditionate the action of causes and effects; and causes and substances mutually conditionate each other.

This relation obviously depends upon the ideas of substance and cause. But if substance and cause are synthetic and *à priori*, then this relation must have an *à priori* ground.

The relation, indeed, could never be known, without the chronological antecedence of phenomena; but as the phenomena do not contain the ideas of substance and cause—as these last cannot be analytically evolved—so, likewise, the phenomena cannot contain, and there cannot be analytically evolved from them, this judgment of a mutual conditionating.

If we confine ourselves to bare observation, we not only fall short of the idea of cause, and rest in mere succession unaccounted for; we also substitute the conditions of the development of substance, and of the activity of cause, for the ideas themselves. But when we admit the synthetic *à priori* judgments of the Reason to have their place, then the distinction between the relation of mere conditions, is distinguished clearly from the relation of substances and causes to their developments and effects.

Finite substances and causes conditionate each other: the condition is not the substance nor the cause, and yet the substance cannot reveal its properties, nor the cause its effects, without the chronological antecedence of the condition. Motives are not the causes of volitions, and yet the Will cannot act without motives. Sensations are not the causes of cognitions, and yet the Reason cannot form cognitions without sensations, either in immediate or remote antecedence. The wall or the pavement is not the cause of the rebounding of the ball, but the rebounding could not take place without it, or some similar condition.

But the distinctive idea of condition, given in respect of the finite, although a logical antecedent of our particular cognitions, must itself have an absolute ground. The relation of cause and effect, has its ultimate ground in cause infinite and absolute : and the relation of substance and property has its ultimate ground in substance infinite and absolute. In like manner, the relation of reciprocal action must have its ultimate ground in an infinite and absolute concurrence. The movements of finite mind, and the movements of nature, cannot at once be resolved into movements of the infinite and the absolute, without creating a system of Pantheism. But all these movements must be conditionated by the infinite and absolute—the infinite and the absolute must concur with them. In this way it holds true, that "in God we live, and move, and have our being."

It appears, then, that RELATION, in its three-fold form, is an Idea of the Reason.

From the sensations it cannot be educed ; but the Reason, upon its own inherent fullness and capacity, forms cognitions from the sensations, in the relations of substance and property, cause and effect, action and reaction. It comprehends, evolves, and employs the idea of relation, when the appropriate phenomena require it.

VII.—MODALITY.

Modality contains,

POSSIBILITY AND IMPOSSIBILITY ;
EXISTENCE AND NON-EXISTENCE ;
NECESSITY AND CONTINGENCE.

Every thing which the mind conceives of, is conceived of as possible or impossible ; as existent, or non-existent ;

as necessary or contingent. Mode has respect to causality and substance. The enquiry of the mind is, whether a given conception can be realized, or whether it is impossible to causality: whether it is actually existent, or not: whether it appears of necessity, or contingently? The answer to this enquiry gives us the mode or manner of the conception.

No one will deny that we can think of that which we know to be impossible, as well as of the possible: that we can think of that which does not exist, as well as of that which does exist: that we can think of that which exists necessarily, or of that which exists contingently.

But how do we come to think of the possible, contrasted with the impossible—the existent, contrasted with the non-existent—the necessary, contrasted with the contingent? Can these ideas be analytically derived from the sensations, or are they synthetic, *à priori* judgments of the pure Reason?

I. The Possible and the Impossible.

Our sensations are simple, actual phenomena; they are nothing more. Whether any thing beyond, or different from these sensations can exist, is a question which the mind starts, and thus shows that it has an idea of the possible; but this idea is not a sensation, nor can it be comprehended within a sensation; it is something which supervenes from the mind itself upon the sensations.

The idea of the possible cannot but imply its opposite, the impossible; as the latter cannot but imply the former. The idea of the possible and impossible shows the mind leaping beyond the bounds of actual experience: so far from being confined to the bare sensations, it is not even confined to the cognitions of the actual, formed upon the sensations; but multiplies forms of being in time and space indefinitely, both of the possible, that is, such as in accordance with rational laws might exist; and of the impossible, or such as imply a violation of all law, and therefore cannot be supposed to exist. It affirms, also, the inherent impossibility of certain conceptions, *e. g.*, that $4+5=12$.

II. Existence and Non-existence.

That we think of non-existence, as well as of existence, is undeniable. And that we form conceptions of objects under the mode of non-existence, as well as under that of existence, is equally undeniable. A point which has neither length, breadth, nor thickness; a line which has length, but no breadth nor thickness; a cube which is formed of six planes united at right angles, but without solidity, and bodiless; the properties of a geometrical arch without a possible realization in any material arch; the conception of a shadow; the conception of empty space; combinations of the imagination in endless diversity; the conception of creation out of nothing; and again, the possible annihilation of creation—all these, and the like conceptions, imply the opposition of existence and non-existence, as a mode of thought.

But it is quite obvious that non-existence could never be contained in any mere sensation. As our sensations do not directly give us reality, neither do they give us non-existence. Here, again, we must refer to the pure Reason, which, from the fullness of its own ideas, gives out cognitions and supplies the forms of knowledge.

III. Necessity and Contingence.

Two conceptions mutually imply each other, when the one cannot be thought of or defined without the other. It is thus with possibility and impossibility; with existence and non-existence; and again, with necessity and contingency.

That these conceptions are in the mind is plain, because we are now speaking of them. That we are continually applying them is equally plain. There cannot be more than one straight line drawn between any two points—*there cannot be*—that is, it is impossible. But how impossible? Is it impossible, because there is no power or skill adequate to draw more than one line? No, it is impossible in itself—it cannot be conceived of under any conditions—it is necessarily impossible.

Again: we conceive of existence absolute and necessary, namely, the existence of God. God cannot be supposed not to exist, for if he did not exist, there would be no existence whatever. We have thus necessary truth and necessary being.

There are also necessary relations. The relation between the substance of any being and the attributes which go to make up our conception of that being, is necessary. The relation between Infinite Cause and the effects which it wills, is necessary. So, likewise, the relation between a finite cause determining itself to effects, and the effects determined, is necessary when these are both in its constituted energy.

Necessity is absolute, when there is no conceivable condition. It is relative, when there is a conceivable condition. The being of God is absolutely necessary. Pure mathematical truths are absolutely necessary. The movements of the planets are relatively necessary; because they continue to move upon condition that the system of nature remains unchanged: but it is conceivable that it may be changed.

The opposite idea of contingency is clearly applicable likewise. That which is, but which may be conceived of both as not having been, and as having begun to be, under the possibility that it might not be, is a contingent existence. Hence, whatever is created, is contingent existence. Hence, also, all volitions are contingent.

The distinction between natural and moral necessity, which has been frequently attempted, is absurd. Necessity is a simple idea, and entirely independent of the distinction between the natural and the moral. Besides, the distinction between the natural and the moral cannot be made out without implying the ideas of necessity and contingency; for that alone is moral which is free; and that which is free cannot be necessitated. Hence, again, the terms moral necessity are contradictory.

SECTION III.

NOMOLOGICAL IDEAS.

I AM reminded of the extensive field of thought I have yet to travel over; and since under the preceding head, I have been particular in illustrating the laws which determine the evolution of Ideas, it will be admissible under the present head to bring the explication within narrower limits.

I.—LAW.

Law manifests itself in the orderly succession and the stated recurrence of phenomena.

Phenomena, as barely existent, demand causality. The fixed relations and the uniform succession demand Law.* How beautiful and glorious to thought is Law! Law governs the sun, the planets, and the stars. Law covers the earth with beauty, and fills it with bounty. Law directs the light, moves the wings of the atmosphere, binds the great forces of the universe in harmony and order, awakes the melody of creation, quickens every sensation of delight, moulds every form of life. Law governs atoms, and governs systems. Law governs matter, and governs thought. Law springs from the mind of God, travels through creation, and makes all things one. It

* Doctrine of the Will, pp. 28, 29.

makes all material forms one, in the unity of system; it makes all minds one, in the unity of thought and love.

The observations of the senses yield us only limited successions and recurrences of phenomena. These have an antecedence in the order of time. But Law, eternal, absolute, and universal, has antecedence in the order of necessary existence, and is an Idea of the Reason. It is the Idea of Ideas, under the Nomological conception.

II.—MATTER AND SPIRIT.

Is Spirit the negation of Matter? With equal force, at least, we may say, Matter is the negation of Spirit. Do we know one better than the other? Then do we know Spirit best, for we ourselves are Spirit, and Matter is *without* us. But neither Matter nor Spirit are contained in the phenomenal. Here, again, the phenomenal is merely the condition, the antecedent in the order of time. But Matter and Spirit is a general cognition founded upon an Idea of the Reason. It is an Idea which comprehends the whole actual and possible sphere of cause and law. Whatever exists and is governed, is either matter or spirit.

III.—PERFECTION.

Where phenomena are compared—and by experience we can compare nothing else—it is impossible to judge even of relative perfection, unless there be in the mind principles and archetypes with which in the first place to compare the objects of experience. For how shall we say of this particular, It is more beautiful than the other; or of this, It is better, wiser, more just, unless there be in the mind a conception and archetype of beauty, and a conception and archetype of the good and the just, by which to determine the intrinsic character of each particular, in order to judge of their comparative perfection? But the conception of Perfection appears not merely in the comparison of qualities in particular objects. We think of an absolute justice, truth, wisdom, and goodness, an absolute beauty, an absolute order, harmony, and fitness. It is absolute law attaining an absolute development. We think of God as Infinite Perfection—a form and measure of being to which nothing can be added, and from which nothing can be taken. But even in finite modes of being, we conceive of a Perfection which relatively to their archetypes, is absolute. There is an absolute beauty of the human form ; an absolute truth and justice in human action ; and an absolute loveliness in nature, which, if not realized in experience, is nevertheless represented in the imagination. We may deny absolute perfection to the mode of being, because it is finite : but we can represent it to ourselves as filling out its measure, as reaching the excellence, glory, and beauty of its archetype.

Now, so far from absolute Perfection, under the form of the Infinite, being a presentation of the senses, not even in finite modes is it such a presentation. Actual experience gives us the limited and variable phenomena, and nothing more. But how do our minds come to leap beyond the actual realities of finite being, and to shape out an unseen perfection of truth and beauty ? How do they ascend up to the conception of Infinite Perfection ? There is but one satisfactory solution : the Idea of Perfection in the Reason.

Thus constituted, when the antecedent conditions in time are supplied by experience, the Reason forms those Ideal cognitions, through its function of the Imagination, which inspire to works of art, to self-cultivation, and to all great and good deeds ; and stretching its eye beyond all created being, sees the Infinite himself in his ineffable greatness and beauty.

The Idea of Perfection thus attaches itself to the whole sphere of human activity. It is the leading Idea. In the particular development, however, we have several Ideas which we shall proceed to consider.

IV.—RIGHT AND WRONG.

This antithesis is universally recognized. Men, indeed, have disagreed as to the particulars to be placed under the two terms—some placing under the first what others place under the second ; but the two terms themselves, as necessarily and absolutely opposed, is a universal conception : all men think of Right and Wrong. There are, also, many particulars which men agree in placing under the same term of the antithesis : there is a code of ethics embracing cardinal principles, which is well nigh universal.

Again : the diversities of sentiment which actually exist, can be explained in the same way that human error is explained on subjects confessedly admitting of exact determination, namely, the want of sufficient education in general, and the want of the requisite examination and thought in respect to the particular subject, unbiassed by prejudice and passion.

The Right has been confounded with the Useful. The Useful is an Idea, or it is a mere induction of consequences. If the latter, then certainly it cannot be identified with the Right. By a bare induction of consequences, we can never attain to an absolute and fixed judgment, since the induction can never be complete. But the judgment of Right and Wrong is absolute, fixed, and universal. The Reason affirms that the two terms can never be transposed ; and where any particular has received a clear and positive assignment to one of the terms, no possible consequences can ever change its character. Thus, lying, injustice, malice, cruelty, blasphemy, adultery, murder, and many other particulars, have received an assignment which is seen to be necessary and unalterable. And the same is true of the opposite virtues.

But if we take the Useful as an Idea ; the impossibility of identifying it with the Right is equally apparent. Ideas are distinguished by their aims. Now, the Idea of Utility aims at the improvement of the external world, so as to multiply the accommodations and comforts of man in his physical relations. But the Idea of Right and Wrong aims to fix the great law of duty in respect to both God and man, in the imperishable relations of moral obligation. The one determines what will minister to physical comfort and enjoyment ; the other determines simply what is Right, in distinction from Wrong, irrespective of all physical comfort and enjoyment. Nay, it commands the Right in opposition to physical comfort and enjoyment, and exalts self-denial into one of the most glorious and majestic forms of virtue. It indeed promises to persevering virtue ample rewards in the ultimate issue ; but it at the same time reveals virtue as pursuing its end, charmed by its own convictions and sweet consciousness, and in this way alone gaining its title, and establishing its meritoriousness. The judgment of Right and Wrong then could be derived from experience only as a distinct induction of consequences, since Utility as an Idea transcends experience ; but an induction of consequences being inadequate to account for this judgment, with its actual characteristics of necessity and universality, we are here again led to the conception of an Idea of Right and Wrong in the Reason.

Phenomena comprising the volitions of a free and responsible being, together with their sequents, form the antecedents in time conditional to the development of the Idea. Constituted with this Idea, no sooner does an act of such a being appear in the consciousness, than the Reason affirms of it, *it is Right*, or, *it is Wrong*. Upon this particular judgment, it forms the axiomatic judgment. Every act of a free and responsible being must be Right or Wrong: and thence proceeds by reflection to recognize its own Idea.

The Idea of Right and Wrong, projected in the various relations of humanity, determines a moral law for the government of human conduct. The highest determination of a moral law is that made by the Divine Reason. A moral law, thus determined, is called, in respect to its origin, Divine law. The human Reason, although it may fail to determine, of itself, an adequate moral law, nevertheless, no sooner reads the Divine law with a clear and open eye, than it beholds the marks of eternal and necessary truth, and bows to the august and awful authority. The moral Idea within determines to the recognition without. The voice which speaks from Sinai, and the voice of the Divine Word, who walked among men, find their echoes within, in thoughts which seem to connect our being with a past Eternity.

V.—FREEDOM AND RESPONSIBILITY.

Right and Wrong can be affirmed of the acts of a free and responsible being alone.

The conception of Freedom is involved in that of Contingence, which has already been considered. A free being is one endowed with the power of contingent determination; that is, the opposite of a necessary determination.*

Responsibility is involved in Freedom and Intelligence. A being who knows Law, and is capable of obeying or disobeying, is bound to account for his acts; and is worthy of praise or blame, according to the account which he legitimately renders.†

Freedom and Responsibility are affirmed by the Reason upon the consciousness of self-determining acts, because it is constituted with the Idea of Freedom and Responsibility.

The Reason, as evolving the momentous Ideas of Moral Law, of Right and Wrong, of Freedom and Responsibility, is technically called the CONSCIENCE.

VI.—PERSONAL IDENTITY.

The phenomena of consciousness present us, in themselves, neither Personality nor Personal Identity. They are a bare flow of variable appearances. The personality is the subjective simple, in whose consciousness all these appearances pass along; and who knows himself both as a cause and recipient of them. The identity of this personality is its unchanged substance and properties in all time and circumstances, amid every variety of phenomenal presentation. It is the conception of identical and indivisible oneness. The phenomena here again take ante-

* Doctrine of the Will, Ch. II., Sec. III. and VII.

† Moral Agency, Ch. III., Sec. I.

cedence in time; while the unchanging subject holds the antecedence of necessary existence.

When the conditional phenomena make their appearance, the Reason, furnished with the Idea of Personal Identity, knows itself and its cognates in their simplicity and oneness. The cognition of Identity does not appear under any limitation of time. The Reason affirms, What I now am I always have been, and always shall be, in the whole circuit of my being.

VII.—IMMORTALITY.

It needs no argument to satisfy any mind, that immortality cannot be a conception of experience. Indeed, many affirm that it is not even a truth of philosophy, but purely a doctrine of revelation. It appears to me that the history of this doctrine affords unanswerable proof that the conception of Immortality is developed in the human mind independently of a Divine Revelation. But, if we grant as a matter of fact, that it was not developed in the human mind until it was formally announced by Divine Revelation, it is nevertheless necessary that the Idea of Immortality should belong to the Reason, in order to make the acceptance of the doctrine possible, unless it can be shown to be comprehended within elements of thought furnished by the senses. Whatever new doctrine is taught us, must be contained under facts or principles, and forms of thought which we already have. If, therefore, the sense cannot give us the conception of Immortality—as confessedly it cannot—and if we have no constituted principle or Idea within to give it, then the doctrine cannot be taught us; just as a moral law cannot be taught us unless there be a Reason or Conscience, furnished with Ideas of law and moral obligation, to respond to it, by forming the corresponding conceptions.

Some seem to entertain the very strange notion, that Divine Revelation is dishonoured by granting to human reason the possibility of arriving at the cognition of Immortality by its own innate powers. Now, it ought to be recollected that the human reason is no less the work of God than the written Word, and hence, that the acknowledgment of the glorious constitution of the former is doing honor to God in the same sense as the acknowledgment of the latter. The latter assumes that we have the former, by appealing to it. The mission of Divine Revelation is special, to renew to human thought truths which sensuality and sin had lulled to repose ; and to bring to light that extraordinary system of grace which could belong neither to Logic nor to Observation ; but which, when brought to light, appears all over inscribed with those moral characters which meet the moral Ideas as the light meets the eye of the new-born infant—a blessed visitation, for which it is prepared.

The above are strictly the *Moral Ideas*. We next proceed to the *Esthetical*. These, also, are allied to Perfection as the leading Idea.

VIII.—THE BEAUTIFUL.

The PERFECT is the conception of the utmost development of Law in general. Appearing in different spheres, it takes different denominations. In *The Morale*, it is RECTITUDE ; in *Logic*, it is TRUTH ; in *Somatology*, it is THE USEFUL ; in *Esthetics*, it is THE BEAUTIFUL.

The Useful relates to the physical sensibilities and well-being of creatures that can enjoy and suffer.

The Beautiful relates to a peculiar class of emotions belonging only to creatures endowed with Reason—a Reason constituted with Ideas determining to cognitions which stand in a causal relation to the emotions.

The Useful determines the constitution, forms, and relations of bodies in respect to physical life and enjoyment.

The Beautiful determines the forms, relations, and properties of bodies in respect to its peculiar emotions. These emotions are explained by referring simply to consciousness.

Emotions are clearly distinguishable from sensations, in this, that the latter precede, while the former follow cognitions. Emotions of beauty obviously, therefore, cannot arise out of simple sensations. A judgment of forms, relations, and properties, intervenes between the two.

The simple cognition of objects which we pronounce beautiful, is made on the general laws of sensuous perception. The question is, Why do we add the jugdment, *they are beautiful?*

It may be replied, we experience the peculiar emotions to which, likewise, we apply this epithet; and then, by analysis, ascertaining the peculiar forms and qualities which are invariably connected with these emotions, we accordingly pronounce them the *Objective Beauty.*

Even according to this, the conception is not derived from sensations, but from emotions. But the emotions are preceded by cognitions, and these not merely the cognitions of the beautiful objects by the laws of ordinary perception; but cognitions of those very forms and qualities as beautiful, which produce the emotions. It is, indeed, true, that the experience of the emotions claim antecedence in time ; and a particular judgment of beauty assumes the appearance of a result of a mere analysis of properties ; but the conception which springs up in the mind, is of the Beautiful as applying universally and determining the forms to which the emotions correlate. We think of Beauty as a principle on which the Creation was constituted and ordered. We are conscious of conceiving of a Beauty far transcending that which we behold. Nay, the Imagination forms ideals and archetypes of specific forms unrealized in nature. The mind proceeds still farther, and conceives of an Infinite and Absolute Beauty. The Beautiful, therefore, has its constitutive Idea in the Reason.

The Beautiful is the generic form of the Idea. It is the Perfect, determining outward forms, relations, and properties, in respect to the esthetical sensitivity. But when we come to the particular spheres in which the Idea goes out as Law, we find it under several specific forms.

The Beautiful is connected with the objects of two senses, the Eye,* and the Ear.

The Beautiful in the World of the Eye becomes specifically :

1. SYMMETRY, or the proper relation of the parts entering into an organic whole, determined by a common measure. Thus, the parts of the human body are symmetrical, when in size and form they seem to melt into a visible harmony. Thus, too, the parts of a building are symmetrical, when the dimensions, in relation to each other, and the pillars and ornaments, in relation to the

* The Eye, of course, is assumed to have been informed by the muscular resistance respecting distance and motion.

main structure, flow into one common unity and harmony. Symmetry, as an Idea, determines the Ideals of the Imagination, which constitute the Archetypes of the Artist. Mathematical ratios and proportions are employed to determine precise measures and rules of mechanical execution. These, however, without the Idealized eye, would present a stiff and ungraceful outline.

II. Grace.—Grace appears in motion. Graceful lines are those which a beautiful, animated body naturally and spontaneously describes in space, from the moving power energizing within. Grace is symmetry in motion. Nevertheless, the expression of Grace does not always demand actual motion; it appears no less in attitude. But this always relates to motion. It expresses the point where motion has ceased, and where motion is just about to begin. There is Grace in a motionless statue, because the attitude expresses the motion which has been, just as it is passing into the motion which is about to be. This grace, this *moveable beauty*,* is the life of painting and sculpture. A dead body has a heavy, painful beauty, because every muscle is relaxed. There is here a total and final cessation of motion, and no prophecy that it shall begin again.

III. Regularity, Uniformity, Variety.—Regularity is the indication of law, and is opposed to confusion and disorder. Uniformity expresses the recurrences and relations which indicate the presence of extended system, and is opposed to isolation and accidental production. Variety expresses the multiformity and richness of the beautiful. These three are ever united in beautiful productions. There is no beauty in a straight line,—it has regularity and uni-

* Schiller.

formity, but no variety. But a curved line, as it possesses all, is beautiful. A simple color cannot be called beautiful: for example, look at colors as disposed in a paint-box. Nor yet is a confused jumble of colors beautiful. It is when beheld in connection with form, and regularly blended, as in the flowers, the foliage, the rainbow, and the 'human face divine,' that they claim to be beautiful. The great system of Nature is constructed upon these Esthetical Ideas.

IV. Determinate Form.—All forms are composed of straight or curved lines. The curved line is beautiful. The spiral line is a composition of curves. The straight line, in its simplicity, is indifferent, or it is the line of utility. When two or more straight lines are joined together in the construction of regular forms, the esthetical properties begin to appear. But, what determines the different forms of bodies and the lines of their motions? Unquestionably, somatological necessities and laws enter extensively into the determination. The world is made as it is, because it is designed for use. This is one solution, but not of itself sufficient. It is not difficult to show how mere use might be attained without a thousand particulars which appear both in the works of God and man. Man is but copying the Great Maker, when he aims to make beautiful, as well as useful. The union of the two is the perfection of the universe. The Idea of the determinate form of beauty, in the mind of God, evolved all the varieties of beautiful form in the creation. These forms are not arbitrary; nor are they merely the best for use; they are the proper forms of the beautiful likewise. The human reason hath the same Idea; and hence, it both recognizes the beauty of actual form, and projects new forms of beauty in the creations of Art.

V. The Sublime.—This is usually embraced under Esthetics. The fundamental Idea, however, is not the Beautiful, but the Infinite. Strictly, esthetical properties are gained, when the Infinite unites itself to the Beautiful, or to the higher Idea of the Perfect. This, indeed, is the common form; and hence the reason why the emotions of grandeur and sublimity are assigned to Esthetics. Infinite Beauty—Infinite Perfection,—these are the highest sources of the Sublime.

Sublimity and grandeur are scarcely distinguishable in the emotion. In the natural world, usage has applied the one to the lofty, and the other to vast extent.

Those objects of either kind which awaken the emotion, are objects which suggest the conception of the Infinite, by reason of their magnitudes, or the amazing power, wisdom, or perfection which they display.

The Moral Sublime can be traced to the same element. Prometheus upon the rock, fills the mind with a sense of its own greatness and nobleness; and we think on in the long track of our immortality until we seem lost in infinite being.

The objects and beings of our experience cannot reveal to us the Infinite directly; but when presented under forms of indefinite greatness—a greatness which surpasses the ordinary standards of comparison—the mind instinctively springs forward to meet the realization of its own Idea. It seems to see the skirts of the glory of the Infinite.

Majesty and *dignity* belong to the same category. They are expressions of mental power and greatness, in the corporeal person of man. In the Arts of Sculpture and Painting, they are capital qualities.

Thus far with respect to the World of the Eye. We proceed to the beautiful in the World of the Ear.

Beauty unquestionably relates to sound. The emotions of sweet music and of the sight of loveliness, melt together into one harmonious emotion.

The esthetical qualities of sound are manifested in three ways: in Music, in Language, and in Tone.

Beginning with Music, we have,

I. MELODY.—As a constitutive Idea, it determines the cognition of beauty in the relations of sounds flowing on in succession; the laws which are to govern the succession; and the movements of the Creative function in endless musical production.

II. HARMONY.—The Idea of Harmony determines the cognition of beauty in two or more successions of sound flowing on in the same time; the laws which govern their union; and the creative function in new and varied productions.

Sensations cannot give the judgment of melody and harmony. If the judgment were derived from the mere sensitivity, it would belong to the emotions. But emotions are always preceded by cognitions; and the cognitions must have their determinative Idea.

LANGUAGE has sound for its material. The Idea of melody determines the construction of Language likewise. This appears in the selection of elementary sounds, their combination into syllables and words, and the arrangement of words in propositions. Smoothness, euphony, elegance, and energy of style, all proceed from this Idea.

RHYTHM, whether in music or verse, is comprehended in the general Idea of melody. It expresses the relative proportion of sounds as measured by time.

VERSE is language, which, while used as the proper vehicle of thought, and retaining its laws as such, is wrought into the highest form of melody, of which the capacities of the constituent sounds will admit.

TONE, in music, respects the intervals of sound, and is comprehended under the general Idea of melody.

TONE, in speech, comprehends the universal language of thought and passion, superadding itself to the articulate and conventional sounds of language ; and contains the esthetical properties of Oratory. Accent, emphasis, and all the inflexions accompanying the expression of thought ; majesty, melody, tenderness, and force, accompanying the words of passion, make up its varieties.

We here end our outline of the Esthetical Ideas. It is by these that we know and enjoy the beauty and sublimity of Nature. It is by these also, as the powers of creative thought, that all the wonders of art are produced.

The Ideas which follow next are the *Somatological.* In the general philosophical classification already given in Part I., I have adverted to the difficulties attending the determination of this class of Ideas.* What follows I wish to be regarded as an indication, or an attempt, rather than a pretension to be a complete evolution. Besides, a full development of this very extensive subject, were it possible, would inevitably lead me to transcend the proper limits of an elementary treatise. A strictly primordial logic, also, requires mainly the laws which regulate the determination of Ideas, and not their application, except so far as may be necessary for the purpose of illustration and a clear understanding.

Before giving Somatological Ideas, we ought to suppose the Dynamical Ideas already to have been deter-

* Pages 82, 83.

mined. But a reference to the Metaphysical Ideas will show that no further determination has as yet been attempted, save those included under the category of Relation. By reflecting, however, we shall perceive that every form of Dynamical Conception is embraced by this Category. All movement and change lie in cause producing effects, in substance developing properties, and in action and reaction. Advancing into the world of bodies, we are introduced to various classes of secondary phenomena; and these, while generally connected with the Cardinal Ideas above named, are still farther, in their peculiarities, conditional of the development of particular Dynamical Ideas.

The most important particular Dynamical Ideas, are the Idea of centripetal and centrifugal forces; the Idea of polarized forces; the Idea of chemical affinity and repulsion; the Idea of vital powers, or the grand Idea of LIFE, as the organific power; and the Idea of instinctive activity. All these are powers and forces recognized in the Science of Nature. When I speak of the Ideas of these powers and forces, I mean that they are not determined by the mere observation of phenomena; but that the Reason contains within itself the constitutive elements which grasp, distinguish, and arrange the phenomena, and reduce them under their respective powers.

Cause conceived of in its universality is metaphenomenal, known on condition of phenomena. If, then, there be specific causes, they likewise, as causes, must be metaphenomenal, and therefore capable of determination only by the supervention of Ideas.

Cause, however, is an Idea of the utmost simplicity. It is that which accounts for actual existence, and all changes or phenomena.

The diversity of causes apprehended and described under Dynamics arises from the diversity of the phenomena.* But in reality have we, under all this diversity, more than one cause in nature—a cause universal? Admitting this, the diversity of phenomena arises from the various spheres in which cause acts, and the various laws which direct and govern its activity. And then, in evolving the Idea of Cause simply, we have really given all necessary consideration to pure dynamical philosophy; and what remains to us legitimately, is the evolution of the Somatological Ideas, or the Ideas which go forth into the world of bodies, and give the law to all its forms, relations, and changes.

All Ideas have some form of reality answering to them, although not adequate to them. The great law of their development is, that the reality must first move certain phenomenal conditions in the consciousness, and then the Ideas come forth to determine cognitions and laws. There may be in the human Reason, Ideas yet undeveloped, because the realities to which they relate have not yet come within the field of Experience. And especially may this be true in respect to the world of bodies where there is such vast diversity and possibility. Mind does not penetrate matter as it penetrates itself. Hence the laws of bodies appear under two kinds or degrees:

THEORETICAL AND POSITIVE LAW.

The first is the conception of a possible constitution of bodies, and one which will embrace and account for a certain number of the phenomena presented. But the

* Doctrine of the Will, pp. 30–32 and 294.

Mind still remains in doubt, first, whether its conception be realized in any system, or be a mere appearance; secondly, whether, if realized, the elements of universality and necessity can be connected with it. While these doubts remain, it is relatively to the Mind-judging, a *Theory*, or a mere view taken for the occasion.

When we speak of possible systems, we speak according to a limited observation. We think of vast diversity and possibility only in particular spheres. In the great universe there may be but one possible system determined by absolute and necessary laws, comprehending the whole, and yet permeating the minutest particulars: and all that we see may be but parts of this grand system, appearing imperfect in particulars, because these are imperfectly seen in their separation from the whole. Space is thus the infinite field in which the Infinite Being plants the perfect elements of worlds, which, under perfect and necessary laws, are led forth to perfect developments in long successions in Infinite Time.

But if there be a diversity of principles possible, on which worlds can be projected into being, and linked together on this extended scale, must we not believe that the Infinite and Perfect Being has chosen the best? Can his work be less than the best and the perfect?

The absolute and perfect laws—if such they be—which are embodied in the Creation, must have their corresponding Ideas in the Divine Mind; and therefore, as far as we are constituted to apprehend them, must have their corresponding Ideas in our minds likewise.

According to this view, every law realized will appear under the characteristics of universality and necessity. The first it certainly must have, and the last can be suspended only upon the question, whether Somatological laws in the Divine determination are of fixed and absolute perfection, or are arbitrary, and of various degrees of perfection. And again, on the other hand, every conception of law appearing under these characteristics, even if supposed not to be realized in any known system, must find its reality somewhere,—either in some other part of space, or in some other period of time;—it must be a prophecy of the distant or the future. But such a prophetic Idea could be developed only in connexion with some form of reality in some degree symbolising with it. Could this be called Theory? I think the mind would repose in it as something higher than Theory. Newton's mind grasped the great law of gravitation before he verified it. He did not yield to it as the actual law of our system, until he had verified it: but it always seems to me to have lain in his mind from its first conception, as a law which must find its verification somewhere. It was a law penetrated by an Idea.

Theory strictly is an ingenious conjecture—a tentative act—a feeling after a law, determined by the mere nascent development of an Idea, and serving the purpose of generalizing the phenomena, reducing them to order, and preparing them for exact and proportionate expressions. This is exemplified in the Theory of Atoms, employed to represent the determinate proportions of chemical affinities.

In attempting an enumeration of cardinal Somatological Ideas, I shall begin with

IX.—THE USEFUL.

I have already introduced this Idea in distinguishing between it and the Beautiful. It comprehends the final end of Material Creation in respect to creatures endowed with natural sensibilities—with the capacity of physical enjoyment and suffering. The Useful, as an Idea, reaches to the perfect constitution and development of the world under this point of view.

The universe, as far as presented to our observation, does not fully meet this Idea. When we reflect upon the character of the Great Creator, and the beneficent designs which every where appear, taken in connexion with the glorious prospects opened to our view in Divine Revelation, we must believe that the universe is constituted upon this Idea, and that all things are tending to its realization. Nay, may it not be already realized in other parts of the vast whole; and is not the Christian's heaven those perfected worlds?

This Idea has stimulated human industry to work its wonders. Man finds the world a rude uncultivated wilderness before he begins to exert his industry. He fills it with comfortable dwellings, transforms it into smiling harvest fields, appropriates its mineral resources in a thousand useful arts, and even controls its powerful elements, to accomplish his designs. He refines and multiplies his wants, and by contriving to gratify them, multiplies his enjoyments.

God has made his highly endowed creature the skilful instrument of perfecting for kindly uses, a world which he has filled with ample resources. Human industry has not yet attained its limit: the resources of the world are not yet exhausted: this beneficent Idea has new wonders yet in store.

The world was made under the Idea of Utility, as one of the constitutive elements; and the improvements which are in progress, whether by physical laws in their necessary development, or by human industry, are governed by this Idea. But this Idea is general and comprehensive ; and gives only the most general form of Somatological law. We have yet to enquire into the Ideas which determine its interior forms, relations, and qualities.

X.—CENTRALIZATION AND DIFFUSION.

The Idea of Centralization is that of perfect dependency and union. The conception of body involves the conception of parts and a whole. But no whole is possible without centralization.

If there were but one vast Whole existent, a law of centralization would be sufficient. But if distinct wholes are to be arranged into a system with mutual relations and dependencies, and with one common and universal dependency constituting the unity of the system ; then there must be likewise a law of diffusion, harmoniously opposing itself to the law of centralization, and preventing a universal consolidation. This is the grand Idea upon which the universe is constituted. *Gravitation,* or the Centripetal force and law, is the great principle of centralization ;—the *Centrifugal force,* the great principle of diffusion.

That it is an Idea, and not a mere theoretical conception, cannot well be questioned ; for the characteristics of universality and necessity seem plainly to belong to it. In the wide space, beyond the utmost limits of observation, whatever worlds and systems may there exist, we believe, under all the force of a commanding Idea, to be arranged and governed on these two stupendous and all-sufficient principles. The history of science shows the constant tendency of the human Reason to the evolution of this Idea: and now that it is evolved, no other can be admitted as the Idea of the Universe.

XI.—AFFINITY AND REPULSION.

This is akin to the preceding, and perhaps comprehended within it. There is this important distinction, however, which is obvious: centralization and diffusion relate to cosmical masses; whereas, affinity and repulsion relate to the constitution of the generic and specific varieties of the particular and minute masses which enter into the great wholes which are governed by the former.

Affinity is of two kinds: First, the cohesion of homogeneous matter; secondly, chemical affinity. The first is permanent affinity, existing independently of change; the second takes place through change.

Repulsion is likewise of two kinds: First, mechanical; secondly, chemical. The first relates to the motion of bodies by mechanical force; the second, to the motion of chemical decomposition.

No less universal and necessary is the principle of Affinity and Repulsion, than that of Centralization and Diffusion. One is the Idea of the great harmonious and all-comprehending system; the other, the Idea of the minute and interior composition of the forms and orders of particular bodies. One determines the laws which grasp the wholes, without respect to their interior constitution; the other determines the laws of this interior constitution.

XII.—LIFE.

Life is the Idea of the Organific power. Organic bodies are distinguished from inorganic in three ways:

First, they possess determinate, generic, and specific forms, which remain unchanged amid the ceaseless flux of the particles which enter into them. Secondly, the actuating or moving power here tends to an unceasing change of particles; while mechanical forces tend to equilibrium, chemical to composition or to decomposition, and then pause. Thirdly, in inorganic bodies accretions are made either by a simple cohesion of homogeneous matter, or by a simple union of particles, determined by inherent affinities; while in organic bodies, a new power, acting from within, resists cohesion and affinities; and, by a process of assimilation, projects, as from a centre, distinct particles metamorphosed into substances of qualities and forms determined by its own inward law.

Wonderful is the law of life! Under the myriad varieties of vegetable and animal bodies, it still preserves its identity. Observation gives us only the phenomena: the law is metaphenomenal. We think of it too as a law universal and necessary. It springs therefore from an Idea of the Reason.

XIII.—POLARITY.

Polarity, as thus far determined, is magnetic, electric, chemical, crystalline, and optical. It is the conception of disturbance, repulsion, and separation, produced by the attempted union of like kinds; and of harmony and repose, produced by the actual union of unlike kinds.

That an Idea lies behind all the observations which have been made respecting polarity, determining their processes and results, is manifest: and that the conception of polarity, as an attempted expression of the Idea, has been the guiding star to the most eminent philosophers in their investigations in magnetism, electricity, chemistry, crystallization, and light, is abundantly attested: nevertheless, it does not yet appear, notwithstanding the confident assertion of Schelling, that the conception fully embodies the Idea, and leads it forth to the determination of a universal and necessary law. As yet, it is a theory, like a thin and almost transparent cloud, with the sun behind it.

XIV.—INSTINCT.

In vegetables we have vital forces, and the law of life, in its beautiful and wonderful variety of manifestation. In animals, as the genus, we have life and instinct. In man, the thinking species, we have life, instinct, and spirit. Instinct and spirit manifesting themselves in the sphere of observation, are not organific, but motive. Vital forces produce motion, but it is the motion of the organific process. Instinct and spirit produce muscular activity in the accomplishment of an end.

The motion produced by spirit, or voluntary motion, belongs to psychology: Instinctive motion belongs to somatology. Instinct is not volition, it is the shadow of volition in the animal sphere. In both activities, ends are proposed, intelligential ends. In volition, the ends are deliberated upon and estimated by the agent himself, and selected by an act of freedom. In instinct, the ends are proposed by the infinite and all-governing intelligence, just as ends are proposed by this intelligence for all the movements of nature: and then the activities of the animal are determined to these ends by necessary laws manifesting themselves in the constitution of the animal, unaccompanied by deliberation and exclusive of choice. The all-comprehensive law of the mere animal nature is instinct. It is a universal and necessary law, governing a mode of being, and springing from a constitutive Idea.

XV. REGULARITY, UNIFORMITY, VARIETY, SYMMETRY, AND DETERMINATE FORM.

These have already been considered in their esthetical relations. They exist likewise in somatological relations. They bear a relation to the useful, analogous to the relation which they bear to the beautiful. They all necessarily result from determinate and yet diffusive law. This appears palpably in the action of centripetal and centrifugal forces, in vital forces, and in crystallization.

In the absolutely perfect, they will not appear in conflict under the two Ideas of Beauty and Utility. In the actual nature submitted to observation, they do appear in conflict. In the arts cultivated by man, this conflict is constantly experienced ; for example, in the form and apportionment of buildings. The Grecian Temple is a pure development of beautiful symmetry ; a commodious dwelling-house is a development of useful symmetry. There is a constant struggle in human art to unite the two ; and they appear together, in consequence, in a union of compromise.

The determinate form of nature viewed on a grand scale, as in the shapes of the planets, the line of their orbits, and the vast arrangements of the starry heavens, present us a perfect union of the two Ideas. It is only in the details of the particular orbs that we perceive the opposition, and especially in the sphere of human activity. In these details, we judge under the light of Astronomy and Geology, that a mighty progress is making from lower to higher states. The intelligential activity, too, in being brought to task itself in the field which it occupies, is at the same time developing its own greatness, and reaching forward to its ultimate destiny.

XVI.—IDENTITY, DIFFERENCE, RESEMBLANCE.

Identity and Difference are antithetical conceptions. Resemblance is the union of the two, in two or more objects compared together. Personal Identity is the sameness of the individual being in substance and essential properties, taken in different and indefinitely distant times and places.

In material particles or parts, there is no necessary identity, for matter, under the forces and laws of nature, is liable to indefinite change. The identity of bodies is an identity of certain forms and qualities, admitting differences in other forms and qualities. Here an identity of substance cannot be considered, for the reason above stated —the constant flux of matter.

Identity and Difference actually existing in nature, lays the ground for the classification of bodies into genera, species, and individuals. Generic forms and qualities are those which are the most general and comprehensive ; thus *animal*, for example, embraces only the forms and qualities which distinguish all animals from all other living organisms. But in *man*, forms and properties are added which, as *differentia*, distinguish him from all other *kinds* or *species* of animals, and, at the same time, identify all the individuals of his own species : while in the *individual* man George, or Thomas, forms and properties are added which distinguish him from every other individual of his kind, and of course identify him with no one.

It has been said that genera and species are names of general conceptions, which we may form and vary at pleasure; and that consequently they have no corresponding realities. It is indeed true that we have no such living and real being as *animal*, comprising only *generic* forms and qualities; and no such living and real being as *man*, comprising only *specific* forms and qualities. It is true, also, that we can widely vary our classifications by uniting together different particulars under new points of agreement. But let it be recollected, that the words *animal* and *man* do express *forms* and *qualities* which really exist: The forms and qualities indicated by *animal* are found really existing in every particular animal; and the forms and qualities indicated by *man*, are found in every individual man. And when we vary our classifications, we are still conversant with realities, for our classification still corresponds to real identities and differences. We indeed view them in different relations, and invent new names to represent our new views; but, nevertheless, we cannot view them out of actually existing relations.

The truth is, that the determinate forms and qualities of bodies exhibit both identity and difference; and these in their universality constitute the possibility of all classification. If there were all difference, there would be all variety, and of course no classification. On the other hand, if there were all identity, there would be no variety, and here again no possibility of classification. Identity enables us to bind together in classes and systems: Difference enables us to separate the classes, systems, and particulars: so that, when we view parts, we still assign them their general relations: and when we view wholes, we still distinguish and comprehend the particulars which go to make them up. We thus know the harmony and variety of the Universe.

If any one were to remark, that universal identity would not be incompatible with some diversity, inasmuch as the identical forms and qualities might be presented in different relations of time and space ; it would be sufficient to reply, that as we should in this case have continually the same recurring perception, we in reality would be unable to distinguish different points in space, and different periods in time.

On the other hand, if any one were inclined to merge identity into mere resemblance, by calling it the most perfect resemblance, he might be convinced of the utter impossibility of this conception, by reflecting, that resemblance cannot be constituted without identity. There must be sameness in some forms or qualities, to enable us to bring them together ; and the union of points of sameness with points of difference, in fact, makes resemblance.

The conception of Identity and Difference, and their common relation in resemblance, is a universal and necessary conception. We extend it not only to what we see, we know it must pervade all worlds. As a necessary somatological conception, it must find in the reason its corresponding and constitutive Idea. Hence, when phenomena are given as the required conditions and antecedents in Time, the Reason under this constitutive Idea—the Idea from which sprang forth the perfect system and the manifold variety of the Universe—begins to cognise resemblance, to classify the objects of perception, and to seize upon the glorious unity reigning amid the glorious diversity.

XVII.—DESIGN, FINAL CAUSE, MEANS AND END.

These are only different ways of expressing the same Idea. The great Architect of the Universe forecasted his design ; this design, contemplated by himself, is the final cause of the Creation ; and the Creation itself is a great system of means and ends, in which the means are ends, and the ends means, in a long chain of linked and harmonious subordination, and all connected with an ultimate end which is not a means, upon which the eye of God reposes in infinite and quiet delight.

This Idea of the Infinite Reason, is found also in the human reason. Hence nothing is more natural and spontaneous than the enquiries which the mind makes after final causes in the structure of plants and animals, nay, in the whole order of Creation.

As a principle of philosophical research, the conception of Final Causes has been adopted chiefly in respect to organised bodies, because here more manifest and certain ; and here unquestionably it has achieved stupendous results, of which the labors of Cuvier alone are a sufficient attestation.

The conception of final causes, like other universal and necessary conceptions, accepts the observations of the senses as its condition and antecedent in time ; but it can rest upon an Idea of the Reason alone as its constitutive element. Phenomena fleeting and apparently irregular and confused, are grasped by this idea and reduced to orderly and beautiful relations. And it is not only in fields of observation actually presented, that it arranges and composes phenomena, and educes system ; as a watchful and expectant eye, it is ever looking about to find phenomena that shall fall in with its own preconceptions. It is a necessary prophetic thought, which wanders through the universe Where no observation can reach, it has full assurance there is design.

I here close my view of Somatological Ideas. Howeve

brief and imperfect, it will answer the end I have in view, namely, Logical Construction.

I will complete this outline, with the Logical Ideas.

XVIII.—TRUTH.

Truth is an antithetical idea : its opposite is Falsehood.

The great aim of the Reason is Truth : and Logic comprises the Laws which govern the Reason in its searches after, in the processes by which it arrives at, Truth.

Truth in itself is identical with the highest form of Reality—with absolute and necessary Reality ; and it is the parent of all other reality—the Reality of actual objective Being. The Ideas, and the necessary and universal conceptions which immediately spring out of them, are the essential body of Truth : Actual Being is the exterior embodiment of Truth. Hence Truth is that in which the Reason ultimately, necessarily, and securely reposes.

When the Reason, contemplating Ideas and necessary conceptions, and their exterior embodiment in the constitution of the Universe, gives the judgment of Truth, it does so under the great Idea of Truth. Mere phenomena contain no truth, because they contain no reality, and consequently they cannot contain the judgment of Truth. The phenomena being given as conditions or occasions antecedent in time, the Reason under the Idea of Truth forms the conception of the subjective and objective Realities—it affirms that they are true.

Falsehood is the opposite or negative of Truth, with the appearance or pretension of being Truth. In the highest—the pure region of Truth, Falsehood cannot well find place. Ideas, and primary absolute conceptions, have such decided characteristics that it is difficult to imagine how a falsehood can disguise itself in their habiliments. They are necessary, universal, and intuitively clear. How can a falsehood put on the appearances of these? The very supposition seems to involve an absurdity. If it were so, could we ever have a certain and infallible test of truth? Is not this the great distinction between a presumed truth and a presumed falsehood, that when carried up to the primary conceptions and their determining ideas, the first quietly flows into these as a congenial essence, while the latter is repelled and flows back to seek its home elsewhere? The necessity, the universality, the intuitive clearness, of the conception, are what give it the character of absolute Truth. Unless it attain these characteristics it cannot be absolute Truth; and when it does attain them, it cannot but be absolute Truth. Falsehood here then must be excluded. In this pure region, a mind may mislead itself by bringing along with it the gross prejudices, the wild and baseless theories, which it has collected in a lower region, and dogmatically investing them with the attire of Truth. But it is a wilful act—the act of a professed Sophist and Sectarian. But to the humble, sincere, open-eyed, and pure-hearted child of Truth, falsehood can find no entrance among these primary ideas and principles. It is in the lower region itself—the region of observation, induction, and deduction, of human will and human passion, that falsehood finds a wide and natural field to walk in. Here the sense may be deceived by appearances, and the intellect amused and led astray by "Idols of the Tribe, the Den, the Market-place, and the Theatre."

But in whatever region of Knowledge the Reason takes its stand, Truth is its great and legitimate object. The Idea of Truth is the spring of all its activity.

XIX.—THE PHILOSOPHICAL IDEA.

This is the Idea of *accounting for* the development and progress of humanity in science, art, government, and religion. It is the Idea of *accounting for* every thing perceived or thought of.

Enquiry supposes that the mind cannot rest satisfied with phenomena, whether of immediate consciousness, or taken in their secondary state, and representing the actual objects and events of the external world. No enquiry would indeed be made, if there were no phenomena presented. But why is not the mind satisfied with its sensations, and spontaneous and natural perceptions? Why does it raise enquiries respecting causes and laws? Not only is the Idea of Cause and Law here presumed, but also the Idea, that if causes and laws can be assigned, the phenomena will be accounted for. This restlessness of the human mind, when dealing with mere phenomena; this conception, that there must be causes and laws; this firm conviction, that science is gained, when the causes and laws are determined; and this quiet satisfaction in the result—all show the working of the philosophical Idea, or element of our being.

That this is an Idea, cannot be doubted, for it is both necessary and universal. The Reason affirms that all phenomena are to be accounted for; and that the principle of every phenomenon really and necessarily exists, or the phenomenon would not be possible.

The connection between this Idea and the preceding is very close: and some, at first thought, may even look upon them as identical. There is, however, one obvious distinction: Truth embraces all absolute and necessary principles, and, although gained upon phenomenal conditions, it may be contemplated separately from all phenomena: the philosophical Idea, on the other hand, always connects itself with phenomena, as determining the activity of the Intelligence in respect to them. Truth is the cardinal Idea of Primordial Logic; the philosophical, the cardinal Idea of Inductive Logic. Truth is the simple Idea of the primal and absolute authority; the philosophical, the Idea of reducing every thing under that authority.

XX.—INTUITION.

Intuition has already been represented as one of the functions of the Reason—the function of immediate insight. Now, connected with this function, is the Idea of the perfect and the absolute authority of such an insight. Hence we assign the name of the function, to express the corresponding Idea. Thus the Reason, by the function of Intuition, perceives, directly, that there are three, and only three, dimensions in space. Such is its immediate and necessary perception. Now, this is a particular perception, or one instance of Intuition: but, upon this one instance, or upon any similar instance, there appears the universal affirmation, that Intuition is an absolute and perfect law of cognition,—that whatever is known by Intuition, is ultimately and certainly known. All axioms—all first principles, and all primary sensuous perceptions, are thus legitimated. But the universal affirmation, or conception, itself reposes upon an Idea of the Reason,—namely, the Idea of Intuition, as the primal and highest and most authoritative form of Cognition. This Idea permeates Primordial Logic, and governs all its particular determinations.

XXI.—INVOLUTION AND EVOLUTION.

Besides Intuition, there are two other forms of cognising truths or realities. These are Induction and Deduction. In the inductive form, we cognise universal truths through particular phenomena in which the truths are embodied. In the deductive form, we cognise particular truths through universal truths which comprehend them, and out of which they are evolved. The two forms, in relation to each other, may be represented under the following formulæ:

Induction {
a, *b*, *c*, *d*, &c. are X
Z is *a*, *b*, *c*, *d*, &c.
Therefore Z is X.

Deduction {
Z is X
a, or *b*, or *c*, or *d*, &c. is Z
Therefore *a*, or *b*, &c. is X.

The first is an involution of inducted particulars, into a general expression. The second is an evolution of the general expression to a particular determination.

According to these formulæ, it is evident that the Induction must precede the Deduction, and that the latter is a return to the elementary particulars of the former.

If the mind be supposed to be placed at the point of observing the particulars, then, by the Inductive formula, it arrives at the general expression. If the general principle, or expression, be already gained by a previous Induction, and the mind be placed at this point, then it can perceive each particular through the Deductive formula.

But here the question may be started, what value is

there in the Deductive formula, since it is a mere return to particulars which were grasped by the Inductive at the outset?

First. There is a more perfect comprehension of the general truth when viewed under the two forms, in their reciprocal relation.

Secondly. The Induction, as an *inference*, does not measure itself by the Induction, as a mere *bringing in* of the facts. The grounds of the general inference, made upon the limited colligation, will be hereafter explained. But this general inference upon the limited colligation, is the fact which shows the necessity of deductions, subsequent to the induction which establishes the general principle from which the deductions are made; for, since all the particulars were not really brought in and colligated, the general principle, when once established, becomes an authority for conclusions respecting particulars not originally inducted.

Thirdly. The Deductive formula does not invariably connect itself with the Inductive, as above exhibited. General principles are not universally the result of Inductive inferences, but are often *à priori* and intuitive. The first principles of morals and mathematics are palpable instances. These principles are established as *à priori* and intuitive judgments; and then sciences, vast, complicated, and momentous, are evolved by the Deductive formula.

Fourthly. In the practical affairs of life, there are received principles which are constantly applied by all men, without instituting anew enquiries respecting their origin and basis. Indeed, multitudes who are capable of applying the principles, are unfitted for the investigations through which they were originally obtained. This practical application is made in a series of deductions, which, although not assuming, in the common language of men, the syllogistic form, nevertheless admit of being reduced to it.

These considerations are sufficient to show the value of the Deductive formula.

The fundamental Ideas of the Inductive and Deductive formulæ, and of the modes of cognition which they represent, are Involution and Evolution. On the one hand, the Reason does not contemplate any phenomenon or fact apart and isolated. It must be colligated with some other fact, and these again with others, and so on until we have a mass of facts bound together in the unity of system, and involved in a great central law.

On the other hand, when the Reason seizes upon any law, axiom, or first principle, it does not contemplate it as dormant, unproductive, or ever revolving within itself. It feels impelled by its own Idea to look out for an exterior sphere in which the great truth shall unfold itself in manifold varieties.

The Reason takes these two directions necessarily and universally; and hence manifests here again the determinative power of Ideas.

XXII.—ANALYSIS AND SYNTHESIS.

According to a general definition, Synthesis is the conception of the composition of systems—of systems of Truth according to logical principles and formulæ; and systems of bodies according to natural and mechanical laws: while Analysis is the conception of the decomposition of systems reversing the order of the Synthesis, and running back in the chain of principles, formulæ, and laws. Geometry is a completed synthesis of principles and consequences. When taught, the synthetical order is observed—the pupil being instructed how to put together the several theorems in a way to show their dependence upon the axioms and definitions, and upon preceding demonstrations constantly accumulating in the progress of the synthesis. A watch, also, or any piece of machinery, when its separated parts are taken up and put together according to the laws of the mechanism, presents us a synthesis. On the other hand, we may begin with the remotest deductions of Geometry, and enquire upon what grounds they rest; these grounds, in part at least, will prove to be other propositions deduced from something still going before: in this way we may continue to unwind the whole concatenation of dependent demonstrations until we arrive at the self-evident principles. So, likewise, we may take in pieces the watch in the order of the mechanical dependency, until we arrive at the main-spring. We thus accomplish an analysis. He that has a perfect knowledge of Geometry, and of the watch, can readily synthesise or analyse both; and the same kind of knowledge enables him to do one or the other. To one ignorant of Geometry, and just setting out to gain a knowledge of it, the synthetical mode is the true and certain mode; for every step here is made according to established principles and demonstrations, which are continually evolving. Here the analytical mode, by constantly referring to previous demonstrations which are not yet comprehended, is liable to produce perplexity and confusion. In respect to the watch, also, an ingenious learner would more safely make experiments in putting together than in taking apart.

In the construction of scientific systems, and in mechanical constructions, a synthesis of the parts necessarily precedes an analysis of the whole. The natural mode of constructing is likewise the natural mode of learning. But where wholes are presented us, as in pieces of machinery which are strange to us, and in natural organisms such as animals and plants, and in the subtile combinations of chemical affinities, analysis of necessity precedes synthesis. In such cases analysis cannot at once proceed with the nice accuracy of geometry and the watch, where the geometer and the mechanician know precisely where to begin, and how to separate, because they know the beginning, the continuity, and the completion of the systematic and the organic wholes before them. Instead of this, many tentative, and even destructive and futile experiments are made before the laws and the harmony of the construction appear.

Analysis and Synthesis do not correspond to Induction and Deduction, but precede or accompany them. In geometry there is, in the progress of the evolution, a constant synthesis of axioms, definitions, previous demonstrations, and new forms and relations. The whole putting together must be made accordingly to a rigid logic: but nevertheless, there is an ingenuity exercised in the combinations and ordering of the parts, for the purpose of eliciting conclusions or evolving proof, which is not provided for in the rules of deduction. This belongs in reality to another function of the Reason, which we have named *Invention.**

Analysis precedes Induction with experiments which are often the starting point; and then accompanies it, by evolving in the continued experiments new and important phenomena.

Synthesis also accompanies Induction, arranging and

* Supra, p. 131.

combining the discovered truths so as to form a compact and harmonious system.

Analysis and Synthesis are thus subsidiary to Induction and Deduction. The Inductive Function is striving to see the general truth through the manifold particulars in which it is manifested, in the unity of system. The Deductive Function is striving to see the particular and remote conclusions comprehended in the general truth, in the unity of system also. The Inventive Function, by its analysis and synthesis, presents the requisite media of the Inductive and Deductive cognitions, and preconceives and suggests the systematic construction.

All these functions are related in their operations to the Intuitive Function, as will appear in subsequent developments.

Analysis and Synthesis, considered as Ideas in the Reason, are certainly nearly akin to, if not identical with, the Ideas of Involution and Evolution. If the Ideas be regarded as Identical, then Analysis and Synthesis are only conceptions under the common Ideas distinguishable from Induction and Deduction by the characteristics above given.

It appears to me, however, that Analysis and Synthesis are distinct Ideas determining Invention; while Involution and Evolution determine Induction and Deduction. Involution and Evolution are Ideas which determine the conception of phenomena running together and colligated in general laws, and general laws reciprocally governing the development of phenomena; and the conception of particular truths and conclusions comprehended in general truths, and general truths evolved into the particular truths and conclusions. But Analysis and Synthesis, taken as Ideas, determine the conception of a system of laws governing a system of bodies—where the whole implies constituent parts, and the parts imply an harmonious whole; and the conception of a system of truths, where each particular truth with the long chain of consequences which it involves is interlinked with other truths and consequences, constituting the unity of absolute science, and where the particular truths and consequences ultimately lead back to pure intuitions.

It thus becomes plain how Analysis and Synthesis aid Induction and Deduction. While inducting facts for the purpose of finding a law in relation to any subject of enquiry, there must be some preconception or Idea to guide in the selection of phenomena, and the form of the experiments: and now the Inventive function is busy in arranging and combining, and in various tentative suggestions. But what governs the Inventive function? Is it not the great Idea of System, where constituted wholes and constitutive parts are reciprocal; or, in other words, is it not Analysis and Synthesis? And so again, when engaged in demonstrating theorems, and solving problems, the Idea of the wide-spread relations of truths and principles—the Idea of their synthetical and analytical capacity—determines the Inventive function in searching for, and finding, the material of the ratiocination.

The same appears also in our reasonings on moral and all practical questions. We find arguments, because, under the Ideas of Analysis and Synthesis—the Ideas of the wide-spread and systematic relations of truth—we know where to look for them.

It is sufficiently obvious that the Ideas of Analysis and Synthesis are necessary and universal. Whatever be the scope or the subject of our reasoning, they inevitably make their appearance. Nor is it conceivable that any course of reasoning can be conducted independently of them, since truth, in its very nature, is analytical and synthetical.

I here close the outline of Ideas. Next in order will be the consideration of axioms, and of primary cognitions and definitions—those which belong to the Intuitive Function. We shall thus complete Primordial Logic.

SECTION IV.

PRIMARY SENSUOUS COGNITIONS, OR COGNITIONS OF THE EXTERIOR CONSCIOUSNESS.

THE primary sensuous cognitions, in general, are those which are formed intuitively by the Reason, respecting the exterior world, through the force of its constitutive Ideas, and upon condition of sensuous impressions in the exterior consciousness.

When these impressions are received in the exterior consciousness, the Reason, under the Idea of objective exteriority,* conceives of an outer world. This is its first sensuous cognition.

Exerting the muscular activity under the Idea of our personal causality, and experiencing a resistance in this outer world, we now, under the Ideas of cause, space, limitation, and substance, cognise body. In this cognition are involved at once what are commonly called the *primary qualities* of body, namely, hardness or resistance, extension and form. They are primary, because they comprise the necessary contents of the cognitions. Indeed, the cognition is now complete. *Secondary qualities* are cognised in particular bodies through the appropriate organs, under the Idea of Cause, or of determinate law.

* Supra, p. 155.

When body is known, then the sensations of which we are immediately conscious, are referred to causes inhering in bodies, or to their specific constitution, correlating with the human sensitivity.

The cognitions of body involving the primary qualities, are thus primary sensuous intuitions.

The knowledge of specific forms, of relative magnitudes, and of relative distances, implies acts of memory, in connecting the successive impressions made upon the muscular organism, in handling bodies, and in locomotion. There are also various acts of calculation, and inferences from comparison.

Introduced into the external world, phenomena now put on their secondary* form: we are no longer engaged with the simple sensations of our being, but with the realities from which they spring; and which, in the case of the secondary qualities of bodies, we name from the very sensations which they supplant in our habitual thought.

Next in the order of this development of sensuous cognition, is to be noticed the remarkable transfer which is made of the knowledge originally belonging to the muscular organism, as the medium, to the organs of the secondary qualities, and, as chief of these, to the eye. The colors of objects, and the varieties of light and shade, become early associated with the primary qualities of bodies, with their specific forms, relative magnitudes, and distances; so that, the simple sensations of color become such ready and familiar signs of the external world, that we now know every thing by the eye alone. Next to the eye, in importance, is the ear, in this acquired system of

* Supra, p. 59.

signs. The other senses, however, play a part by no means insignificant.

Thus, by the power of Ideas, man steps out from his internal sensations into the world which is correlated to him ; and so appropriates these sensations, that every act of consciousness becomes an act of observation.

SECTION V.

PRIMARY SUBJECTIVE COGNITIONS, OR COGNITIONS OF THE INTERIOR CONSCIOUSNESS.

THESE are the cognitions which are formed intuitively by the Reason, respecting the simple subjective, through the force of its Ideas, and upon condition of the phenomena which arise from the subjective activity.

When these phenomena are recognised in the interior consciousness, the Reason, under the Idea of subject,* conceives of the simple subjective, or *the Me*.

Under the appropriate Ideas, we are next determined to cognise *the Me* as the spiritual substance, antithetical to the material substance which we have cognised without.

Here the same remarkable transfer of phenomena, which we have noticed in the preceding Section in respect to bodies, takes place in respect to the spiritual being.† Having cognised the subject, we no longer think of bare phenomena of the consciousness, but of effects and manifestations of spiritual faculties; and the intelligence, causality, and sensitivity which constitute our triune being, are known and distinguished. The Ideas of personality, Right and Wrong, Freedom, Responsibility, and Immortality, now clothe this being with lofty and glorious attributes; and through the simple consciousness of interior phenomena, as conditions, we have the intuitions of self-knowledge.

* Supra, p. 155. † Supra, pp. 56, 57.

It will be understood both in respect to sensuous, and to subjective intuitive cognitions, that when I undertake to point out their progressive development; and the transfer of phenomena from the consciousness to the objective and subjective realities—thus associating the phenomena with the causes which produce them, instead of viewing them in the field of their immediate manifestation,—I nevertheless do not mean to aver that this progressive development and this transfer are really recognised in the consciousness in relation to successive and marked periods of time; but only to indicate the logical order and relations of the facts. In the very dawn of our being in the world of the senses, our faculties open their play unitedly and harmoniously; and ere we begin to exercise reflection, we find ourselves in a world already realized. But when we attempt to know ourselves, we must of necessity represent to ourselves in clear propositions the logical order of the cognitive development. In doing this, we assume periods of time corresponding to the order of this development for the sake of distinctness, while yet, in relation to time, there was actually simultaneity.

SECTION VI.

AXIOMS.

AXIOMS* are those truths which depend neither upon Induction, nor upon previous deductions; but which are intuitively cognised under determinate Ideas.

It is evident that before deductions are possible, there must be judgments expressed in propositions. Now these judgments must of necessity be resolved either into intuitions, or into Inductions. If into the latter, even then, in the last result, we come to intuitions, since all facts of observation, whether belonging to the interior or exterior consciousness, must ultimately rest in simple intuitions.

The consciousness of phenomena, if regarded as a form of perception, is manifestly immediate and intuitive. But beyond this, the primary sensuous and subjective cognitions, as we have seen, are intuitive likewise. The Real is not an induction from the phenomenal: The latter is a condition; the former an Intuition.

But Axioms, while they are independent of Induction and Deduction on the one hand,—on the other, must not be confounded with the primary cognitions whether sensuous or subjective. These primary cognitions relate to the Reality of Being; axioms relate to the Reality of Truth.† A primary cognition expressed, becomes a pro-

* Greek 'Αξίωμα, Authority, Worth. Hence, an established principle—one the authority of which cannot be called in question.

† Supra, p. 140.

position which affirms existence. Thus a primary sensuous cognition expressed, becomes an affirmation of the existence of bodies and their qualities : and a primary subjective cognitive expressed, becomes an affirmation of the existence of the simple subjective with its faculties and functions.

But an axiom is a proposition expressing a judgment of universal and absolute truth—of truth which indeed holds important connexions with actual Being, when actual Being is given ; but which, nevertheless, is no less true, if being be not given, or only hypothesised. For example, the axiom, *If equals be added to equals, the sums will be equal*, is a truth no less, if there be no actual Being. And the axiom, *every body must be in space*, demands merely a hypothesis of body, and not an affirmation of the existence of body. It is true, indeed, that the mind does not proceed to form axioms antecedently, in the order of time, to judgments of actual Being ; * but still, when the axioms are formed, they are seen to have a necessary and independent existence, and a logical antecedence.

Axioms are determined immediately by Ideas. The judgments which they express are the first judgments of Truth ; and they in themselves are the first propositions of Truth.

Axioms may be classified, according to the philosophical divisions above given, into the metaphysical, and the nomological. The Reason, with its Ideas entering into the world of Reality, forms not only its cognitions of that which is, conceived of as mere facts of existence, but affirms also truths universal and absolute. The Reason again, by its

* Supra, pp. 60 and 140.

Ideas, not only determines the laws which actually govern the Real, but here likewise makes universal and absolute affirmations respecting the necessary forms of law. These axiomatic affirmations reach the spheres of determinate science, and constitute the starting points of the scientific construction.

METAPHYSICAL AXIOMS.

I. AXIOM OF SUBSTANCE AND ATTRIBUTES.—The Reason not only cognises particular substances and attributes, but upon such particular cognitions as the chronological conditions, makes the universal affirmation, *Every substance implies attributes, and every attribute implies substance.*

II. AXIOM OF CAUSE AND EFFECT.—The Reason first cognises a particular cause upon certain phenomenal conditions; and then upon this particular cause, taken in its turn as a condition, it affirms the axiom, *Every phenomenon implies a cause.*

III. AXIOM OF BODY AND SPACE.—Body is a primary sensuous cognition; but no sooner does the cognition take place, than the Reason affirms, *Every body must be in space.*

IV. AXIOM OF TIME AND SUCCESSION.—The cognition of some particular succession is the conditional starting point; upon this the Reason affirms, *Every succession must be in time.*

V. AXIOM OF THE FINITE AND THE INFINITE.—Time and Space and the Deity are cognised under the Idea of the Infinite. In the antecedence of Time, the limited and finite are indeed first cognised; but it is only by the Idea of the Infinite that it becomes possible for us to affirm of any thing, *It is finite.* Thus a particular instance of the Finite becomes to us a condition of the judgment of the Infinite. The axiom which immediately follows this judgment in the order of Time is, *Every Finite implies the Infinite.*

VI. Axiom of the Objective and the Subjective.—The Subjective and Objective are cognised on the condition of particular phenomena, and their relations seen in particular instances. But here again the Reason affirms, *Universally the Objective implies the Subjective.*

VII. Axiom of Universal Being.—The Reason cognises matter and spirit in the particular, and then goes on to affirm, *All being must be either matter or spirit.*

These are the fundamental and most general metaphysical axioms. My object, however, in the above, as well as in what follows, is not to give a complete enumeration of the axioms, but only so far as shall serve to illustrate their peculiar characteristics, and the law under which they are determined. The characteristics of axioms are manifest: they are, absoluteness, independency, and universality. The law of their determination is equally clear; they are affirmed by the Reason, under the comprehension and force of its Ideas. In the general view already given of the evolution of Ideas,* the axioms will be recognised in the separation of the universal from the particular. In the order of time, we have the phenomenal, the particular, and the real, before we have the Axioms and Ideas; but when we have arrived at Axioms and Ideas, we perceive that in necessary existence they claim antecedence. Ideas determine those universal judgments of truth which are expressed in axioms; and these univer-

* Page 154.

sal judgments make the particular cognitions logically possible. For example, although I cognise a particular body in space, before I affirm the axiom, *Every body must be in space,* nevertheless, the potential existence of this judgment in the Reason constitutes the possibility of the particular cognition. This two-fold order,—the order of actual development in time, and the order of logical determination,—is the all-important principle to be kept in mind.

NOMOLOGICAL AXIOMS.

I. Axiom of Universal Law.—The Idea of Law determines this axiom, in the same way that the Idea of Cause determines the axiom of Causality. When particular phenomena are given, the Idea of Cause determines to the assignment of a particular cause ; and then upon this determines the affirmation, *Every phenomenon must have a cause :* so here, likewise, when particular phenomena are given, the Idea of Law determines to the assignment of some law ; and then upon this determines the affirmation, *Every phenomenon must have a law.* The Reason does not admit the possibility of chance. *No-Law* is as great an absurdity as *No-Cause.* A violation of law is conceivable only in the case of free, and therefore moral, agents ;* but even here the violation takes upon itself a form of law—a law of evil.

II. Axiom of the Uniformity of Nature.—Involved in the Idea of Law is that of order, harmony, and system. Order, harmony, and system are the developments of law. The Reason, therefore, not only affirms on the presentation of phenomena, there must be law govern-

* Moral Agency, Chap. VII., Sec. 1.

ing them; but still farther, these phenomena, thus governed, must present uniform recurrences and adjusted relations. The judgment thus formed is as universal and absolute as law itself. The axiom which has obtained as the expression of this judgment is as follows: *Nature is uniform in her operations.* By this axiom, we are led to bring together the homogeneous phenomena under the laws; and to expect with certainty the reappearance of phenomena.

III. Axiom of Universal Design.—This Axiom is determined by its appropriate Idea, and is as follows: *Whatever exhibits marks of design, is the work of an Intelligent Creator.*

The Ideas of Law and Design being developed, upon the condition of particular phenomena, the Axiom is thereupon immediately affirmed by the Reason, and becomes thenceforth the starting point and guide in all subsequent observations and experiments. This Axiom lies at the foundation of the so-called *à posteriori* argument for the existence of a God. Hence the ultimate basis of this argument is an *à priori* principle. But the ultimate basis of all cognition and ratiocination is, as we have seen, composed of *à priori* principles.

IV. Axiom of the Correspondence of Ideas and Reality.—*Every Idea implies a Reality of Actual Being or of Truth; and every Reality of Actual Being or of Truth, implies an Idea.* Every Idea developed is developed in connexion with some form of Reality,* in the effort of the Reason to grasp Reality. On the other hand, let us place ourselves in the world of Reality, and all our attempts at rational explanation lead us back to the Con-

* Supra, Part II., Sec. 3.

stitutive Ideas.* Now, upon the particular instances of this two-fold movement, the Reason supervenes with the universal affirmation which we have given above. All Ideas must attach themselves to Realities. All Realities must correspond to Ideas. It is the cardinal Axiom of pure Philosophy.

V. Moral Axioms.—I have given the cardinal moral Idea, namely, the Idea of Right and Wrong; but have not, for obvious reasons, entered into an explication of the particular Ideas of Justice, Benevolence, and so on, contained under it. It would, in like maaner, transcend the objects of this elementary Treatise to attempt, in detail, a presentation of the Moral Axioms. I will only remark, that the Divine Code announced at Sinai, and afterwards expounded and exemplified by the Redeemer of men, is in truth a collection of the fundamental Moral Axioms. They are indeed given under the form of laws, but they, at the same time, contain the affirmation of great and universal truths, uttered by the Infinite Reason, and responded to and re-affirmed by the Reason of every moral being.

VI. Esthetical Axioms.—These are determined by the Idea of Beauty, and comprise the first principles of Esthetical Science and of the rules of Art. I will adduce only two or three. These will answer the end of illustration. And I propose nothing further.

1. Beauty of every species and form has its Ideal or Archetype in the Imagination.

2. Every particular form of Beauty presents a union of regularity and variety.

3. Nature and Art are homogeneous; but the former does not limit the latter.

* Supra, Part I., Sec. 10.

VII. Somatological Axioms.—A complete exhibition of these would strictly belong to a Philosophy of Nature. Here, also, I am aiming only at an illustration of the great law of determining Axioms by the Ideas of the Reason.

1. *Axiom of the Inertia of Bodies.*—This Axiom is determined by the Idea of Matter, as a passive, and not a self-moving substance. Our actual experience is limited; nay, as to one part of the Axiom, we have no experience whatever, namely, *that a body, when put in motion, will continue to move on for ever in the line of the impulse, unless it meet with resistance from another force:* for we have no example of a body moving on without meeting with a resistance, tending either to bring it to a state of repose, or to change the direction of its motion. Besides, the universality and absoluteness of the entire affirmation must carry it beyond the possibility of experience.

2. *Axiom of Action and Reaction.*—The equality of reaction to action in an opposite direction, is an affirmation of universal and necessary truth, and therefore transcends the reach of experience. It is determined by the Idea of Relation under the third form.*

3. *Axiom of the Centre of Gravity.*—That every body has its centre of gravity, or a point, around which, when supported, all the parts of the body are balanced by the gravitating force, is unquestionably a universal and necessary conception. By mere experience it could not be determined; nor has any one ever attempted to determine it by experience. On the other hand, the Ideas of Action and Reaction, and of Centralization, cannot but determine it. It is a truth with which we begin our investigations in Nature, and of which no subsequent experience renders us more certain and confident.

* Supra, p. 171.

It will be seen by reflecting upon these and other axioms, which might be adduced from mechanical science, that the order of development is as follows:

First. The Reason, by its function of consciousness, comes, in the order of time, in connection with the phenomena of the external world.

Secondly. Its constitutive Ideas now form the original sensuous cognitions.

Thirdly. Thus introduced to particular Realities, the Ideas determine the universal judgments, which, when expressed in clear and convenient language, become axioms.

VIII.—Axioms of Pure Science.—These belong to the Mathematics. They are universal and intuitive affirmations of the Reason respecting the two forms of quantity, namely, *continued* and *discrete*.*

The most remarkable of these Axioms are those generally laid down in mathematical treatises as Axioms of Equality and Inequality. The Ideas which determine these Axioms are Quantity, Identity, and Difference.

Unity, multiplication, and diminution are the fundamental conceptions of the Science of Numbers: and these are contained in the Idea of Quantity. Equation is the fundamental conception of Geometry and Algebra; and this is given in Identity. Proportion, as an equation of ratios, is embraced by the same conception: and Ratio is but a comparison of quantities in respect to a common unit.

What remains to be remarked respecting axioms of this class will naturally come up under the following section.

* Supra, p. 92.

IX.—LOGICAL AXIOMS.

Axioms of this class relate to the processes of the Reason in general in its truth-seeking activity. We have seen that there are three cardinal forms of this activity, Intuition, Induction, and Deduction. Logical Axioms, therefore, may be classed under three corresponding heads.

AXIOMS RELATING TO INTUITION.—1. *Whatever the Reason intuitively knows, it knows under the characteristics of Universality and Necessity.* Intuitive truths are universal, that is, true without any exception ; and necessary, that is, their opposites are impossible.

2. *Whatever is known intuitively neither requires nor admits of demonstration.* Demonstration always presumes something going before which is already known. An endless retrogression of demonstrations is an absurdity. There must be some first truths which do not require demonstration ; and which, because they are first, do not admit of demonstration, since there is nothing by which to demonstrate them.

3. *Whatever is known intuitively must reach beyond any induction of particulars, and be antecedent to them in the order of necessary existence.* All induction is to us unavoidably limited, and must be led on by some antecedent and guiding principle. Induction without a purpose does not belong to philosophy.

AXIOMS RELATING TO INDUCTION.—Axioms relating to Intuition properly belong to this division of our Treatise. Axioms relating to Induction cannot be discussed here without anticipating what properly belongs to the next division. I shall, therefore, adjourn any statement of them.

AXIOMS RELATING TO DEDUCTION.—The reason above

given applies to this class of Axioms likewise. I shall accordingly adjourn them to the appropriate division, only remarking, that the "*Dictum de omni et nullo,*"—that *whatever is affirmed or denied of any term distributed, or, taken universally, is affirmed or denied of every particular comprehended under it,*—which Aristotle employs for explaining the validity of Deduction,—is a cardinal Axiom of this class.

SECTION VII.

OF THE CHARACTERISTICS OF AXIOMS IN GENERAL.

THESE characteristics have appeared in the course of the preceding section; they are Universality, Necessity, and Logical Antecedence to Induction and Deduction. My principal object in presenting them in a separate section, is to meet certain objections which have been urged against them.

It has been said that Axioms are merely statements of general observations. For example, that "Every body *must* be in space," means nothing more than that "Every body," as far as observation goes, *is* in space;" and that the Axiom, "If the same or equal quantities be added to equal quantities, their sums will be equal," and all the other Axioms of Equation, are merely of the same nature —expressions of general observations, unattended by any exception. Here, it will be perceived, that *universality* is merged into *generality;* the necessary into the inconceivable; and absolute truth into phenomenal conditions. That "Every body is in space" is thus merely a fact in the experience of all men; and it is inconceivable that any body should not be in space, because no fact of this kind has ever appeared in human experience. And if it be affirmed in opposition to this, that our thought at least surpasses our observation when passing beyond the possibility of actual observation—beyond all visible stars,—we think that if bodies be there also, they must there also be in space;—then it is replied that we make to ourselves in this case an imaginary representation of facts, which are merely copies of real facts, and that we are thus still in the region of observation:—The imagination takes the place of the sense, and wherever it goes, it only represents facts of the sense;—wherever it goes, it still makes for itself locality and particular facts. It does not fill immensity, nor grasp the universal,—it is only extending observation, and multiplying facts in another way.

The above is the argument fully stated. The answer does not appear to me difficult.

First. Before we can determine the validity of Axioms as necessary, universal, and intuitive truths, we must determine the validity of Ideas. Have we ideas of Space, of Necessity, of the Infinite, and so on? It does, indeed, seem, that if we have any positive cognition whatever, space is such an one. Equally positive is our cognition of its characteristics. Space is necessary and infinite, and having no limits, it has no form. And when we affirm that it is infinite, we do not mean to express merely our incapability of conceiving of limits; but the utter impossibility of limits. And, again, when we affirm that space is necessary, we do not mean to express merely our incapability of conceiving of no space, but the absolute being of space independently of all conception whatever. To make all cognitions personal and relative—deriving their characteristics from the individual constitution, is to deny to Truth any independent and absolute foundations. Then are we, for aught we know, only entertained with shadows, and without any fixed certainty of Reality. But we cannot yield to such doctrines; because we have that within us which assures us of their falsity. Our cognitions are facts, which are explained, and can only be explained by referring to the Ideas of the Reason.

Secondly. It has been shown in the preceding pages that the primary phenomena are simple sensations and affections of our own being revealed to consciousness; and that they assume their secondary character as manifestations of Reality, only through the supervention of Ideas. Without Ideas we should never attain substance, cause, or law, nor the exterior sphere of their manifestation. The very cognition of Body, therefore, depends upon Ideas which assign it substance and qualities, connect it with causes, and give it limits, and form and place. Not even a particular body can be cognised in space without Ideas.

Now, when we have the Idea of Space and the Cognition of Body with their opposite characteristics, the Reason cannot but affirm 'Every Body must be in space.' It is by no means an affair of observation and induction—it does not depend upon looking at this body and that body, in order to see whether they really are in space, and thus from multiplied observations drawing a general conclusion: On the contrary, no sooner do we cognise Space and Body, than we affirm absolutely and necessarily, 'Every Body must be in space.' So far from requiring imagination beyond actual observation, actual observation itself is anticipated.

The same reasoning will apply to all other Axioms. Take the Axiom, 'If equals be added to equals, the sums will be equal.' This Axiom is not a general conclusion from repeated trials and observations; but no sooner have we cognitions of Quantity, Identity, and so on, under the corresponding Ideas, than we make this and the kindred affirmations as universal and necessary affirmations. Here, again, instead of multiplying observations by imaginary cases, we pause for no observation whatever, but directly determine the Axioms by the Ideas.

Take another Axiom: 'If two straight lines intersect or cross each other, they can never meet again; but if produced, must go on diverging for ever.' Now, having formed the conception of two straight lines, drawn in space in the position above stated, we require no observation along the course of their production, either actually or by the imagination, in order to gather facts for a general conclusion: the instant the thought is fixed upon the lines at the point of intersection, the affirmation is made under the characteristics of Universality and Necessity.

The distinction between a conclusion gained by extended and careful observation, and a truth which at once flashes upon the mind—between the result of a long drawn out induction, and an immediate determination of the Reason, —is clear and palpable. The phenomenal conditions, under which such a truth is given, are easily separable from the truth itself; since they neither contain nor measure it: for example, the sensation of hardness which is conditional to our cognition of Space, neither contains nor measures Space. Again, the universality of such a truth is clearly distinguishable from the generality of an observation;—for the truth is affirmed without admitting the possibility of limits or exceptions, as that 'Every body must be in space;' but an observation, as that of the rising and setting of the sun, and that of the rising and falling of the tides, admits of the possibility of limits and exceptions. Omnipotence can change the whole order of the system, but not even Omnipotence can form a body not in space. Once more, the inconceivableness of a fact, and the necessity of a Truth, are also clearly distinguishable. A fact is inconceivable, when it is both removed from the sphere of our observation, and unlike any fact which has come under our observation. Thus a person residing within the Tropics, and who has never seen ice, cannot conceive of freezing water. The Cartesians rejected the Newtonian doctrine of the gravitation of bodies, on the ground that it is inconceivable that a body can act where it is not. Their error lay in adopting a theory of causality which made the causal activity a matter of sensuous conception. The Newtonian doctrine is inconceivable as a sensuous fact, if causes act only in the contact of material particles. But the doctrine was to be determined on other grounds than the possibility of observing the attractive force itself. A necessary truth, on the other hand, is not received, because it is conceivable as an observed fact, nor because its opposite is simply inconceivable: It is received because it is absolute and fixed as a cognition of the Reason, and its opposite impossible. That 'Every body must be in space, that 'Two straight lines cannot enclose a space,' are necessary truths, because seen by intuition to be such that their opposites are impossible. You may say, if you please, that their opposites are inconceivable, taking this term in an intense and superlative sense, and, indeed, identifying it with the impossible: but the term is objectionable, because ambiguous, and liable to confound pure intuitions of the Reason with facts of observation.

SECTION VIII.

GENERAL RELATIONS OF AXIOMS.

I. Axioms, in themselves, primary universal and necessary *intuitive* truths, are related as logical antecedents to universal and necessary *deductive* truths. The science of Geometry affords us a perfect and stupendous example of this relation.

II. Axioms are related also as logical antecedents tc our cognitions. The Axiom 'Every body must be ir space' offers an illustration. When we come to cognis any particular body, we of necessity must cognise it ir space; but we can cognise it in space only upon th ground of the Axiom, 'Every body must be in space. As the idea of space is the logical antecedent of the cog nition of the body, so also the universal affirmation is th logical antecedent of any particular designation, for a pai ticular designation implies the general truth. The sensa tion of resistance is the antecedent in time—the conditio or occasion of the cognition of both body and space: ar as comprehending the cognitions in their relation to eac other, appears the Axiom, 'Every body must be i space.' The same course of remark applies to the Axiom 'Every phenomenon implies a Cause,' and 'Every ph nomenon implies a Law,' and other similar Axioms. 'I attempt to establish these Axioms by induction, is for ever to travel in a circle, since every fact inducted implies the Axioms themselves.

III. Axioms either take immediately the form of Laws, or determine Laws. As instances of the first, we may adduce the great moral laws announced at Sinai. I have already referred to these. Every one of these utters a universal and necessary moral truth. Duty as here presented is not arbitrary, but rational.

In the department of Physics, we have a striking illustration in the Three Laws of Motion. The first Law is the Axiom of the inertia of bodies, the Axiom itself being determined by the Idea of Cause: The second law is the Axiom of Effects proportioned to their causes, and is determined by the same Idea: The third law is the Axiom of Action and Reaction. These are Axioms, because universal and necessary truths determined by ideas.

They are universal, for no exception is admissible; they are necessary, for the Reason affirms the impossibility of their opposites. They are true on a mere hypothesis of bodies. But when taken in their relations to actually existing bodies, they become actual primary laws.

All primary laws are Axiomatic: but there are secondary laws which proceed from the Axioms. All ethical laws for the specific regulation of human conduct, and all civil jurisprudence, are thus derived.

All the secondary laws of Physical Science are dependent, in like manner, upon the primary Axiomatic laws. Here, too, the Mathematics are applied, inasmuch as the motions, magnitudes, distances, times, weights, and forces of bodies are representable either as continued or discrete quantities.*

* Supra, pp. 92—5.

I have already shown* that science in general is constructed out of phenomena by the aid of Ideas and Axioms. In the pure Mathematics, the phenomenal material belongs to the interior consciousness—that is, is given in reflection—and comprises particulars comparatively few in number, simple, and definite.

In physical science, on the contrary, the phenomena belong to the exterior consciousness, that is, are given in sensation, and are various, complicated, and multitudinous. In the latter, therefore, observation and experiment, nice, laborious, and extensive, are required. And here it is that Inductive Logic receives its widest and most important application.

* Part I., Sec. XII.

SECTION IX.

DEFINITION.

"THE end or scope of all definition, is to make any given object clearer, plainer, and more distinct to the Intelligence. Adopting the usual division of logicians, we represent definition as either nominal or real. A nominal definition is merely substituting one name for another,—the name substituted being supposed to be better understood. A real definition aims to explain the nature of the thing, by enumerating its parts, assigning its classification, pointing out its substance, describing its properties and relations, or fixing its limits and distinctions.

"A real definition may be accidental or essential. When accidental, it explains merely those accidents or properties of an object which are not constitutive of it, and without which it can be conceived;—for example, the name, time, place of birth, and employment of an individual, are accidents. When essential, it explains the essence and properties of an object which are constitutive of it, and without which it cannot be conceived;—for example, mind and body are essential parts of an individual man.

"Again: an essential definition is logical, when it assigns the object its place, under generical and specific classification. Thus man is logically defined an intellectual animal—animal being the *genus*, intellectual the *differentia,* or that which distinguishes him essentially from all other animals.

"An essential definition is physical, when, where the objects admits of it, the physical parts are enumerated, meaning by physical parts those which are presented to the observation of the senses.

"An essential definition is metaphysical, when it assigns essence and properties to the object, which are metaphysical—meaning by metaphysical that which is not known by observation of the senses, but by intuition of Reason;—for example, Man is a *spiritual* being; body is a resisting *substance.* From this it appears that a logical definition is dependent upon antecedent, physical, and metaphysical definitions.

"Now, it is plain, that in order to define, we must have some prior conceptions by which to define. In a mere nominal definition, we must have a prior word already better understood than the word we are about to define. In a real definition, we must already have a clear knowledge of the essences, properties, and accidents we may make use of for this purpose. A definition, therefore, which we are at this moment framing, must be preceded either by definitions already made, or by conceptions which do not require or admit of antecedent definitions.

"When present definitions presume antecedent definitions, these antecedent definitions must be preceded by other antecedent definitions, or by conceptions which do not require or admit of antecedent definitions. We must, therefore, in all cases, at length come to conceptions which do not require or admit of antecedent definitions; for a retrogression of definitions *ad infinitum,* is an absurdity.

"These starting points of thought—these primary

conceptions and beliefs, are logically necessary to account for, explain, and define all our other knowledges. They are like the light, which, while it reveals all objects of sight, can find nothing by which it itself can be more plainly revealed. That we cannot analyse light proves nothing against its existence : we know it must exist, because we see all things by means of it. Indeed, we must affirm in general, that whatever is clearest to our minds, and really best known, must be incapable of explanation, definition, or demonstration : for if these were required in reference to the objects supposed, then it would follow that there must be something beyond these still clearer, and still better known, namely, that by which the explanation, definition, or demonstration is to be effected,—which is contrary to the hypothesis." *

The distinction above made between a nominal and a real definition is palpable ; for to give the signification of one word, by means of another more familiar, is widely different from pointing out what is designed to be expressed by the word itself. But inasmuch as a real definition is designed to point out what is expressed by the word itself, it has been contended that no definition can properly be said to explain the nature of a thing ; but only to determine the appropriation of a word : Thus, to define *Man* is not to point out the nature of man, but to show what is intended to be expressed by it.

Now it seems to me that to determine the appropriation of a word is equivalent to defining the nature of the thing for which the word stands. Take the usual definition of a circle, for example :—' A circle is a figure contained by one line, which is called the circumference, every

* Doctrine of the Will, Ch. II., Sec. 1.

point of which is equally distant from a common point called the centre.' Here it is evident that the word circle cannot be defined, or, in other words, its appropriation determined without explaining that for which it stands. In the course of this real definition we give also two nominal definitions, when we call the containing line the circumference, and the common point the centre. We may also nominally define a circle by saying, 'it is a figure bounded by a circumference.' But taken together as above, we have a real definition of circle. In this definition we have undoubtedly an intuitive cognition expressed; for in defining a circle it is implied that it is an actual magnitude. We may indeed define that which has no real existence, as a griffin, a centaur, or a harpy; but then it is understood that we are referring to imaginary beings.

Real definitions, in so far as they contain or imply judgments of truth, are authoritative. This is true of geometrical definitions, with the exception of those which are merely nominal. 'A surface is that which has length and breadth without height or thickness,' is a real definition, because it points out and affirms two dimensions in space; and it is authoritative just to the extent of this affirmation. Strictly nominal definitions can be made out only by synonymes or by a circumlocution.

A real definition is complete or incomplete. It is complete, only when all that is comprehended by the word which represents the object of thought is expressed. Thus that 'Man is a rational animal' is a real definition, but still an incomplete one; for the object of thought represented by the word 'Man' comprehends more than is expressed by the genus 'Animal,' and the differentia 'Rational.'

Definitions are varied according to different ends proposed. The definition is always adequate when it meets the end proposed. To define 'Man' as a 'rational animal' is sufficient in ordinary classification to distinguish him from all other animals. According to a distribution which Cuvier made of the species of the Animal Kingdom, he found it necessary to define 'Man' "a mammiferous animal having two hands." Both definitions are real, because giving in part what really belongs to Man: both are incomplete, considered in respect to the whole subject 'Man;' and yet both are adequate when considered in respect to their particular ends. Indeed, what are technically called *definitions* must of necessity, in numerous instances, be incomplete, either from our imperfect knowledge of the subject, or from its manifold richness; so that to give a complete definition would be equivalent to a scientific disquisition.

In Geometry, and in all absolute science, the definitions are complete. They express a complete and perfectly clear cognition, and give a name to the object of the cognition. That 'a straight line is the shortest distance between two points,' and that 'a curve line is one which changes its direction at every point,' are cognitions clear and full, while the objects of the cognitions are distinctively named. Were not this the case, the definitions could not be received as a basis of the exact and rigid scientific construction.

There is one enquiry which yet remains. What distinguishes an Axiom from a real Definition? An Axiom has been shown to be a universal and necessary truth determined immediately by Ideas. A real definition is the explication of a cognition represented or expressed by some particular word or phrase. Cognition may be primitive and intuitive, or secondary and derived. If the latter, it plainly cannot be axiomatic. But suppose it be the former, like the definitions of Geometry? Then, in this case, it is unquestionably authoritative as an original intuition:—the definitions of a straight and of a curve line, of a circle, of a triangle, of a right angle, of a parallelogram and so on, must be rigidly adhered to in all the subsequent demonstrations; but still they are only cognitions, of certain magnitudes. Now, an Axiom does not respect any particular magnitude, but comprehends all alike. Thus when it is affirmed that 'things which are equal to the same thing, are equal to each other;' that, 'if equals be added to equals, the wholes will be equal,' no respect is had to any particular magnitude or quantity: the Axioms are true alike of all Geometrical magnitudes, of all real quantities, or of quantities represented generally under Algebraic Symbols. We have thus a very plain distinction—the distinction between an original intuitive cognition in relation to a particular subject, and a universal judgment limited to no particular subject. The definition of a circle is authoritative, but it is so only in relation to a circle; while the Axiom, "If equals be added to equals, the wholes will be equal," is so manifestly universal, and independent of any particular subject, that it not only appears just as clear in the general expression as in the particular, but really takes logical antecedence in the general expression, and determines by its authority the truth of the particular.

I here complete the view I proposed to take of Primordial Logic. Next in order is Inductive Logic. Before we can proceed to Deduction, we must have truths and principles from which to deduce. These are furnished by Intuition and Induction. Hence the two corresponding forms of Logic.

BOOK II.

INDUCTIVE LOGIC.

SECTION I.

INTRODUCTION.

It is sometimes said, that to an Omniscient Being neither Induction nor Deduction are necessary; but that to such a Being all truth and knowledge are intuitive. Induction and Deduction indeed are not necessary to an Omniscient Being, considered as indispensable means of knowledge. Such a Being must have the power of seeing all truth directly. It is told of Newton that his mind grasped the conclusions of Geometry without laboriously passing through the usual process of reasoning. This indicated a mental energy superior to that of men in general. But, nevertheless, the truths and knowledges, at which we arrive by Induction and Deduction, do not stand in the same relation to the mind with intuitive truths. An intuitive truth is not only—in respect to the mode of knowing—seen directly;—it is also seen to be true in itself—true independently of all antecedents. But a deductive truth, even if—in respect to the mode of knowing—seen to be true without passing through the deductive process; still, if a reason be given for its truth, and it be minutely analysed, it must to every mind be seen to be true, not in itself and independently of all antecedents, but true, because something going before and upon which it depends, is true. So also an inductive truth, although known directly by the power of an Omniscient mind, must be known in all its relations and dependencies; otherwise it is not truly and perfectly known. It thus appears, that when we speak of Intuitive, Deductive and Inductive truths, we refer not merely to modes of knowing, but to the intrinsic character of the truths themselves.

What, then, are those truths and knowledges, which are arrived at in the way of Induction? In other words, what is the field of Induction?

The field of Induction is that in which we find the secondary phenomena.

The primary phenomena are simply the conditions of the primary cognitions. In these we attain objective reality. Then, the phenomena—thenceforward recognized as the phenomena of objective reality—become the materials of Induction.

Phenomena have Cause and Law as necessary antecedents. The phenomena do not by generalization make up the Cause and Law; but the Cause and Law are the ground of the phenomena. The mere classification of phenomena under Resemblance and Difference, for the purpose of affixing a common name, is widely different from assigning them Cause and Law. In attempting to account for the resemblance and difference, we of course have to proceed to Cause and Law; but the classification itself gives us neither the one nor the other.

In the Divine Mind, cause and law existed before phenomena were developed. Here was the actual necessary antecedence. The mind which conceived and created, conceived and created from its own plenitude. The Divine Mind, therefore, foresaw the phenomena in the cause and law which it contained within itself. The phenomena must have been connected with cause and law in the Divine Conception, since the connexion is necessary to the completeness of the knowledge. But here we see that the order of knowing is identical with the order of necessary existence.

It is conceivable that the Divine Being might have constituted finite minds with such lofty powers as directly to know the causes and laws of the Universe, and through them the appropriate and necessary phenomena. Now, that these causes and laws are attained, phenomena through them can be known in regions of space where the eye has yet made no observations, and predicted in periods of time lying far away in the future. And these lofty minds, in possession of the causes and laws by a superior intuition, might in like manner grasp the phenomena springing out of and depending upon them. But man is not a being thus constituted. The order of his development presents us—First, simple sensations: Secondly, the realization of the objective world by Ideas appropriating the sensations: Thirdly, the observation of the phenomena of this objective world in order to determine its causes and laws. Now, under the last, we have the field of Induction as before stated: and the great point to be determined is, how by the observation of phenomena the causes and laws are arrived at.

SECTION II.

CAUSES AND LAWS.

THE philosophical distinction between Cause and Law is perfectly clear. Cause is that which accounts for the existence of being and phenomena: Law is that which accounts for the order and relations of being and phenomena.

Cause may be divided into two grand classes, spiritual or mental, and physical; the former presenting two grades, the infinite and the finite, the latter presenting the finite only.

Now, in philosophical strictness, the only enquiry that can arise here respecting Cause is, Whether the physical cause is really distinct from the spiritual. In respect to all our enquiries into the constitution of the objective world, every end is answered by granting at once—First, that in every finite intelligence there is a proper Cause which accounts for all the voluntary acts: Secondly, that in the universe of matter all causality is resolvable into the First and all-comprehending Cause. Physical causes, viewed in philosophical simplicity, are invisible powers lying behind the phenomena of the universe. Whenever we attempt to classify these, we in reality classify only the phenomena which are received as the signs or expressions of the Causes.*

* Phenomena, and phenomena alone, are classed into genera and species on the grounds of resemblance and difference. We, indeed, speak of a mag-

What are ordinarily termed physical causes are merely phenomena which are stated and invariable antecedents, or fixed conditions of other phenomena: for example, the sun and moon in the changes of the tide; visible fire in combustion; water and steam as propelling powers, the conjunction of substances in chemical changes; light, heat,

netic cause, a healing cause, a consuming cause, and so on; but these *differentia* really refer to the phenomena;—the phenomena of magnetism, of healing, and of combustion, all differing from each other; but Cause is one simple Idea, the Idea of that which accounts for the possible and actual existence of these various phenomena. Indeed, we can conceive of the same cause as producing them all; as when we conceive of the Divine Being as the universal and sole Cause. This plainly is possible: and in the case of second causes we do actually attribute a vast variety of phenomena to one cause; the phenomena being capable of being reduced to genera and species, while the cause retains all its simplicity.

"Human power, taken under any point of view, is one of perfect simplicity; it is nothing that can be described under any form; it can neither be physically separated into parts, nor logically distributed into genera; it always manifests itself by volition; and yet how various are the phenomena produced —the phenomena of which volition is the immediate antecedent!

"There may, however, be differences in degree; one cause may produce a greater variety of phenomena than another; and thus, causes which produce certain phenomena, and act in relation to certain substances only, may be conceived of as simply limited in power without implying difference in kind. If, for example, I were gifted with the power of regulating my digestive functions, or the circulation of my blood, or of moving my ears after the manner of a dog or a horse, it would argue no new power differing in kind, but merely the extension of my causality. My volition now is limited to the movement of certain members, and cannot influence others; if I could move my ears as I do my hands, then my volition would do one thing more than it is now capable of doing.

"Again, water is known to hold salt in solution: Now, if we were to suppose water to have the additional power of dissolving wood and holding the potassium in solution, we would not be altering in our conception the nature or kind of solvent power in water:—We would only be enlarging that power. It is manifest that if we had made the experiment of the solvent power of water only upon sugar, we might with as much reason conjecture that, if further tried, it would dissolve wood, as that it would dissolve salt."—*Doctrine of the Will*, pp. 31, 32. See also p. 301.

air, and moisture in vegetation, and so on. In making out a science of nature it is immaterial, as before intimated, what we conceive the invisible and real causes to be; or whether we conceive of only one universal cause producing all this variety of effect. On the other hand, the very determination of such a science depends upon observing the order and relations of the phenomena. But the order and relations of the phenomena do not truly belong to cause, but to law. Hence the aim of Induction, when expressed with philosophic precision, is not to arrive at causes, but to arrive at laws. Thus in gravitation, the great enquiry did not so much respect the nature of the cause, as the fact of the regulated central determination of bodies. The expansion of steam is a phenomenon; and other phenomena are connected with it as invariable consequents: We know there must be cause lying behind the phenomena—of this we are satisfied—whether it be a physical cause, distinct and measured in its own sphere, or the all-pervading universal Cause: but the great points of interest to us in science and practical mechanics are the order and relations of the phenomena; in other words, the law which governs the evolution of the phenomena.

If the undulatory theory of light be established, the interest of the thing does not arise from having arrived at an ultimate cause; but in having gained new phenomena with wider relations and more comprehensive laws. An ultimate cause we have not attained; the ethereal undulations precede the sensations of light, and the presence of the sun precedes the undulations; and thus we have a succession of related phenomena;—while enquiries still arise respecting the correlation of the sun and the all-pervading elastic ether which may bring to light other antecedent phenomena. The real enquiry then is, not after the ultimate cause of light, but after the whole succession of inter-dependent phenomena connected with the sensation under all its phases. Throughout the whole succession of phenomena there is cause acting, cause developing the phenomena; but that which we seek after—the characteristics of phenomena, their order and relation, is comprehended by law. We can conceive of one universal cause producing from its own fulness every variety of phenomena; but this variety itself denotes diversity of design and therefore diversity of law.

The attraction of gravitation draws bodies towards the centre of the earth. Suppose it were ascertained that an exceedingly subtile ether exists between the particles of matter, having in itself a central determination by which all bodies are made to tend toward the centre: Then indeed we should have a new class of antecedent phenomena; but the tendency of bodies towards the centre would be no more explained than before, as far as cause is considered; we would only be carried one step farther back in our observations; and we might now institute enquiries respecting the force acting upon or in the particles of the subtile ether. Unquestionably, however, were such an ether discovered, we should enlarge our view of the laws and order of creation.

To revert to the theories of light. By the common theory, luminous particles are supposed to be thrown off in straight lines from the luminous body, the phenomena of this emission being the antecedent phenomena deemed sufficient to account for the consequent phenomena. By the undulatory theory, the sensation of light and all the phenomena are supposed to find their sufficient antecedent phenomena in the undulations of the elastic medium;

that is, the ethereal undulations being granted as the invariable antecedent to the sensation of light, and the cessation of these undulations as the invariable antecedent of darkness or the absence of this sensation, then the movement of these undulations will serve to explain all the phenomena of vision. In both theories we have in part a hypothesis of phenomena, and in part a statement of actual phenomena; and the object in both is so to connect the hypothetical with the actual as to exhibit not the cause of the actual phenomena, but the law. That light consists of fine particles thrown off from luminous bodies and moving in straight lines with an inconceivable velocity, is a theory which legitimately connects itself with the phenomena of reflection and refraction as exhibited in speculums, prisms, lenses, and so on. These phenomena can also be legitimately connected with the undulations of the imponderable medium. Other phenomena, however, are deemed by philosophers to be legitimately connected only with the last theory. But in neither theory do the hypothesised constitute the cause of the actual phenomena, but only the required conditions of their manifestations. If now we conceive of the great and all-comprehending Mind designing to produce the phenomena of light and vision, whether by his direct agency, or by second causes permeating and acting in material substances, then the manner in which different substances are related to each other, and the fixed order and dependency of the phenomena, become to us the exponent of the law, which the Great Designing Mind ordained for his own efficiency, or for the governance of the secondary powers. The two theories present us in part, two different orders of phenomena, and hence two different laws of light and vision. In the minute and complete determination of these laws, so far as the conception of quantity comes in, the mathematics, as the science of quantity, is employed to give the expressions.

What then is law? Is it only the invariable succession of phenomena? May the Creator, by his omnipotence, fix the succession of phenomena in any order he pleases, and is this fixed and arbitrary succession the law of Nature?

Law is not arbitrary in *the morale.* Hence that succession of phenomena which comprises the conduct of responsible beings can be right and fit only when conformed to one law.

Equally clear is it that the law of the Beautiful is not arbitrary.

But how stands this question in Somatology? This is the point now to be considered.

In the first place, in any system of bodies there can be no room for arbitrary laws, so far as the conditions of the system bring the bodies under mathematical formulæ. And bodies, since they must have magnitudes and determinate forms, and be related to each other, and have motion as the resultant of forces, cannot escape these formulæ. It is inconceivable and impossible, that a universe of bodies should have been constituted in violation of the principles of the science of quantity.

In the second place, the very notion of arbitrary law is absurd. Law is the work of the Reason—the necessary outflow of its Ideas. The will may institute arbitrary rules, as the word *arbitrary* indicates. The Will may violate the Reason; but the institutions of arbitrary choice in opposition to Reason, or in the mere freakishness of Fancy, are not to be dignified with the name of laws, in the high and proper sense.

In the third place, arbitrary choice cannot be ascribed to Infinite Intelligence. He who is the Fountain of truth, law, beauty, benignity, and order, cannot be thought of as creating the universe otherwise than under the light of his Eternal Ideas. And when we come to look into his works, we find everywhere the resplendent marks of law: and the farther our observation penetrates, the more varied, resplendent, and positive do these marks become.

The axiom, "that every phenomenon presumes a law," or that every phenomenon is the result of intelligent design, is affirmed by the Reason in the clear insight that Infinite Intelligence, and not arbitrary choice, decided the system of Nature.

There might indeed have been a variety of systems governed by laws more or less benign and perfect, a conception which we allow in the various theories by which we attempt to express the laws of given phenomena; but nevertheless, we are constrained to believe that an infinitely perfect Intelligence could not but have projected the best possible system, taking it in all its relations. When we look therefore into Nature, we expect not only to find laws properly so called; but we expect also to find the wisest and most benign laws.

SECTION III.

THE HUMAN REASON AS RELATED TO THE OBJECTIVE WORLD.

ľHE great and all-wise Being, who constituted the outer .vorld, constituted also the Mind which is to investigate its aws. The Mind does not go to its work unfurnished. √Iade after the likeness of the Creator—after the likeness ›f that Reason from whose Ideas all law sprang forth ;— ›onstituted therefore with Ideas, and thus having sources ·f law within itself, it cannot go out into the world where ɿw is embodied and realized, without waking up the ˌlorious recognition. Having eyes to see, the light which ›ours in upon it seems not a strange, but an expected and enial visitation. The human mind is prepared to know world which had its origin in mind. As an artist comrehends the works of art, so does the mind of man comrehend the works of God.

I have already, in the preceding Parts, said so much ˇ the Ideas of the Reason, that I need here barely allude › the subject, or call it up again only so far as to apply it › the matter in hand.

The development of the Ideas, as we have seen, does ›t take place separately from Reality ; but when the reity is present in relation to which they are to act, then ey manifest themselves. The manifestation is spontaneous—the earnest outflow of the mind to reach its proper objects.

In the first place, Ideas of cause and law, and of consequent system and order, Ideas psychological and somatological, as soon as phenomena are given, determine the mind to undertake investigation, and hold up the objects to be attained.

Then, inasmuch as Ideas comprehend the constitution of the universe, just so far as in the presence of the conditionating and quickening Reality they are developed, does there appear a prophetic power of the Intellect preconceiving, suggesting, theorizing, and sometimes, as in the case of Newton, seeming to grasp at once the great system of things. It is impossible to express the extent tc which the spontaneous inspiration of Ideas carries thc mind, or all the modes of their action. Like the forma tion and growth of a common Language in masses oi mind, like the development of Music without rules of ar in popular tunes, or the growth of Poetry from rude bal lads to the Iliad of Homer, like the spontaneous invention and discoveries of man before he began to philosophise from the results we feel assured there is law exact an beautiful; but still, as in the fine vibrations of the air, an in the more subtile oscillations of the ethereal medium o light, no representation is possible: The movement lies s far behind all ordinary and familiar forms, and is so muc more delicate and subtile than any thing we are accu tomed to handle, to speak of, or to represent, that we ca find nothing by which to convey it. In the germinatio and growth of plants, how many fine influences are work of which the physiologist presents us no diagram and which he can command by no formula; so likewise mind, the germs of thought, their first springing fort and their infinite and beautiful complexities in reasoning, invention, memory, imagination, and taste, while exhibiting in their result the commanding presence of law, surpass the finest skill of the analyst.

The superior power which some minds display in inductive reasoning may be accounted for mainly by the remarkable degree in which they are endowed with three qualities, Clearness, Candor, and Patience. Clearness of mind, the result of exact and laborious discipline, prevents uncertain, confused, and inapposite observations and experiments, and leads to accurate and sound judgments. Candor purifies the mind from all "idols," and makes it an honest truth-seeker. Patience disposes to undistracted attention, quiet and protracted thought, cheerfulness in undertaking labors, perseverance in overcoming difficulties, and willingness to wait until investigation shall ripen the harvest of knowledge.

But Ideas not only impel the philosopher to undertake ıvestigation, and suggest the route he is to pursue, and)reshadow the results at which he is to arrive,—they also etermine the Method of Investigation.

There are three particulars in relation to which this ıethod requires to be expounded :

I. The induction of phenomena for the purpose of assifying them into genera and species.

II. The induction of phenomena for the purpose of riving at the expression of a general fact, or a general der of sequence, but without determining a fixed and ›solute law.

III. The induction of phenomena leading to the de-rmination of a fixed and absolute law.

SECTION IV.

GENERAL VIEW OF CLASSIFICATION.

CLASSIFICATION is dependent upon abstraction and generalization. When phenomena are realized under thei secondary form, the first impression must be that of an undistinguished totality. By abstraction the mind fasten upon a particular quality or feature, and separates it fro the mass. This quality, or feature, is then noted in othe objects ; and at length *generalized* as a common sign fo the whole class to which it belongs. In the next place, name is given to the common sign, which thenceforth be comes the name of the class. When there is but on quality generalized, the class must be exceedingly general and described in great incompleteness. As we add o qualities, we narrow the limits of the class, and at th same time describe with greater completeness.

The most general arrangement of classes is that o GENUS and SPECIES. The Genus, or *kind*, expresses onl the particular, or particulars, in which all the species com prehended under it are identified. The Species, or *th particular forms of the kind*, express all of the Genu and in addition to this, the *differentiæ*, or points of diffe ence between one species and another. The Genus is th divided into Species by the addition of qualities. Eve Species is made up, in the last analysis, of INDIVIDUA

An individual is that which admits of no farther division, because all the qualities belonging to the object are supposed to be indicated by the name assigned to it. The above may be conveniently represented as follows :

Genus=The common Essence or Quality.

Species=Genus+Differentia.

Individual=Genus+Differentia+Accidents.

By *Accidents* are meant the individual peculiarities. We will illustrate by an example :

Genus Animal=The common property or essence by which animals are distinguished from vegetables.

Species Man=Animal+Rational.

Individual Cæsar=Animal+Rational+All the qualities which distinguished Cæsar from all other men, and made him particularly Cæsar.

There are different orders of *Genera ;* for a genus may ɔe a species* in relation to some higher genus, while a ,enus truly in relation to orders comprehended under it. Thus *Animal* may be said to be a species of *Creature*, ınderstanding by *Creature* any thing created ; *Vegetable* ɔeing another species of creature. The distinction thus rises between a *Maximum* and a *Proximum Genus,*— *laximum* denoting a genus which is not a species, and *'roximum* a genus next above a species, but yet not the ighest genus. It is evident, however, that in our Classication we are not necessarily limited to a certain number f divisions : on the contrary, we can multiply them acɔrding to our convenience. Hence we find naturalists ıaking Orders and Classes, in addition to Genera and pecies.

* Species here is taken in an imperfect sense.

Classification is either NATURAL, SCIENTIFIC, or ARBITRARY.

I. NATURAL CLASSIFICATION. This is that spontaneous Classification which appears in all language, independently of scientific investigation. Thus all the objects of nature, as Animals, Vegetables, and Metals, in their different kinds, and all the products of human art, are distinguished and classed.

II. SCIENTIFIC CLASSIFICATION. This is the result of scientific and elaborate investigations, and appears in books of Science and Natural History. The terms here employed are invented for the purpose, and are generally unintelligible to the vulgar, because remote from common use.

Scientific Classification is strictly natural, also, in onc point of view; that is, it is conformed to the actual Sys tem of Nature. Natural spontaneous Classification arise: from that striking, palpable, and *outside* view of Nature which all men readily and unavoidably take: Scientifi Classification arises from a more intimate and curious, an an *interior* view of Nature, determined by philosophica aims and principles, formally laid down and reflecte upon.

III. ARBITRARY CLASSIFICATION. This is an inten tional violation of natural identity and difference. I consequently is altogether distinct from the two precedin forms of Classification. It is an incongruous and grotesqu assemblage of particulars produced by the sportive fanc for humorous and witty effect.

SECTION V.

PRINCIPLES DETERMINING THE INDUCTION OF PHENOMENA IN CLASSIFICATION.

IDEAS of Identity and Difference, Ideas of Synthesis and Analysis, belong to the common human mind, and impel it, whether spontaneously and without reflection, as in the first form of Classification, or whether through reflection and investigation, as in the second form, to classify and distinguish the objects of perception. The world without, made after the Ideas of the Divine Architect, derives from these Ideas its diversity and unity. And here, again, the mind of man, made after the likeness of its great Original, is prepared to read this diversity and unity. The Identities and Differences of all created things, the beautiful variety amid perfect system and order, find within our reason the key of interpretation. *We* do not really classify: the Classification is already made in the constitution of the world; *We* only read and comprehend it.

And even Arbitrary Classification has its law within ourselves; for it is only the nice perception of natural and rational identity and difference which enables us to make those violations of congruity which produce the humorous and ludicrous effect. Hence we find that minds of the most delicate and perfect structure are most keenly alive to genuine wit and humor. In Addison, we have a striking exemplification of this fact.

After pointing out the Ideas which lead us to classify all, it still remains to explain the principles on which the different classifications arise.

The conception of general Classes, such as *Genera*, comprehending other Classes such as *Species*, the conception of divisions and subdivisions, until we arrive at Classes composed barely of *individuals*, naturally arises out of the Idea of the unity and variety of system. But the particular question to be determined is, How do we select the distinct characteristic of the Genus and the Species? In other words, Why, amid many identities and differences, do we fix upon the particular ones?

I. We have seen* that the Idea of Determinate Form, both esthetically and somatologically, enters into the structure of all things. Hence the identities and diversities of the world appear in the forms of things as limited in space. Nothing is more obvious to the common eye than these, and therefore no classification springs up more readily and spontaneously. Thus animals and plants are known, distinguished, arranged, and named. Th Idea of Determinate Form within the human mind pre pares and predisposes it for the actual knowledge of th generic and specific forms of nature. The conception o the determinate forms of objects, however, is connecte with that of interior functions and properties; and eve in the most unreflective and spontaneous judgments, th two are not entirely separated. Thus the distinctio between the animate and inanimate never lies wholly i form, but in the Idea of Life, as an organific power dete

* Pages 189, 202.

mining the difference. And, again, the distinction between animals and plants never lies wholly in the form, but in sensibility, locomotive activity, voluntary appropriation and skill, and various functions belonging only to the former. There is, in fine, a conception of different laws governing these different forms of life.

Specific identity may be defined by the form alone. It is the Identity of the outline drawn and limited in space, and the Identity of proportion and of mechanism, making together one distinct picture for the imagination.

Generic Identity, on the contrary, lies not in the collective outline of form, but in the outline of capital parts, and in connection with this, in the oneness of relations, ends, and functions.

The Individual embodies the generic and specific identities, and superadds all the lineaments, shades, and expressions, which combined constitute the finished and unique picture.

II. Another ground of Classification is found in the Identities and differences of the order of antecedence and sequence of phenomena. The important ideas which govern here are Cause and Law. But nevertheless we have not in the mere classification, the determination specifically of causes and laws, but only the arrangement and naming of phenomena, from the fact that they uniformly precede as immediate antecedents certain other phenomena, or uniformly succeed them as immediate sequents.

This, like visible form, is a principle of ordinary classification: for although the uniformities imply Law, and would not excite attention unless the Idea of Law were in the mind, still they are not contemplated in particular reference to Law, or with a view at once to establish Law, but simply to obtain a convenient arrangement and nomenclature. Such a classification is indeed subsidiary to the determination of Law—a preparatory process of the highest moment. We have a striking exemplification of its importance, as well as of its mere subsidiary character, in the history of Chemical Science. Experiments were multiplying from the age of the alchymists, and the observed uniformities of the phenomenal sequence as they continually became enlarged and modified, suggested new classifications and new terms. The facts were thus preserved, disseminated, and handed down; philosophical meditation had distinct objects before it; new investigations had their obvious starting points; and a widening avenue of knowledge gave still more inviting prospects. But it was reserved, at a late period, for Dalton and Faraday to propound Theories which, if indeed still theories, approach very near the line where theory merges into law, and proclaims the ultimate end of human thought attained.

III. The highest ground of classification is the con ception of a fixed law comprehending and governing th phenomena.

The determinate forms of bodies spring from som law, whether somatological or esthetical, or from a unio of both; and the uniform sequences of phenomena hav likewise their law somewhere. Now, before any law i distinctly conceived of, the classification, as we have repre sented, takes place by the mere marks of likeness and un likeness in form, and the mere correspondency of th sequences. Thus arise the classifications which obtai commonly among men, and which are expressed in th general terms of ordinary language. Thus also arise th earlier classifications of Science, while, by various tent tive efforts, it is groping its way to stupendous and sure results. But no sooner have conceptions of general and fixed laws become developed, than the human mind attempts classifications from a higher point of view. Now the law which is conceived of as binding together the widely diffused and multiform parts of an extended system, gives the generical designations; while the species show the complete unfolding of formative powers, whether by a plastic force impressed from without, or by an organific energy acting from within. If the laws which govern the widely extended systems in their unity, and those which control the specific developments in their completeness, be accurately discovered, then the classification will attain its highest perfection. And just, as under theoretical conceptions, an approximation is made towards the point of accurate discovery, will an approximation be made towards a perfect classification—a classification which at the same time is the most philosophical and the most natural.

The history of Natural Science affords us abundant illustrations of the progress of classification. I have already referred to Chemistry. Botany and Zoology afford perhaps the most striking illustrations, since on account of the multitude of particulars, classification becomes at once an object of paramount importance. The earlier classifications in these sciences were formed by arranging the particulars according to their external parts. Hence they were merely descriptive; and as description must vary according to the accuracy and variety of the observations, new systems were continually appearing, and endeavoring to supplant one another. Linnæus, by introducing the *sexual* principle, henceforth gave to the classification of plants a phytomological character, and advanced Botany to the dignity of determinate Science. Cuvier accomplished a similar reformation in Zoology. With him the interior organization, as manifesting a wise and harmonious design, became the great object of research. Under this great Idea he not only arranged the tribes of animals at present existent, but even called forth into beautiful and rational symmetry, the fossil and fragmentary remains of ancient and extinct generations. It was the apprehension of the rational design and of the organific law, which led these great philosophers to their invaluable and immortal achievements.

Having distinguished the cardinal principles of classification, we may next proceed to enquire particularly into the distinctive characteristics of genus and species.

I have already remarked, that we are not necessarily confined to the particular classes of genus and species. In reality, wherever a number of particulars have any common characteristic, they may be classed together on this ground. And so also, on the other hand, any point of difference between particulars may be assumed as a ground for separating them, and seeking for them some other distribution. But we have seen that there are principles, which, amid the vast number of possible classifications, demand a limitation; and even spontaneously constrain the common mind to conform to it. Besides genus and species, which have universally obtained, and which therefore seem to be a most natural division, we have Orders of a widely comprehensive character, including genera; and again, Orders of a limited character, included under species. The comprehensive orders however, are only a higher description of genera, and the limited orders a variety of the species; so that an exposi tion of genus and species must include the main principles of logical division.

I shall begin with Species. In respect to form, I have already defined species, a completed picture for the imagination. If we take the species on the higher ground of law working in the interior organization, the same conception of completeness becomes the governing conception. In the species we have the completed organization. Every individual, of course, is a completed organization. But the individual contains no organism, powers or properties, which do not belong to the species. Indeed, every individual may be taken as a representative of the species to which he belongs; and the species is but a collection of individuals identified in the whole organism, and in all the powers and properties which go to make up the distinct and complete being under its organific and determining law. The individual is justly said to be distinguished from the species only by *accidents*, and not by essential constitution and properties. These accidents are either circumstantial and separable, that is, they stand around the individual, describing locality, position, and exterior relations generally, but forming no part of the essential being; or they are modifications of the essential and constitutive organism and properties of the species. The clear conceptions of Identity and Constitutive Law enable us to compare and limit the species; and the equally clear conception of difference enables us to detect those higher modifications which do not affect the identity of the species, and only form the accidents which serve to distinguish the individuals. These conceptions are developed under their proper Ideas in the process of making comparisons of phenomena. There is thus the union of a certain tact acquired by experience, and of rational *à priori* determination. It is this union which makes classification truly philosophical.

The orders formed under species are based upon modifications more remarkable, yet not destructive of the palpable identity of the species.

Genus differs from species in this, that while the last expresses a completed organization, and all the essential properties, and is capable of full representation in the individual, the former comprises only a part of the organization and properties, and cannot take the individual as its representative. It is true, indeed, that the common mark by which several species are united under one genus, must be found in every individual of the several species; but then it appears in the individual in the unity of all the parts, while in the genus it is abstracted from them.

The all-important inquiry here is, what shall govern us in the selection of the generic mark? Having a clear conception of species as determined by the identity of the constitutive law of the complete organization, and of the essential properties, we now, under the idea of system, proceed to consider the relations between the several species. Here identities are also perceived; and it is possible to select any one of them as the generic mark. But suppose an identity be perceived in a certain number of instances, with respect to a particular mark, how can we be certain of its universality? We cannot be certain of its universality, unless it be a mark which is the exponent of a universal law. The occurrence of the mark in a great number of instances, and to the extent of our observation, would lead us to suspect the presence of a law; and therefore the selection of this mark as a generic designation becomes a convenient and wise expedient, until we are enabled to reach a higher ground. A proper generic classification then cannot be based upon a trivial and doubtful mark. It must be one, which, by its importance and prevalence, points at least towards a law. But where the law is gained, there the generic mark becomes permanently fixed, and there alone. We may take as an illustration, the generical distinction between the *animate* and the *inanimate*. Here the great Idea and the laws of life are the ground of the distinction; and here we are assured that it is fixed unalterably. Of equal clearness and fixedness is the distinction between the animal, and the vegetable, because we comprehend clearly the peculiar laws of their organizations. And so universally, wherever we perceive a common mark in several species, which stands as the exponent of a law working in all these species, there we have the sure and proper element of the genus.

As several species are embraced by a genus under a common mark, so again several genera may be embraced by a higher genus under a common and more comprehensive mark. This mark is the exponent of a higher and more comprehensive law, binding together laws, which, in their particular spheres, govern and explain the phenomena. The human mind is ever intent upon system, and hence is ever seeking for higher generalizations. By synthesis, it aims at a universal unity, and by analysis, developes unity into constituent parts harmoniously colligated.

From the foregoing, I think it must be clear that classification has its starting-point in Ideas of the Reason; and that definite laws already known, or the theoretical conception of laws, form the determining principles.

These principles undoubtedly obtain an expression in the form of axioms and definitions, which, if they have not been formally laid down, have nevertheless, as current and generally understood judgments, formed the immediate authority and guide of all just and philosophical classification.

A statement of the leading axioms and definitions belonging here will close this part of our subject.

I. Every universal is made up of particulars identified either in their determinate form, or in their cardinal properties, or in their organific or constitutive law, or in all conjointly.

II. Every particular is comprehended within a universal by the identity either of determinate form, or of cardinal properties, or of organific or constitutive law, or of all conjointly.

III. Species is the identity of determinate form, cardinal properties and organific or constitutive law, conjointly, where all these exist in the subject, so that every particular is essentially complete in the description of its species.

IV. Genus is the identity of several species in a cardinal form, property, or law, which comprehends them in the unity of system.

V. The unity of nature lies in identity ; the variety of nature lies in difference.

VI. Where difference consists in the opposition of determinate forms in the organisms compared, and in essential properties, while at the same time there is an identity in some constitutive law comprehending all alike, there arises the distinction of species.

VII. Where the difference consists in the oppositior of determinate forms in the organisms, and of essentia properties, without identity in some general comprehend ing law, there arises the distinction of genera.

VIII. Where several genera are comprehended within an order or higher genus, the identity which binds them together, appears also in the several species under each particular genus ; but then it appears *alone* in the higher generalization, leaving behind in the lower classes the other points of identity.

Scholium. Species is an identity throughout. Genus is an identity in part. As the points of identity diminish, the generalization advances. Thus from the individual we advance to the species, from the species to the proximum genus, from the proximum to the maximum. The universal law sits like a sovereign in lofty state, regulating all ; but having under it a multitude of subordinates, which it binds together in an intimate and harmonious co-working.

SECTION VI.

DISTINCTION BETWEEN A GENERAL FACT AND A FIXED AND ABSOLUTE LAW.

The relation between Ideas and Laws has been treated of in a preceding Part.* If the views there presented are just, then that alone is entitled to the name of law which finds its correspondent and basis in an Idea. Moral laws thus answer to the Ideas of right and wrong, freedom and responsibility, personal identity, and immortality. Esthetical laws answer to the Idea of the beautiful, under its different modifications. And so, likewise, somatological laws must answer to their appropriate Ideas. This I have attempted to exhibit under Primordial Logic. The characteristics of Ideas are necessity and universality in their proper spheres. Hence the axioms, definitions and laws, must be necessary and universal likewise in their proper spheres.

The Intuitive Function, in connection with sufficient observation, perceives these laws. The law is seen to comprehend the facts of observation, and thus to be *the* law of the facts; while, as a law, it is seen to be universal and necessary.

Now, on the other hand, a general fact is the mere statement of a series of facts, appearing to the extent of

* Part I., Section VII.

our observation in a uniform relation of sequence. We may proceed to give a theory, or even to determine a law of the facts ; but this is another affair. Taken as a mere general fact, the series is neither theory or law.

But the enquiry may here be made, How, then, does a general fact differ from generalization under genus and species? Generalization is a grouping of phenomena on the ground of identity in one or many particulars, for the purpose of assigning a common name, which may thenceforth be employed in our thinking and reasoning, as the sign of all contained under it. But the general fact is the affirmation of the identity itself as a truth belonging to the whole class of things contemplated. The identity affirmed in the general fact, however, is not always the one upon which the generalization is based. For example: upon the observation of certain identities and differences we have classed certain animals under the terms sheep, ox, deer. Upon a farther observation of these animals, we find that they are deficient in the upper cutting teeth, and that they ruminate. We extend our observations, and we find that all animals, deficient in the upper cutting teeth, ruminate. Now, upon these identities we may class together all these animals as *ruminating* animals. But the general fact is the affirmation that all sheep, oxen, deer, and so on—that is, all animals already classed by certain identities and differences—have this additional identity, of being deficient in the upper cutting teeth ; and again, that all animals thus deficient, ruminate. So, also, in chemistry, we call all substances which change vegetable blues into red, *acids ;* and those which change them into green, *alkalies ;* but the general fact is the affirmation that all acids, and all alkalies, possess these respective properties; and again, that acids and alkalies neutralise each other. In the general fact is contained the affirmation of a uniform order of sequence, upon which we may base a classification or not, as we please, *e. g.* when we observe that the animals above described ruminate, we are under no necessity of classing them as ruminants : but whether we do so or not, the general fact remains. In fine, in the one case we are aiming simply to arrange and name : in the other, we are affirming a truth and the semblance of a law. To name all animals which have the above-mentioned characteristics, *ruminating animals*, is plainly different from affirming, generally, all animals which want the upper cutting teeth ruminate.

I call the general fact the *semblance* of a law, for the general fact, as such, is not a law. But, nevertheless, it answers the most important ends in calling before the mind the stated connections existing between phenomena. "Bakewell, the celebrated cattle-breeder, observed, in a great number of individual beasts, a tendency to fatten readily ; and in a great number of others, the absence of this constitution : in every individual of the former description, he *observed* a certain peculiar *make*, though they differed widely in colour, &c. Those of the latter description differed no less in various points, but agreed in being of a different make from the others. These facts were his data : from which, combining them with the general principle that Nature is steady and uniform in her proceedings, he *logically* drew the conclusion, that beasts of that specified make have universally a peculiar tendency to fattening." * This was the general fact at which Bakewell arrived, a fact of great practical moment to all cattle-breeders. But as announced by him, it was no law,

* Whateley's Logic, Book IV., ch. ii., § 2.

because connected with no Idea. Now let us suppose that the peculiar make was one connected in respect to climate, food, &c., with the freest and most genial development of the organific power of life; and also, that it combined the finest esthetical proportions, so that the conclusion might have been announced as follows:—The most genial culture gives the highest animal beauty, and the highest animal beauty is connected with the highest animal utility, exhibited in strength, activity, and a tendency to fattening. Should we not here be advanced beyond a general fact to the conception of a universal law, and that because we have brought in points of consideration connected immediately with Ideas?

That bodies fall to the earth, was a fact of general observation before Newton saw the apple fall; and as a general fact, it was of eminent and daily use among men; but it was not until this general fact had been elaborated in the mind of Newton that it became the exponent of a law. But what gave to gravitation now the characteristics of a law? Was it not the Idea of centralization—the Idea of the universal and necessary arrangement of matter in order to form a system? The centrifugal law is no less based upon an Idea; for the Reason sees with intuitive certainty that without a diffusive movement harmoniously united with the central movement, matter could not exist in space in separate masses.*

Chemistry has, until very recently, been a science of general facts, and, therefore, an imperfect science. Now, the great advance made by the combined labors of Dalton, Davy, and Faraday, and especially by the investigations and acute reasonings of the last, are just an advance from

* Supra, p. 198.

a mass of general facts to a comprehensive law, developed under the force of an Idea : at least, it is a near approximation to such a result. The identification of chemical and electrical attractions is a lofty generalization. But the Idea and the law are indicated, if not fully expressed, in the conception of Polarity,* or, to use Faraday's language, in the conception of "an axis of power having equal and opposite forces." In the law of gravity and of the centrifugal force, we have the law of the cosmical masses : in Polarity, or the "axis of power," we have the dawn at least of the law which governs the interior constitution of bodies. These are the great laws of the universe.

The method of arriving at general facts is the empirical method. It is the method of the earlier processes of science, and preparatory to the determination of laws. On many subjects the human mind has not advanced beyond these general facts. This is true of medicine, for example. From accident and investigation, certain substances have been found to possess a remedial effect; until at length something like general rules have been instituted for the treatment of various diseases. The whole history of Therapeutics exhibits a conflict of theories, and a mass of conjectures often sagacious, but more frequently wild and loose. The subject is one of extreme difficulty, on account of the multitudinous influences which have to be taken into the account. Even at the present day, more reliance, perhaps, is to be placed upon individual experience, judgment, and tact, than upon any established general principles. Curious and hopeful generalization may have been made, but no law has as yet appeared.

* Supra, p. 200.

But the defect in Therapeutics is not merely the want of laws, but the want of clearly ascertained general facts; for were it certainly known that certain substances could expel disease, for instance, as certainly as that a particular breed of cattle fatten easily, we should obtain practical rules of the highest value.

General facts, when once established by a sufficient number of experiments, show the presence of law, although the law has not yet attained to an expression, and they may, therefore, be applied as authoritative. Numerous chemical compositions and decompositions were settled as unquestionable facts, before the later great chemists appeared. Rules of practical mechanics obtained before the laws of the science were discovered. On all subjects open to common observation, the uniform order of sequences has been noted among the multitude, and general facts have been attained with more or less accuracy.

But notwithstanding the many beneficial results arising from spontaneous observations of the uniformities of Nature, it must be confessed that errors have likewise arisen in this way. Observations may be defective in many ways: They may be made hastily and inaccurately; they may not be sufficiently varied, nor often enough repeated; and they may be made under prejudice, with an excited imagination, or with a concealed, obstinate determination to arrive, at all events, at a particular conclusion. These defective observations have been so rife in Therapeutics, that the word *empiricism* has in common usage become diverted from its original and just meaning, and is applied to express those loose and baseless methods of treating disease which are enveloped in mystery, at once to excite the imagination of the multitude, and to conceal their own absurdity. Popular beliefs, also, in dreams and omens, are only another form of empiricism, or loose and insufficient observation. And yet, even these errors show the noble constitution of the human mind; for it is the strong sense of law which creates the tendency to draw general conclusions, wherever uniform sequences appear.

The importance of establishing principles and rules of observation in view of arriving at general facts and laws, is apparent to every one. This, indeed, comprises, in the main, the Logic of Induction. To this we shall now proceed. In the first place, we shall speak of observation in respect to general facts; and in the next place, in respect to laws. The distinction between the two which I have attempted to draw, I think, will not be misconceived. It may, indeed, be summed up as follows: General facts are the uniform sequences of phenomena—or the uniform dependence and involution of phenomena, so that a given consequent cannot exist without a certain antecedent, nor a given antecedent without involving a certain consequent: Law, in distinction from the orderly sequence itself, is that which governs it and accounts for it, and without which the sequence would not have been possible.

SECTION VII.

THE LOGIC OF GENERAL FACTS.

THE great Francis Bacon, the first who labored at a full exposition of the Inductive Philosophy, himself signally failed in all his attempts to give an exemplification of its principles. The catalogues of facts which he has left are of little or no value. The reason is obvious :—The facts are heterogeneous, mixed, scattered, casual, and often trivial. The observations appear to have been governed by no principle, no definite aim, no prophetic thought, in fine, by no Idea. As the observation of facts and ideas are both demanded in a philosophy of Nature, so the omission of one or the other must be fatal to any attempt to arrive at such a philosophy. Bacon exposed the errors of those who had attempted this work by Ideas alone. He himself failed, because he attempted it by observation alone.

The point now distinctly before us is to ascertain the true logical grounds of deciding when phenomena have a real and fixed connection, as antecedent and consequent, so that we may affirm, as a general fact, that they are thus connected.

The connection of phenomena, as stated antecedent and consequent, is the exponent of law. Hence, we are determined to the observation of orderly sequences as naturally presented, and to make experiments in order to enlarge the field of observation by the Idea of law. If we do not find the law itself, we shall find its beautiful manifestations—we shall know at least that we are dwelling in the light of its countenance.

The Idea of law gives rise to the axioms of universal law and of the uniformity of Nature.* These axioms are like the voices of the Idea, ever speaking to our thoughts as we search about and pry into the phenomena of Nature.

Thus, then, in seeking to establish general facts, we are looking out for the uniformities of Nature.

The phenomena which we examine and compare, must stand in the one or the other of the two relations of antecedent or consequent, for phenomena are in a continual flux, and conditionate one another in this way, the same phenomena being consequents of antecedents, and antecedents to consequents. The flux of phenomena, however, is not a lengthening chain of succession, ever presenting new particulars, but is composed of cycles, where the end returns into the beginning: and the complexity of Nature presents us cycle winding within cycle, cycle crossing cycle, and all in perfect harmony; for not only are the particulars of each cycle related, but cycle also is related to cycle in the unity of one vast system. The acid which is itself a consequent of the union of two simples, returns by one cycle into these simples again; and by another relation, becomes an antecedent in another cycle, and aids its movements, as in double elective affinity. General facts, therefore, may be more or less extensive. The perpetual relation of a particular antecedent and consequent is in itself a general fact; an established cycle of antecedents and consequents is a general fact; and

* Supra, p. 228.

the established connexion between different cycles is another form of general fact. But the principles are the same which govern the whole; for the observation in all is the observation of recurring antecedents and consequents.

There is one thing here worthy of being remarked, namely, that when we are seeking for the stated consequent of an antecedent, we may employ experiment as well as observation, since being already in possession of the antecedent, we can place it in different relations in order to see what consequents are connected with it; but that, on the contrary, when we are seeking for the stated antecedent of a consequent, we can employ observation only, for the consequent being subsequent to the antecedent, we cannot place it in different relations in order to see how it arises, since it already is; and, therefore, we have to watch for new instances where the consequent in question is presented together with its proper antecedent.

Our object being to establish the fact of uniformity, it is necessary to settle, as a preliminary question, how many instances are demanded to this end. As Nature is governed throughout by exact law, if it can be shown, in respect to any succession, that a given consequent does take place when a certain antecedent is present, all other antecedents being excluded, then if there be only one instance, this one is sufficient to establish the fact of the sequence. Suppose, for example, that we exclude, in the combustion of a metal, all antecedents but oxygen gas, then it becomes certain, upon the axiom of the uniformity of Nature, that the presence of oxygen is a condition of this phenomenon. But it does not appear from this that oxygen is a general condition of combustion. We may, therefore, proceed to observe and experiment other combinations, excluding oxygen—and if we find that in all such instances no combustion takes place, *then*, and not until then, we infer that oxygen is a general and indispensable condition of this phenomenon. Here one instance is not sufficient, since, although oxygen is a supporter, there may be other substances which act in the same way. When several instances concur, the conclusion becomes strong; and when all known observation and experiment give the same result, no doubt is any longer entertained, for the uniformity seems now fully developed. The case in which we determine that oxygen is a condition of combustion, and the case in which we determine that it is *a general* condition, are widely different, since one instance is sufficient for the first, whereas the induction must be extended in the second.* Wherein lies the distinction between the two cases? Is it not that in the first case we take a given antecedent, and excluding from it all other antecedents, we observe it in circumstances where, if any consequent ensue, it alone can be the condition and antecedent of that consequent; while, in the second case, we take a given consequent, and observe it as it occurs in a variety of circumstances, in order to see whether in all these circumstances there is a general difference, and but one uniform point of agreement, and that point the presence of the oxygen?

Here, then, we see the greater advantage we possess in following the sequence from the antecedent to the consequent, than in the reverse order. In the first, having the antecedent, we can, as before remarked, by experiment

* Oxygen, for some time, was considered the only supporter of combustion This was the general fact until subsequent discoveries brought to light other supporters of combustion. In no *general* fact, therefore, do we attain the *necessary*—this belongs only to law.

place it in different circumstances and isolate it; but in the second, we cannot experiment, but must merely observe the instances in which the consequent appears in connection with an antecedent: and here the circumstances may be so numerous as to require many comparisons in order to detect the particular antecedent required. But, on the other hand, the antecedent itself may be complex, and require analysis in order to determine the force of the different elements. Where this analysis is possible, so that we may separate the elements, we can reduce the experiment again to the utmost simplicity. If we have established that common air is necessary to combustion, and afterwards find that combustion takes place in another gas different from common air, we may be led to enquire whether this gas is present in common air; and when by analysis we have arrived at the composition of the atmosphere, we may test the elements in order to determine whether one element alone is the condition of combustion.

But it often happens that we cannot analyse the complex antecedent. For example, a certain remedy appears to be efficacious in a particular disease; now, if all the circumstances are precisely the same in any other case of the disease, the remedy may here be expected on the general uniformity of Nature to be equally efficacious. But the complexity of the antecedents creates a two-fold difficulty. Do we have such a perfect knowledge of all the circumstances in the first case—the constitution of the individual, the influences of regimen, &c., the nature of the disease itself, and the force of the recuperative power of nature, as to be confident to what extent, or even if at all, the remedy is to be taken as an antecedent to the recovery? And if all this were granted, is our knowledge of all the circumstances in the second case sufficiently minute and accurate to enable us to decide upon the identity of the two cases ? Now, it is evident that where antecedents are thus complicated, observations and experiments need to be multiplied in order to arrive at a general expression in any degree satisfactory.

It appears from the preceding remarks, that the number of instances necessary to enable us to decide upon a prevailing uniformity, depends upon our success in eliminating all the antecedents and consequents foreign to the particular sequence we are contemplating. If, in the case of the treatment of disease, we can eliminate every thing but the disease and the remedy, then we shall at once be in a condition to decide upon the sequence. We shall proceed, therefore, to consider the

PRINCIPLES OF ELIMINATION.

I. General difference with uniform agreement in one point.—Here we suppose several instances of conjoined antecedents to be brought under observation, in each instance, all the antecedents being different but one. Now, if in all these instances a particular consequent uni formly appears, then we infer the general fact that the un varying antecedent is connected with the unvarying con sequent. Two instances thus agreeing would, on th axiom of uniformity, lead us to a conclusion. This con clusion, however, attains its greatest force only where th agreement is verified by general observation and experi ment, that is, by all the observation and experiment, nc only of the individual philosopher, but also of the whol fraternity engaged in the same course of investigatio Thus, if in several combinations of elements, all differin except in the single circumstance of the presence of oxygen, and if in all these an acid is uniformly produced, then we would conclude, under the conditions above laid down, that oxygen is the acidifying element.

The same principle applies to the observation of an unvarying sequent appearing amid varying sequents: here, if the antecedents generally appear irregular and indeterminate, but among these there is one antecedent, which, in all the observed instances, is uniformly present, then we infer that it is connected with the unvarying sequent.

There is another mode of applying this principle, which, wherever it is possible to combine it with the preceding, makes the elimination far more perfect. Suppose that, after having determined, in several instances generally unlike, the connexion of an unvarying antecedent with an unvarying consequent, we are able next to compare instances which are also generally unlike, and agree only in the uniform absence of the particular antecedent noted before, and in the absence of the corresponding consequent, or in the absence of the consequent and the absence of the corresponding antecedent,—then we have here an indication of uniformity tending to the same general result. By the first mode of applying the principle, we eliminate all the unlike and varying antecedents and consequents from the particular antecedent, and consequent on the ground of their unvarying co-presence: by the second, on the ground of their unvarying joint absence.

II. General agreement with uniform difference in one point.—By this principle, we effect a complete elimination. There are three modes of applying it.

First: Let there be a number of antecedents and consequents conjoined: remove one of the antecedents, the consequent which disappears with it is its particular consequent. Or if we observe the disappearance in some instance of one of the consequents, and find that a certain antecedent has also disappeared, then we infer again the sequence of the two. In the first case, we may experiment as well as observe; in the second, we can only observe; since we can compel the disappearance of a consequent by the removal of its antecedent, but we cannot act upon the antecedent through its consequent. Where we repeat the experiment or the observation, and in every instance remove, or note the disappearance of, the same element, and in every instance find that the same corresponding antecedent or consequent is likewise wanting, we of course confirm the general fact by a wider induction.

Second: Let there be several antecedents attended with certain consequents; and among these let there be introduced a new antecedent, the new consequent which now appears we infer to be in sequence with the new antecedent. Let this be repeated in other instances, and if wherever we introduce the particular antecedent the same consequent uniformly appears, and there only, then the elimination of all foreign influences is complete, and the sequence under investigation firmly established.

On the other hand, if, among several phenomena, a new phenomenon should make its appearance, and if, upon examination, a new antecedent should be found to be also present, then a connexion between the two would be inferred. If, in repeated instances, the same concurrence takes place, nothing seems wanting to the elimination.

Third: Let there be a number of antecedents, presenting complicated effects, concurrent, opposing, or independent of each other. If, upon examination, we can trace certain of the consequents to particular antecedents, then we may at once subduct these consequents with their antecedents from the sum total. What remains now, becomes the subject of new investigations ; and thus we may successively eliminate antecedents and consequents, until, we will suppose, only one consequent remains. Now, if there be only one antecedent also remaining, then we infer its connexion with the consequent. This remaining consequent is what Sir John Herschel calls the *residual phenomenon.* I borrow from him the following illustration : "The return of the comet predicted by Professor Encke, a great many times in succession, and the general good agreement of its calculated with its observed place during any one of its periods of visibility, would lead us to say that its gravitation towards the sun and planets is the sole and sufficient cause of all the phenomena of its orbitual motion ; but when the effect of this cause is strictly calculated and subducted from the observed motion, there is found to remain behind a *residual phenomenon,* which would never have been otherwise ascertained to exist, which is a small anticipation of the time of its re-appearnces, or a diminution of its periodic time, which cannot e accounted for by gravity, and whose cause is therefore o be inquired into. Such an anticipation would be caused y the resistance of a medium disseminated through the elestial regions ; and as there are other good reasons for elieving this to be a *vera causa,* it has therefore been asribed to such a resistance." *

III. Elimination by corresponding quantities and ntensities.—Antecedents and sequents may be brought

* Discourse on the Study of Natural Philosophy, p. 156.

under the conception of Quantity ; and as Quantity has its exact science, antecedents and sequents are reducible to precise expressions. Now, there are certain antecedents which never entirely disappear, and therefore we cannot effect an elimination on the preceding principles. For instance : heat is always present, so that we can never determine by actual experiment what consequent would disappear if heat were entirely withdrawn. But if, by changing the quantity of heat, we find corresponding changes in the consequents, then we know, as before, that a sequence exists. We do not remove the antecedent, nor change the essential order of the sequence,—we only modify the antecedent, and uniformly a like modification takes place in a stated consequent. Thus, we notice, in the first place, certain changes in our sensations with respect to heat and cold ; then, observing quicksilver, we see that as our sensations of heat increase in intensity, a corresponding expansion of its bulk takes place, and that, as our sensations moderate, its bulk contracts, and that this contraction regularly goes on as the cold becomes more and more severe, until at length we make out an exact scale of temperature. Now, having determined that quicksilver regularly ex pands and contracts, as the temperature increases or de creases, we apply the scale to the observations we mak upon other metals, and then upon bodies indiscriminately and thus the general fact appears, that all bodies are ex panded by heat, and contracted by a loss of heat. In th same manner, we may determine that all bodies, when pu in motion, will continue to move until brought to a stat of rest by an opposing force, taking this in the light of general fact : We continue to remove obstacles, and a the obstacles are removed, the time of the continuatic of motion is increased, and thus, although we can nev remove all obstacles, we may infer that if all obstacles were removed, the body would continue to move on for ever.*

"Sound consists in impulses communicated to our ears by the air. If a series of impulses of equal force be communicated to it at equal intervals of time, at first in slow succession, and by degrees more and more rapidly, we hear at first a rattling noise, and then a hum, which by degrees acquires the character of a musical note rising higher and higher in acuteness, till its pitch becomes too high for the ear to follow. And from this correspondence between the pitch of the note and the rapidity of succession of the impulse, we conclude that our sensation of the different pitches of musical notes originates in different rapidities with which their impulses are communicated to our ears."†

There is another form of the method to be noticed. We may succeed in removing entirely the antecedent, but the consequent, instead of disappearing with it, may only undergo some modification,—perhaps a mere change in the degree of its intensity. If this modification of the consequent be uniform, then we cannot but infer a real sequence; but inasmuch as the consequent is modified only, and does not disappear with the removal of the antecedent in question, it must be consequent to some other antecedent or antecedents also. This, then, becomes a case of *compound sequence;* and the only way to arrive at the several antecedents is by tentative experiments, in

* I introduce this merely as an illustration of the process of elimination under the principle laid down. The proposition is really an axiom—a universal and necessary affirmation, determined by the idea of matter itself.—*Vide supra*, pp. 158 and 219.

† Herschel's Discourse, p. 153.

which we eliminate successively various circumstances of the phenomena, or introduce new circumstances. In this way we enlarge our knowledge of the antecedents, or at length, by making the phenomenon disappear in conjunction with the eliminations, ascertain the entire compound antecedent.

IV. Elimination of the terms of a Sequence, in order to determine which is the Antecedent, and which the Consequent.—Phenomena may be *invariably concomitant,* and therefore be known to have a fixed connexion, as antecedent and consequent, but the order of the sequence may not at once appear. Now, inasmuch as the causal influence acts through the antecedent to the production of the consequent, it follows that a consequent can be made to disappear, or be modified only by the elimination or modification of the antecedent. Hence, if in attempting to eliminate or modify one of the terms of a sequence, we hit upon the consequent, we shall soon find that *it is* the consequent, by being compelled to introduce an antecedent in order to accomplish our purpose: whereas, if we hit upon the antecedent, we shall remove or modify it without introducing the other term, and its removal or modification, immediately acting upon the other term, will show the order of sequence.

We have an illustration of this in the Theory of Dew by the late Dr. Wells, and which Sir John Herschel, in his Discourse already referred to, introduces as throughout "one of the most beautiful specimens of inductive experimental enquiry lying within a moderate compass." *

We propose dew as a phenomenon whose invariable antecedent we would ascertain. "In the first place, we

* Ibid, &c., pp. 159–163.

must separate dew from rain and the moisture of fogs, and limit the application of the term to what is really meant, which is, the spontaneous appearance of moisture on substances exposed in the open air when no rain or *visible* wet is falling. Now, here we have analogous phenomena in the moisture which bedews a cold metal or stone when we breathe upon it; that which appears on a glass of water fresh from the well in hot weather; that which appears on the *inside* of windows when sudden rain or hail chills the external air; that which runs down our walls, when, after a long frost, a warm, moist thaw comes on: all these instances agree in one point, the coldness of the object dewed, in comparison with the air in contact with it." In the above we have an illustration of our first principle, there is here *a general difference with uniform agreement in one point.*

But with respect to night dew, is this the real antecedent? "Is it a fact that the object dewed *is* colder than the air? Certainly not, one would be at first inclined to say; for what is to *make* it so? But the analogies are cogent and unanimous; and, therefore, we are not to discard their indications." The similarity of the consequents argue a similarity of the antecedents. In this case, to settle the question, we have only "to lay a thermometer in contact with the dewed substance, and hang one at a little distance above it, out of reach of its influence. The experiment has been therefore made; the question has been asked, and the answer has been invariably in the *affirmative.* Whenever an object contracts dew, *it is* colder than the air. Here, then, we have an *invariable concomitant* circumstance." But is cold the antecedent or the consequent of dew? The vulgar prejudice would make it the consequent. "We must, therefore, collect more facts, or, which comes to the same thing, vary the circumstances; since every instance in which the circumstances differ is a fresh fact; and, especially, we must note the contrary or negative cases, *i. e.* where no dew is produced."

"Now, 1st, no dew is produced on the surface of *polished metals*, but it *is* very copiously on glass, both exposed with their faces upwards, and in some cases the under side of a plate of glass is also dewed; which last circumstance excludes the *fall* of moisture from the sky in an invisible form." Here, then, according to our second principle of elimination, is a general agreement with a difference in one point, namely, the *substance* of the material. But what relation have the metal and glass to the *invariable concomitant* circumstance of cold in the production of dew? Have we removed the dew, and thus prevented the cold in the case of the metal, or have we removed the cold and prevented the dew? Unquestionably the latter; for the metal being a good conductor of heat, has continually brought the heat from within itself, or from the earth beneath, upon its surface, while the glass, being a poor conductor, has suffered its surface to become cooled. "This done, a *scale of intensity* becomes obvious. Those polished substances are found to be most strongly dewed which conduct heat worst; while those which conduct well resist dew most effectually." We have thus determined that cold is the antecedent of dew, and not dew the antecedent of cold.

The same fact is confirmed by other striking experiments. Thus, *rough surfaces*, which radiate heat most freely, are most copiously dewed, the substance remaining the same. Again, substances of a loose *texture*, such as cloth, wool, eider-down, cotton, velvet, &c., contract dew more readily than substances of a close texture, such as stones, metals, &c., and the former are precisely those which are selected for clothing, since, on account of their feeble conducting power, they do not carry away the heat from the skin to the air.

"Lastly: among the negative instances, it is observed that dew is never copiously deposited in situations much screened from the open air, and not at all in a *cloudy night;* but if the clouds withdraw, even for a few minutes, and leave a clear opening, a deposition of dew presently begins, and goes on increasing." This remarkable fact shows the same order of sequence. "Those surfaces which part with their heat outwards most readily, and have it supplied from within most slowly, will of course become coldest, if there be an opportunity for their heat to escape, and not be restored to them from without. Now, a clear sky affords such an opportunity. It is a law well known to those who are conversant with the nature of heat, that heat is constantly escaping from all bodies in rays, or by *radiation,* but is constantly restored to them by the similar radiation of others surrounding them. Clouds and surrounding objects, therefore, act as opposing causes, by replacing the whole or a great part of the heat so radiated away, which can escape effectually, without being replaced, only through openings into infinite space." We are thus led to the general fact, that any surface "cooling by radiation faster than its heat can be restored to it by communication with the ground, or by counter-radiation, so as to become colder than the air," condenses the moisture of the air upon itself in the form of dew.

Herschel remarks, "In the analysis above given, the formation of dew is referred to two more general phenomena: the radiation of heat, and the condensation of invisible vapor by cold. The cause (antecedent) of the former is a much higher enquiry, and may be said indeed to be totally unknown; that of the latter actually forms a most important branch of physical enquiry. In such a case, when we reason upwards till we reach an ultimate fact, we regard a phenomenon as fully explained; as we consider the branch of a tree to terminate when traced to its insertion in the trunk, or a twig to its junction with the branch; or rather, as a rivulet retains its importance and its name till lost in some larger tributary, or in the main river which delivers it into the ocean." Now, the ultimate fact upon which all enquiry reposes can, in respect to cause, be nothing less than the Divine volition; and the ultimate fact in respect to law can be that law only which rests immediately upon an Idea. We may continue, by observation and experiment, to enlarge our knowledge of the order and relations of phenomena—of antecedents and consequents indefinitely, reaching from one antecedent to another; but no mere antecedent phenomenon gives a place for the repose of thought. The radiation of heat, and the condensation of vapor by cold, are antecedents to the formation of dew. Could we now discover their antecedents, we should only have new phenomena calling for other antecedents again. We thus accumulate general facts, but we want still the centralising, all-comprehending, and necessary Law. An infinite series of sequences there cannot be. But if the ultimate fact be a mere antecedent like the other antecedents, that is, uniformly preceding its consequent, and having no distinguishing characteristic except that of being the last, then must enquiry cease here by a mere arbitrary decision of the Deity or of Fate. It does not cease because the mind feels satisfied, but because it is permitted to go no farther. But if the ultimate fact be not a phenomenon, but a law, affirming, in the light of Ideas, what *must* be, not a *thing of observation*, but an *intuitive thought*, then indeed must enquiry cease, not by a necessity of compulsion, but by a necessity of pure Reason itself.

I have already remarked that the flux of phenomena is not to be represented as a lengthening series of particulars, which, as it runs back, is ever evolving some new antecedent, until we reach an ultimate phenomenon; but that, on the contrary, this flux goes on in cycles where the end runs into the beginning.* In a series of the first kind, the ultimate fact would be either an unconditional phenomenon, which is contrary to the nature of phenomena; or it would be law as we have defined it, removed from the sphere of phenomenal development; whereas the rational conception of law demands that it be everywhere present, permeating the whole development. But, in a series of the second kind, all the phenomena are both conditionated and conditionating, and the law, as from a centre, radiates into the whole cycle, filling out and governing the whole.

It ought to be remarked here, also, that theory applies to general facts as well as to law. In the latter application, the conception has already been given.† In the former application, we mean by it the hypothesis of an antecedent general fact for the purpose of conditionating a known fact, and thus enabling us to give a more full and rational explication of the whole series under consideration. As instances, we may cite the undulating theory of Light; and Dalton's theory of Ultimate Atoms. In

* Supra, p. 269. † Supra, p. 194.

both instances, we have antecedents hypothesised and connected with actual phenomena. We hypothesise, in order to supply undiscovered parts of a cycle of phenomena, the parts which are known suggesting those which are unknown: or the unknown facts may be hypothesised on the basis of a theory or a law, which, already comprehending the known facts, demands certain other facts to complete the cycle.

In making observations, we may hit upon any part of a cycle of facts, and thence be led through the relations of antecedents and consequents to other parts. Herschel remarks, in respect to the induction in the case of dew, "Had we no previous knowledge of the radiation of heat, this same induction would have made it known to us, and, duly considered, might have led to a knowledge of many of its laws." That is, any part may serve as a good starting point. "In the study of nature," he adds, "we must not, therefore, be scrupulous as to *how* we reach to a knowledge of such general facts: provided, only, we verify them carefully when once detected, we must be content to seize them wherever they are to be found." * Now, it is because the development of phenomena moves in a cycle that we may begin at any point indifferently, since, beginning wherever we please or happen to, we cannot lose the connected particulars. If we go back from consequent to antecedent, the last antecedent becomes the consequent of the first consequent, which, relatively to it, becomes an antecedent; and if we go from antecedent to consequent, the last consequent becomes an antecedent to the first antecedent, which, relatively to it, becomes a consequent.

* Supra, p. 174.

Were the cycles of phenomena completed, then observation and experiment would have done their work in respect to establishing general facts; then the uniform antecedents and consequents would all be known.

I shall close this section by summing up the cardinal points.

I. The governing ideas are Cause and Law.

II. The leading axioms are those of Universal Law, and of the Uniformity of Nature.

III. The last named axiom may be conveniently expanded into two particular axioms: *

1. Like antecedents involve like consequents.

2. Like consequents imply like antecedents.

IV. General facts may be determined to an indefinite extent before the law is arrived at, but whenever a law is arrived at, or a theory adopted, the cycle of facts may be enlarged or completed by their necessary demands.

V. Hypothesis relates either to fact or to law. Hypothesised laws are theories.

VI. In the observation of phenomena we must be both general and minute; noting all the phenomena, and all their characteristics.

VII. Uniform antecedence and sequence of phenomena, the semblance and exponent of law, is determined by a method of elimination which excludes whatever is foreign to the particular relation to be determined.

VIII. The formulæ of Induction † comprehends every mode of elimination, since it determines the general expression of the uniform sequences.

IX. When general facts are attained, they may be

* Supra, page 228. † Page 211.

verified by returning to the particular instances from which they were derived, or by multiplying instances. There are often accidental and unlooked-for verifications, which are of great weight, because they seem like a spontaneous testimony of nature.

SECTION VIII.

INDUCTIVE LOGIC OF UNIVERSAL AND NECESSARY LAWS.

LAWS are determined in two ways, either directly in the form of axioms;* or indirectly, through an induction of facts. The ultimate determining power in both cases lies in Ideas of pure Reason.

We have seen that even Ideas and Axioms demand phenomenal conditions for their development; but this is widely different from that induction of facts which at the first leads us to uniform antecedents and consequents, and in the end to universal and necessary laws.

The axiomatic forms of law appear in the most original laws, such as the laws of Logic itself, and The Moral; but the great laws of Nature, those which comprehend the interior constitution of substances, and the constitution of systems of bodies, are laws arrived at by Induction.

The Idea of Law, that sublime Idea so quickening to thought, leads on all observation and experiment, whether the result be merely general facts of uniform sequences, or universal and necessary laws. Uniform sequences are the exponents of law; hence, in seeking for them, we are really seeking ultimately for law. In the progress of our research we pass from one generalization to another more

* Supra, p. 242.

extensive and comprehensive, until at length we seem to reach an ultimate generalization, and this we call the great and ultimate law. But it is not the great and ultimate law simply because it is at present the ultimate point of investigation; it may be only the most general fact, or an antecedent the most remote, which we have as yet reached. To make it law, something is required in its own intrinsic nature, as exhibited to the eye of Reason. Law, taken on its highest ground, lies in the pure Idea; taken under its highest manifestation, it is the determinate purpose or design of the Creative Mind. And in its sphere; in relation to its appropriate phenomena, it is universal and necessary. Thus the great moral law in its sphere, that is, responsible being; in relation to its appropriate phenomena, that is, the conduct of responsible being, is universal and necessary: it is the law without exception and in every instance; and it is the necessary law, no other being admissible. It lies originally in the Idea of Right and Wrong; it appears as the wise design in the Creative Mind which bodied forth this noblest form of being; and it gives birth to every rule of moral action.

So also in Somatology, law taken on its highest ground lies in the pure Idea; taken under its highest manifestation, it is the determinate purpose or design of the Creative Mind. In its sphere—*e. g.* the interior constitution of bodies or their arrangement into system, in relation to its appropriate phenomena—*e. g.* the changes of bodies in composition and decomposition, or their motions in masses through space, it is universal; and, considered as the wisest and the best,* it is necessary. Now, that upon

* Part I., Sect. VII. Also, Part III., pp. 194, 195.

which the Reason fastens when it becomes satisfied that a law is attained, is the correspondence between the outward generalization and its own Idea, and the presence in the generalization of the characteristics of universality and necessity. Thus, Gravitation is an ultimate generalization; but it is more, for the Reason perceives its correspondency with its own Idea of Centralization,* and therefore judges not only that it is the ultimate generalization actually attained, but also that there is no other beyond it that can be attained, and affirms that it is the law, and the necessary law, of all systems of bodies.

The logical process by which we arrive at universal laws is akin to that by which we arrive at general facts. Indeed the establishment of general facts is a part of the process. The principles, therefore, laid down in the preceding Section, are applicable here also.

It is impossible to prescribe the number of general facts which are demanded as conditions of the determination of a universal law. Sometimes the law is preconceived at a very early stage of the investigation; such was the fact in the case of Newton in respect to gravitation. Although believed to be a law, it can, under these circumstances, be received only as a hypothesis, until verified in numerous and decisive applications. But the secret conviction, the earnest hope, and the indomitable purpose of investigation, inspired by the conception from the beginning, proves it to lie deeper in the soul than a fortunate guess or an enticing fancy.

The verification of a law hypothesised is strikingly illustrated in Physical Astronomy. "The law, for example, which asserts that the planets are retained in their

* Page 198.

orbits about the sun, and satellites about their primaries, by an attractive force, decreasing as the square of the distances increases, comes to be verified in each particular case by deducing from it the exact motions which, under the circumstances, ought to take place, and comparing them with the fact. This comparison, while it verifies in general the existence of the law of gravitation as supposed, and its adequacy to explain all the principal motions of every body in the system, yet leaves some small deviations in those of the planets, and some very considerable ones in that of the moon and other satellites, still unaccounted for; residual phenomena, which still remain to be traced up to causes. By further examining these, their causes have at length been ascertained, and found to consist in the mutual actions of the planets on each other, and the disturbing influence of the sun on the motions of the satellites."* And thus these residual phenomena turn out an additional verification of the law of gravitation.

In other instances the law dawns slowly, and is preceded by many vague and inadequate hypotheses, which have to be overcome before the true light can shine clearly. And when it begins to shine, hypotheses appear, which indeed are more or less ingenious and satisfactory, but still indecisive. And thus there appears a gradual convergence from many points to the all-comprehending law. But when the law is attained, whatever be the process by which we attain it, it is known to be the law by its sufficiency in respect to the phenomena to be explained, by its universality and necessity, and its echo to the Idea of the Reason within.

There is also to be remarked a difference in the men

* Herschel's Discourse, p. 166.

tal constitution, by which a superior degree of the intuitive function seems to be awarded to some individuals. These are the chosen interpreters of nature. By a sudden and wonderful leap they are seen to pass from a limited induction to a stupendous conclusion. With a prophetic power they seem to foretel the law, which, before ordinary minds, lies only as the result of an immense and laborious observation. The mere experimenter and observer collects facts, but does not gain laws. On the other hand, a mind of high intuitive energy cannot make itself independent of experiment and observation; for those high prophecies require the verification of facts. It is the union of the two which makes the finished philosopher of nature, for it is the union of the two which constitutes the true Inductive Logic. And indeed, where these high gifts are found, we may generally expect a corresponding skill and diligence in collating facts; for the mind that can penetrate the laws of nature under her simplest manifestations, will be prone to seek the fullest confirmations of these laws from observation and experiment.

In the discovery of laws there is so much that appears like inspiration, and indeed so much that is really inspiration, if Reason be the inspiration of the Almighty in man, that to lay down exact logical rules and formulæ designed to govern and represent the process of discovery, would appear puerile in the attempt, and prove impracticable if attempted.

The great principle, however, can be clearly expressed. It is that which has already been alluded to, namely, the union of Ideas and Observation. It is the force and light of the cardinal Ideas of Cause and Law which at first impel and guide us in investigation. Ideas of Time and Space open to us the possibility of succession and arrangement. But, beyond this, the laws which govern the world, inasmuch as they had their origin in the Divine Mind, cannot be strange to us. While, therefore, the perceptive and inductive functions are busy in collecting facts, the mind is intensely meditative, and intuition is awake. Now it is that the Ideas which are to spring forth into law are quickened and called upon. The orderly and uniform sequences of phenomena are noted ;—these we have called the exponents of law. Generalization follows generalization. Hypotheses are framed. Observation is enlarged, and rendered more exact by experiment. The Reason conceives more and more clearly. All that lies before it in the phenomenal world, having proceeded from the Divine Ideas, is ready to meet corresponding Ideas in the human mind. At length the required Idea is developed, and it projects itself into the external world as the law of the phenomena.

It will be perceived that we have limited the term *law* to the universal and necessary. In common usuage the term is applied to uniform sequences in general. The former is the strictly philosophical use. While we are looking at particular sequences separately from the universal law, or in ignorance of it, it may perhaps be convenient to call them laws of nature ; but when viewed in connexion with the law, they are seen to be only forms of its manifestation or exponential facts. For example, it might be called a law of wood, and of vegetable matter generally, to float in water,—and of metals and minerals, to sink ; a law of vapour to rise, in the atmosphere ; a law of water, to flow down descents of any degree,—and of bodies generally, to roll down declivities when moved off their balance ; a law of the tides, to rise and fall ; a law of the pendulum, to preserve a determinate vibration ; and so on. But when the law of universal gravitation is understood, then these particular laws, so-called, are perceived to be mere uniform sequences determined by the universal law.

And here we may understand the difference in the intelligent apprehension, between uniform sequences and universal laws. All these particular laws, taken in themselves as uniform sequences, are mere arbitrary facts. We come to know them familiarly; and, indeed, we seem to understand them, because we are accustomed to their appearance; but still, all we can say of them is, that such is the order of nature. But when we can refer them all to one universal law, we gain a deeper and more satisfactory insight. Now we perceive a unity and simplicity in nature which awakens admiration, like that which we experience when we view a grand and perfect mechanism. But still more, we now perceive the great comprehending law to be a universal and necessary law—the law of the universe springing from an Idea. Nothing is so intelligible as Ideas, for they are the elements of the Reason itself, "the light of all our seeing." In the Idea of centralization we perceive how the universe *must* be constituted, and in the law of gravitation we find the realization of the Idea. Equally satisfactory is the law of centrifugal force, as the realization of the Idea of Diffusion. *

The human intellect has oftentimes expended its force in hypothesising new and more remote antecedents, instead of directing itself through an induction of unquestionable facts to the discovery of a law. Des Cartes hypothesised vortices as antecedents to the primary phenomena of the planets in their revolution about the sun, and of the

* Page 198.

satellites about the planets. And Bernoulli attempted, in accordance with this hypothesis, to explain the elliptical form of the orbits by the shape of the planets, acting like the rudder of a boat in the stream of the vortices. But how were the vortices themselves to be explained? A mere multiplication of the antecedents only threw the difficulty farther back without overcoming it. Nay, more; it introduced new difficulties, in the necessity of sustaining the hypothesis.

Chemistry, the science of material elements and their mutual relations in the composition and decomposition of bodies, was, until a late period, a mere collection of uniform sequences. As such, it was of immense practical importance. And as the facts of chemistry had to be elicited by nice, ingenious, and difficult, and often dangerous experiments, the discovery of a new fact often formed an epoch in the science, and conferred a just and lasting fame on the discoverer. But still the facts stood out to view simply as facts, unexplained by any central and comprehensive law. They indeed revealed a beautiful and benign constitution of nature—they connected themselves with the idea of paternal wisdom and goodness; but this was accounting for them only under a moral aspect. The same wise and benign ends might perhaps have been reached equally well by a different constitution. What was required, was the intellectual purpose growing necessarily out of an Idea, and projecting itself in the outer world as the all-pervading law of the interior constitution of bodies.

I have already had occasion to refer to the stupendous results to which the genius of Faraday has conducted us. In these results, chemistry attains to simplicity and unity. All chemical changes are now made to appear under one great law, by whatever name we call it, whether of Polarity or of Electrical Induction. Behind the law there lies an Idea.* Neither the Idea nor the law have as yet reached a full development, but to this point we are evidently tending. The Idea must be an Idea of the pure Reason, related to the elemental constitution and changes of bodies analogously to the Idea of centralization and diffusion in its relation to the masses of constituted bodies; and the corresponding law must comprehend and govern in its sphere, analogously to the law of gravitation in its sphere. In Faraday we perceive, in an extraordinary degree, the union of the most exact, elaborate, and extensive experimentation with Ideal conceptions. It is a union of the Senses with the world of the Reason; like the union of those opposite polar forces by which he solves the mysteries of his favorite science, and brings to light the order and harmony of Nature in her elements.

The application of the mathematics to the expression of physical laws arises from the fact that the subjects of these laws are real quantities, such as magnitude, motion, time, and distance. For example, gravitation implies motion, and motion is related to space; the intelligible expression of the law, therefore, requires its expression in the relation of space.

Ere we close this part of our investigation, we must return for a moment to the cyclical order of phenomena, and the central position of law. Receiving this, at least, as a convenient, if not a purely rational conception, it must be evident that the law, as law, cannot be absent from any point of the phenomenal movement; but is like an indefinite number of radii drawn from the centre to the

* Page 200.

circumference, which are many, and yet, in their perfect identity, one ; so that we may regard the circumference as formed either by the extremities of an indefinite number of equal radii projected from a common centre, or by the extremity of one of the radii revolving about the centre. Now, suppose our observation were fixed upon only one point of the circumference, we might account for its existence by conceiving of it as merely the extremity of a straight line : or, suppose we were to observe several points in curvilinear juxtaposition, then we might account for them by conceiving of an angle of which the whole arc formed the measure. But as our observation became more extended, we might be led to the conception of a circle, and then every point would be explained in reference to it alone, and the particular straight line and the particular angle would pass out of thought in the wider generalization. Now, our first conclusions were true, but they did not contain the whole truth ; and when the whole truth is ascertained, we no longer require our first conclusions. In like manner, in a cycle of phenomena, our observation is fixed at first upon a certain antecedent and consequent, and we name the particular end of the uniformity, a law. Here indeed is no error; for the law from the centre radiates into this particular uniformity, and is the true source of it. But, inasmuch as the particular sequence in question is only one of a wide circle of sequences, we require the law of the whole ere we have the sufficient law of the part. This law of the whole permeating every part explains every part ; and like the centre and radii of a circle, is a conception of pure Reason based upon an Idea.

The Reason in its Ideas enjoys a perfect and quie cognition ; and when phenomena are explained by laws which again are explained by Ideas, then we have reached the clearest light, and the highest satisfaction of knowledge.*

The leading Axioms and definitions of the Inductive Logic of Universal and Necessary Laws, so far as implied in the foregoing, may be summarily stated as follows :

I. Every particular phenomenon is both an antecedent and a consequent, taken in different relations; and, as a part of a harmonious whole, is comprehended by a law.

II. Every law is the projection of an Idea.

III. Observation and experiment supply the orderly sequences of phenomena, and thus conditionate the development of law; but the law itself, with its characteristics of universality and necessity, is a conception of the Reason.

IV. A rational hypothesis is an effort to find a law by tentative acts;—it is feeling after a law by rational forethought, if haply we may find it.

V. Observation and experiment, without a rational hypothesis, is like a man groping at objects at random with his eyes shut. But even rational hypothesis, unaccompanied by the former, is only felicitous dreaming.

VI. Inasmuch as the world of the senses was created by the Divine Reason from its own Ideas; and inasmuch as the mind of man is made after the likeness of the Divine Mind, therefore can it truly be said to know the world of the senses only so far as, like the Divine Mind, it finds its Ideas there projected.

VII. Hence the Science of Nature can be determined only by a union of Sensuous Phenomena with Ideal Conceptions.

VIII. The criteria of a law are, its sufficiency in

* Part I., Section X.

respect to the phenomena, its characteristics, viz., universality and necessity, and its correspondence to an Idea.

IX. Law implies Cause. Cause is present wherever law is manifested. Law expresses the rational plan, the wise and fit developments of Cause.

SECTION IX.

THE LOGIC OF ART.

Art depends upon the Inventive Function.* There is a Logic of Science; is there also a Logic of Art?

Art exists before Science. Sometimes it is the effect of accident. Generally, in its earlier stages, it is the effect of human wants inspiring an unreflecting ingenuity to empirical efforts. Art, in its highest state, is an effect of ripened science.

Pure accident and empiricism reach art by mere felicities. But even where there is no science, there is often exhibited an ingenuity and skill which impress us as a manifestation of high and extraordinary powers. Men of this mould seem to invent by a sort of inspiration. They seem prepared for every difficulty, and arrive at results the most curious with wonderful ease and tact. These instances are found both in the mechanical and the fine arts. There must be here an exceedingly vigorous spontaneous development of Ideas, together with a nice and quick observation, and a vivid imagination.

There is, therefore, a true Inductive Logic, leading virtually to important conclusions, although they be not stated in the form of distinct propositions. These conclusions really direct the hand of the mechanician and

* Page 231.

the artist. They are not reflected upon as universal principles, and therefore are not elaborated into a scientific system; they appear to the individual as something belonging to him, something that answers his special purpose, and with this he remains content. In his use they soon become reduced to mere rules of art. This natural and spontaneous Logic plays an important part in the development of humanity; and that which we call Genius, and which so proudly overcomes all obstacles, presenting us the unscientific but skilful mechanician and artist; or leading onward the untutored, as in the case of Ferguson and Corregio, and a multitude of others, to the loftiest eminence of science or art, is chiefly a natural logical power, lying in the proper union of Ideas and external observations—a union of the Ideal and the sensuous. Unite with this the highest form of the imagination, and you have the most splendid form of genius: for it is the imagination which from Ideas creates those ideal representations which constitute archetypes of all that man accomplishes of the great, the beautiful, and the sublime.

Where all the lights of science are enjoyed, invention exhibits a chain of the nicest reasoning, both inductive and deductive. The latter form of reasoning appears indeed in the cases above mentioned; but more remarkably here, inasmuch as the invention sets out with principles already ascertained. In its progress it may have to make many inductions, and to exert that high prophetic power which gives birth to rational hypotheses. Indeed, the imagination is here also tasked in ideal representations of mechanism. The steam engine from its conception to its present state, exhibits a constant series of scientific inventions springing from a rigid logic.

One of the most beautiful instances of scientific invention is Davy's safety-lamp. Here conclusions were drawn from established scientific principles; new inductions were made; a hypothesis formed; an ideal of the invention represented in the imagination, from whence an external model or diagram could be produced; and thus every thing was made ready for that simple effort of mechanical skill which completed the great achievement, —great as a work of the intellect, and no less great as a merciful visitation to poor and laboring men.

BOOK III.

DEDUCTIVE LOGIC.

SECTION I.

INTRODUCTION.

We have hitherto been engaged with the Logic of First Truths, General Facts, and Universal Principles and Laws. We are now to consider the Logic of drawing inferences from a comprehending or containing Whole, to particulars concluded under it. In Inductive Logic, particulars were shown to be involved into universals: In Deductive Logic, we must show that universals may be evolved into particulars.*

Deductive Logic implies, 1. That some first truths, general facts, and universal principles have been established: it implies, therefore, a considerable advance of human knowledge. 2. It implies that a cultivated language exists, one adequate to express truths, principles, and facts, in clear and precise propositions.

It is, therefore, with propositions that we begin in Deductive Reasoning. These propositions may themselves

* Pages 211–213.

be conclusions drawn from antecedent propositions, or they may be primary and underived. They may be analytical or synthetical; and synthetical *à priori* or *à posteriori.** But the manner in which they may have been obtained is not taken into account in the particular deduction with which we may be engaged. Neither do we take into account the subject matter of the propositions; this is referred to particular sciences. If the subject matter be pure quantity, it is referred to the mathematics; if it be composed of natural phenomena, it is referred to physiology, natural philosophy, or chemistry, and so on. In considering any branch of science, or any subject whatever, we may have occasion to make many deductions—these may be a means to one end: but in each particular deduction we have only to pay regard to the proper relation between those propositions which form our premises, and the conclusion we deduce. This part of Logic, therefore, aims to express a universal form of deduction,—one that shall apply to every subject indifferently.

* Vide Part I., Sec. X.

SECTION II.

ANALYSIS OF PROPOSITIONS.

A JUDGMENT is an affirmation of the mind. When expressed in language, it becomes a *proposition*, because it is then propounded to general attention. Every proposition consists of a *subject* and a *predicate*. The subject is that of which the affirmation is made; the predicate is that which is affirmed of the subject.

The affirmation is either *positive* or *negative*; that is, an affirmation of agreement or of disagreement.*

The subject and predicate are collectively called *terms*. Each term expresses an object of thought complete in itself.

That which connects the terms together in a proposition, is called the *Copula*. This copula must always be IS, in positive propositions; and IS NOT, in negative. The reason is obvious, viz., that the verb *to be* enters necessarily into the simple and direct form of affirmation. In the ordinary forms of language, propositions do not, indeed, generally employ the substantive verb; but they are always capable of being reduced to this form, by using a participle or an adjective, in connection with the verb: *e. g.* "Cæsar conquered," may be reduced to the form, "Cæsar *was* victorious," in which the copula appears. A

* Supra, p. 64.

term may consist of one or of several words. No single word is capable of being a term in itself, except a nominative noun, because no other word, in itself, expresses a complete object of thought. The infinitive mood of the verb is not an exception, for this is really a noun: *e. g.* "To be loved is to be happy:" *i. e.*

Sub. "The state of being loved | is | *Pred.* a state of happiness."

When the adjective appears as a predicate, the noun, of course, is understood in connection with it. Where a term consists of one word, it is called a *simple* term; where it consists of several, a *complex* term.

Sometimes no little circumlocution is necessary, in order to reduce a proposition, consisting of complex terms, to its exact form: *e. g.* "If he starts to-day, he will probably arrive the day after to-morrow:" *i. e.*

Sub. "The event of his starting to-day

Pred. an event which makes it probable he will arrive the day after to-morrow."

Again: "I am sure he said so:" *i. e.*

Sub. "The thing referred to by 'so,' | is | *Pred.* what I am sure he said."

Simple terms are *singular* or *common*. A singular term stands for an individual, and can be predicated only of itself. A common term stands for many, and, of course, can be predicated of many.

Propositions are *categorical* or *hypothetical*. The former is an unconditional affirmation; the latter a conditional.

Propositions are distinguished again by *Quality* and *Quantity.*

The Quality of a proposition refers to its positive or negative character: *e. g.* "A horse is a quadruped," is positive; "A covetous man is not contented," is negative. We must be careful to distinguish between a strictly negative proposition, *i. e.* one which connects the negative particle with the copula, and one which contains a descriptive negative particle in one of its terms: *e. g.* "He was conversing with a man not like the one you describe," is positive; "He was not conversing with a man like the one you describe," is negative. Sometimes it is convenient to transfer the negative particle from the copula to one of the terms, and thus to change the negative form for the positive: *e. g.* "Man is not perfect" is equivalent to "Man is imperfect."

The logical use of the negative particles must be distinguished from those uses which obtain in the familiar idioms of conversation. In the latter, they sometimes not only deny, but affirm the contrary: *e. g.* the remark sometimes playfully made, "He is no fool," is intended not merely to deny one kind of quality, but to attribute no common share of the opposite kind; whereas, in the logical use, the negative particles simply deny, and never imply, an affirmation of the contrary.

The Quantity of a proposition expresses the extent of the affirmation or negation. When the predicate is affirmed or denied of the *whole* of the subject, the proposition is *universal;* when it is affirmed or denied only of a *part* of the subject, the proposition is *particular: e. g.* "All men are mortal," "No miser is happy," are universal; "Some men are prudent," "Some animals are not sagacious," are particular.

Propositions, as *positive*, and *negative*, and *universal*, and *particular*, are distributed into four kinds. These are generally, for the sake of brevity, represented by the symbols A, E, I, and O. And since Deductive Logic considers the *form* of propositions, and not the *matter*, we may conveniently represent the subject and predicate by symbols. The whole, then, may be represented as follows:

A, *Universal affirmative.* Every X is Y;
E, *Universal negative.* No X is Y;
I, *Particular affirmative.* Some X is Y;
O, *Particular negative.* Some X is not Y.

In conversational idiom, when we affirm a part, we intend to deny the remainder. Thus, when we say, "Some of the company have arrived," we intend to signify that a part have not arrived. But, in logical language, on the contrary, we intend to signify no more than we express. Thus, when we say some X is Y, we do not mean to imply that some X is not Y; this may or may not be, and no doubtful form of predication is admissible.

Indefinite propositions, *e. g.* "Birds have wings," "Food is necessary for life," "Fish live in the water," are those whose quality is left unexpressed. These do not belong to the province of Logic, for here no proposition can be indefinite, but to that of Rhetoric. The truth is, that indefinite propositions never appear in correct writing —unless the intention be to mislead—except where, from the connection, or from the well-known nature of the matter, every reader at once is able to supply the true quantity. Thus, when it is said "Food is necessary to life," the writer is sure he will not be misunderstood; otherwise, he ought to supply the quantitive particle.

Where the subject of a proposition is a singular term, the proposition is reckoned among universals, because the whole subject is spoken of: *e. g.* "Socrates was an Athenian philosopher," means the *whole* of Socrates.

Propositions may be universal, without having both their terms taken universally: *e. g.* when it is said, "All horses are quadrupeds," the term "horses" is taken universally, but not the term "quadrupeds;" for it is not true that all quadrupeds are horses: but in the proposition, "No merciful man will abuse dumb animals," both terms are taken universally; for, in excluding merciful men from that class who abuse dumb animals, we do also exclude the latter from the former. In the other example, although all horses are affirmed to be contained in the class "quadrupeds," this does not imply that all quadrupeds are contained in the class "horses." In particular affirmative propositions, it is evident that neither term is taken universally: *e. g.* "Some undeserving men are prosperous."

In particular negatives, the subject plainly is not taken universally; but the whole of the predicate being excluded from the subject, must be regarded as taken universally: *e. g.* "Some good men are not prosperous." Here the subject enters only partially; but the predicate composed of the class "prosperous," is entirely excluded from the subject "Some good men." When any term is taken universally, it is technically said to be *distributed.* Employing the symbols already introduced, the whole can be presented at one view.

A, X is Y. Subject distributed.
E, X is Y. Subject and predicate distributed.
I, X is Y. Neither term is distributed.
O, X is Y. Predicate distributed.

SECTION III.

OF PROPOSITIONS AS OPPOSED TO EACH OTHER.

Propositions are opposed to each other when the subject and predicate remain the same; and they differ in quantity or quality, or in both.

I. *Opposition in quantity.* A is opposed to I; and E to O. The nature of this opposition is such, that A being affirmed, I must be affirmed likewise; and the same in respect to E and O: and the denial of I and O respectively involves the denial of A and E; but the denial of A and E does not involve the denial of I and O.

This results from the axiom, That the affirmation of the universal is the affirmation of the particular: and the negation of the particular destroys the universal; but the negation of the universal does not destroy the particular.

II. *Opposition in quality.* A is opposed to E; and I to O. The nature of this opposition is such that A being affirmed, E must be denied; but I being affirmed, O is not to be denied; and *vice versa.* The denial of A or E does not involve the affirmation of the other; but the denial of I or O does involve the affirmation of the other.

This results from the following axioms: 1. A universal positive and a universal negative being contraries throughout their whole extent, cannot both be true. 2. A particular positive and a particular negative being contraries within limitation, may lie upon different parts of the same field, and therefore both be true. 3. The denial of a universal of one quality does not legitimate the affirmation of a universal of the opposite quality, since both universals may be false, and the truth lie only in the particulars: but both the particulars cannot be false, for then both the universals would be true.

III. *Opposition in both quantity and quality.* A is opposed to O; and E to I. The nature of this opposition is such that A being affirmed, O must be denied; and E being affirmed, I must be denied; and *vice versa.* And again: A being denied, O must be affirmed; and E being denied, I must be affirmed; and *vice versa.*

This results from the axioms:

1. Opposition in quantity and quality, inasmuch as it excludes all agreement, amounts to positive contradiction, so that the affirmation of one form of the proposition cannot be less than the destruction of the other form.

2. The opposition of a universal positive to a particular negative, or of a universal negative to a particular positive, constitutes a perfect alternative,—the denial of the one being the affirmation of the other.

The most general form of this axiom is as follows: *To deny a positive, is equivalent to affirming a negative; and to deny a negative, is equivalent to affirming a positive.* In this form, quantity is not taken into the account; but the introduction of the idea of quantity modifies the expression of the axiom, since to deny a universal positive, is not to affirm a *universal* negative, inasmuch as this may also be false, *i. e.*, the *universality* may be false; but it is to affirm a negative, *i. e.*, the negative must be true in some form; and therefore, as it is not necessarily true in the universal form, it remains that it must be true in the particular form: and so also of denying a universal negative in relation to a particular positive.

The following table presents the whole at one view:

AFFIRMING *is equivalent to*		DENYING *and*		AFFIRMING.
A	=	E, O,	=	I,
E	=	A, I,	=	O,
I	=	E,		
O	=	A.		

DENYING *is equivalent to*		AFFIRMING *and*		DENYING.
A	=	O,		
E	=	I,		
I	=	E, O,	=	A,
O	=	A, I,	=	E.

SECTION IV.

OF THE CONVERSION OF PROPOSITIONS.

A PROPOSITION is *converted* by the *transposition* of its *terms: i. e.*, the subject becomes the predicate, and the predicate the subject.

The proposition as given, is called the *exposita;* when converted, it is called the *converse.*

The law which governs the conversion of propositions is as follows: *No converse may assert more generally than the exposita.* This law results from the axiom, that, *A consequence cannot transcend its premises.* Hence, what is affirmed in the exposita of a part only, cannot, in the converse, be affirmed of the whole. The application of this law is very evident.

1. *Universal affirmative.* A, X is Y, does not distribute the predicate, but only the subject: all the X's are in the Y's, but the Y's may contain more than X's; and, therefore, from the affirmative, every X is Y, we can only affirm some Y is X; *i. e.*, as much of the Y as answers tc the X.

2. *Universal negative.* E, X is Y distributes th(predicate as well as the subject. If there is No X in Y then, consequently, there is No Y in X.

3. *Particular affirmative.* I, X is Y distributes neithe one nor the other: If only Some X is Y, then only Som. Y is X.

4. *Particular negative.* O, X is Y distributes only the predicate: only some X's are not contained in the Y, but all the Y's are excluded from the some X's in question. Hence, a simple conversion cannot take place; for this would distribute the X, and, of course, make it to assert more generally than the exposita: From some X is not Y, we cannot infer some Y is not X, for then, by the converse, all the X's are excluded from the some Y's in question. It is true, indeed, that some Y is not X may, in some instances, be consistent with the exposita some X is not Y, but it is consistent, not as the converse of this form, but as a deduction from another form of the proposition: *e. g.*, "Some soldiers are not brave men," is consistent with the exposita, "Some brave men are not soldiers;" but the first is not true, as the converse of the last, which plainly it is not; but as the contradictory of the universal affirmative, "All soldiers are brave men," this contradictory, from our knowledge of the matter, being first denied.

In like manner, the several forms A, Y is X; E, Y is X; I, Y is X, may be consistent with O, X is Y, in particular instances, where the matter is such as to admit of it. But legitimate conversion takes place independently of the matter. According to a strict exposition of the form, therefore, a particular negative exposita has no converse. A negative proposition, however, may be changed into a positive, by connecting the particle of negation with one of its terms: *e. g.*,

Sub.		*Pred.*
"Some brave men	are	not soldiers,"

may be converted as a particular positive, thus,

Sub.		*Pred.*
"Some not soldiers	are	brave men."

Here the exposita and converse are identical, and may be represented under the bare form thus, some X is $\overline{\text{not Y}}$; *converse*, some $\overline{\text{not Y}}$ is X. Where the particle of negation is a component of the term which it affects, the conversion, by a particular positive, is peculiarly graceful: *e. g.*, "Some good men are not fortunate;" *converse*, "Some unfortunate men are good men."

To deny a negative being equivalent to affirming a positive, we may convert a positive, under a form of *negation*, or *contraposition*: *e. g.*, "Every poet is a man of genius." This is equivalent to "No poet is not a man of genius;" which may be converted by "He who is not a man of genius is not a poet." *

The following table contains the different kinds of conversion under the bare form:

EXPOSITA.		CONVERSE.
A, X is Y	=	I, Y is X,
E, X is Y	=	E, Y is X,
I, X is Y	=	I, Y is X,
O, X is Y	=	I, $\overline{\text{not Y}}$ is X.

By contraposition.

A, X is Y	=	E, $\overline{\text{not Y}}$ is X.

Some universal positive propositions, such as defini tions, for example, have *convertible* terms, *i. e.*, *exactl equivalent* terms, and, in this case, are said to admit of universal positive as a converse: *e. g.*, "All equilatera triangles are equiangular;" but to state this strictly, w should say, "All the equilateral triangles are all th

* Whateley's Logic, Book II., ch. ii., § 4.

equiangular triangles." And so, again, the example, "A good government is that which has the happiness of the governed for its object," and which also seems to admit of conversion by a universal positive, if stated strictly, becomes, "All the good governments are all those which have the happiness of the governed in view." But these propositions need not be considered universal, for, in the first example, we are speaking not of "all triangles," but only of some triangles, *i. e.*, those which are "equilateral:" and in the second example, we are speaking, not of "all governments," but only of some governments, *i. e.*, "good governments." We may, therefore, convert them by particular positive propositions, as follows:

"Some triangles, *i. e.*, the equilateral, are equiangular."

"Some triangles, *i. e.*, the equiangular, are equilateral."

"Some governments, *i. e.*, the good, have the happiness of the governed in view."

"Some governments, *i. e.*, all which have the happiness of the governed in view, are good governments." *

* Whateley's Logic, ibid.

SECTION V.

PROPOSITIONS CONSTRUCTED INTO SYLLOGISMS.

A SYLLOGISM * is the formula of the most direct and simple deduction possible.

Let X is Y represent, as before, any proposition. If the agreement of X and Y is directly perceived, then intuition supersedes the necessity of deduction: but if it cannot be perceived directly, then we must enquire for a medium. Now, suppose this medium to be Z, and that we perceive by intuition, or as the result of a previous deduction,† that X and Y respectively agree with Z, then we *infer* that they agree with each other. We have thus the formula of positive conclusions:

X is Z,
Y is Z,

therefore

X is Y. ‡

The axiom which determines this formula is the following: *If two terms agree with one and the same third term, they agree with each other.*

Again: Let X is not Y represent any proposition in which disagreement is affirmed between two terms. If this disagreement be not intuitively perceived, we must once more seek for a medium through which to deduce it

* Vide supra, p. 84. † Pages 64, 65. ‡ Page 211.

Let Z, again, be that medium ; and suppose that either, by intuition, or as the result of a previous deduction, we perceive that X agrees with Z, but that Y disagrees with Z ; then we *infer* that X and Y disagree with each other. We have thus the formula of negative conclusions :

X is Z,
Y is not Z,

therefore

X is not Y.

The axiom which determines this formula, is the following : *If of two terms, one agrees, and the other disagrees with the same third term, they disagree with each other.*

If the two terms both disagreed with the third term, no inference could be made, because no relation could be established between them.

The above axioms are really axioms of pure science.* They apply rigidly to the formula of deduction, because this formula is wholly independent of the matter of propositions.

It is evident that the syllogism can have neither more nor less than three terms. If it had two terms, there would be no deduction, but merely a proposition. If it had four terms, it would have one term more than is required for a simple deduction ; and this fourth term would either be irrelevant, or would be a term in another link of a chain of deduction. A chain of deduction may be of an indefinite length, as in geometry, for example, where the whole science is a chain of deduction from the axioms and primary definitions ; but the links of the chain must each consist of the syllogism,—this being necessarily the ever-recurring form.

* Vide supra, p. 232.

As the syllogism, or formula of deduction, has three, and only three, terms, so also it has three, and only three, propositions. Two of the propositions contain the comparisons of the two terms, respectively, with the third term. The third proposition contains the comparison of the two terms with each other, in which their agreement or disagreement is inferred. The term with which the two are compared is called the *middle term;* the term compared with the *middle* in the first proposition, is called the *major term;* the term compared with the *middle* in the second proposition, is called the *minor* term. The first two propositions are together called the *premises;* and the last proposition is called the *conclusion.* The proposition which contains the *major term, i. e.*, the first, is called the *major premiss;* and that which contains the *minor term, i. e.*, the second, is called the *minor premiss.*

But now the question arises, what determines the order of comparisons, or the major term, and the major premiss? Before we can answer this, several principles must be considered.

1. It is evident that if all the terms were distributed, it would be quite immaterial how we arranged the premises. If all X be contained in all Z, and all Y be contained in all Z, then X and Y cannot be otherwise thar compared through Z, in their whole extent.

2. If the middle term be not distributed, then th two terms or *extremes* cannot be certainly compare through it, for one of them might agree with one part o it, and the other with another part, and thus no relatio between them be established: but a distribution of th middle in one of the premises is sufficient, for if on extreme has been compared to the *whole* of the middl term, and the other to only a *part* of it, a relation

evidently established between them, since *every part* of the middle term, in this case, presents the extreme compared with the *whole* of it, to the extreme compared with a *part* of it.

3. Hence it appears, again, that where there are two particular premises, no legitimate conclusion can be drawn; for we shall then have either an undistributed middle, *e. g.*

Some Z is X,
Some Y is Z;

or we shall fail in establishing a relation between the two extremes; for the only case of a distributed middle with particular premises, is where the middle term is the predicate of a particular negative, *e. g.*

Some Z is X,
Some Y is not Z,

in which some Z and X being first affirmed to agree, and then some Y only being excluded from Z, it cannot follow certainly that some Y is not X, since some other part of X may *not* agree with Z, and some other part of Y may *agree* with Z, for particulars of opposite qualities may both be true; and thus the conclusion is left wholly indefinite.

4. But the case is widely different where one of the premises is universal, and the middle term is distributed, *e. g.*

All Z is X,
Some Y is Z;

here all Z being contained in X, the some Y contained in Z must be contained in X also. Again: in the premises,

No Z is X,
Some Y is Z,

inasmuch as the whole of Z is excluded from X, and some Y is contained in Z, it follows that some Y is not in X.

Hence if one of the premises is a universal, it is sufficient if only the middle term be distributed, and this takes place when the universal premiss is E, or when, if it be A, the middle term is the subject.

5. We may not distribute in the conclusion a term which has not been previously distributed in a premiss, for this would violate the cardinal axiom, that *A consequence cannot transcend its premises.*

6. From two negative premises no inference can be made; for, since in this case both extremes disagree with the middle term, we cannot know, by means of this term, whether they agree or disagree with each other.

7. If one of the premises be negative, the conclusion must be negative also. Here one of the extremes is affirmed to agree, and the other to disagree, with the middle term, and consequently they must disagree with each other.

8. If one of the premises be particular, the conclusion must be particular also; for, although the whole of one extreme is compared in the universal premiss with the middle term, yet, as in the particular premiss, only a part of the other extreme is compared with the middle term, only a part of the first can be compared with the second in the conclusion.

9. Where there are two universal positive premises we cannot draw a universal conclusion, if the two extremes are both predicates in the premises, for then they are both undistributed: *e. g.*

All Z is X,
All Z is Y,

therefore

Some Y is X.

The ambiguity of the middle term is a fallacy arising

from the matter, or the peculiar use of words, and therefore is not to be considered here, where we are discussing the pure deductive formula.

It is evident that only four different conclusions can be drawn, viz.: A, E, I, and O; now the premises which are to determine these conclusions must be constituted in accordance with the above principles. Let us consider them in order.

I. *A universal affirmative conclusion.* This can be drawn where all of one extreme can be inferred to be contained in the other. It is not necessary that the containing extreme should itself be distributed; it may contain the other extreme, and a great deal more; all which is necessary to the universal conclusion is, that all of one extreme should be affirmed to be contained in the other. Now, as the middle term must be distributed, it must be the subject of one of the premises; and as one of the extremes must be distributed, it must be the subject of the other premiss; and again, as it is the only extreme listributed, it must be the subject of the universal conclusion. And, once more, as the middle term is the nedium of comparison, it, on the one hand, must embrace he whole of one extreme, and, on the other hand, must tself be all embraced by the other extreme. The followng arrangement of the terms is the only one which comrises all the conditions of a universal conclusion:

A, Z is X,
A, Y is Z,
A, Y is X.*

Hence the *major term* is here the one which *contains* ie middle, and *the minor* is the one which *is contained* the middle.

* Barbara.

We might arrange the premises thus:

A, Y is Z,
A, Z is X,
A, Y is X,

but the major premiss is generally placed first.

II. *Universal negative conclusion.* Here the two extremes are universally denied of each other. Hence there is only one possible arrangement of the terms, viz.: *so that one extreme shall be universally excluded from the middle term, and the other extreme universally contained in it,* as follows:

(1.)		(2.)
E, Z is X,*		E, X is Z,†
A, Y is Z,	or	A, Y is Z,
E, Y is X,		E, Y is X.

The only difference between the two syllogisms above, is the conversion of the major premiss, in the last.

Or we may express the same thing thus:

(3.)		(4.)
A, X is Z,‡		A, X is Z,§
E, Y is Z,	or	E, Z is Y,
E, Y is X,		E, Y is X.

The only difference between the last two is the conver sion of the minor premiss, in the second. And the onl difference between the first and the last two is, that th extreme which, in the first two, is excluded from th middle term, in the last two is contained in it; and th extreme which, in the first two, is contained in the middl term, in the last two is excluded from it.

* Celarent. † Cesare. ‡ Camestres. ‡ Camenes.

But it is evident that all these different forms satisfy the conditions required, and are virtually the same.

As to the title of the extremes, the term which becomes the *subject* of the conclusion is generally called the *minor* term, and that which becomes the *predicate* of the conclusion, the *major* term. In a universal negative conclusion, however, this is of no account, inasmuch as it is simply convertible. It is quite immaterial whether we express the conclusion by E, Y is X, or E, X is Y.

Indeed, the 2, 3, and 4 forms may all be easily reduced to the first: the 2, by simply converting the major; the 3, by simply converting the minor, and making it to change places with the major, and then simply converting the conclusion; and the 4, by transposing the premises, and simply converting the conclusion.

III. *Particular affirmative conclusion.* This conclusion is drawn where one of the premises is a particular affirmative, or where both premises are universal affirmatives.

1. Where one of the premises is a particular affirmative, *all of the middle must be contained in one extreme, and some of the other extreme in the middle, or*, which amounts to the same thing, since a particular affirmative is simply convertible, *some of the middle in the other extreme.* The form which directly presents this is the following:

(1.)
A, Z is X,
I, Y is Z,
I, Y is X.*

* Darii.

The deduction here is manifestly valid. There are three other forms, viz.:

(2.)	(3.)	(4.)
I, Z is X,*	A, Z is X,†	I, X is Z,‡
A, Z is Y,	I, Z is Y,	A, Z is Y,
I, Y is X.	I, Y is X.	I, Y is X.

All these evidently fulfil the required conditions. Here, again, the 2, 3, and 4 forms may be reduced to the first: the 2, by simply converting the major, transposing the premises, and then converting the conclusion; the 3, by converting the minor; and the 4, by transposing the premises, and converting the conclusion.

Scholium. It will be remarked that the change of the forms, by conversion of propositions, and the transposition of the premises, does not alter the current of the deduction. We have seen§ that a proposition, when lawfully converted, asserts no more than it did before: the transposition of the premises obviously does not change their character, nor their relation to each other; and since, when this transposition is made, what was before called the major becomes the minor term, and *vice versa*, the conclusion is converted, to correspond to it.

2. Where both premises are universal affirmatives. Here, either both extremes are predicates, and of course undistributed, or one only is a predicate, and undistributed.

There are then two forms:

* Disamis. † Datisi. ‡ Dimaris.

§ Supra, Sec. IV.

(5.)	(6.)
A, Z is X,*	A, X is Z,†
A, Z is Y,	A, Z is Y,
I, Y is X.	I, Y is X.

These also can easily be reduced to the first: the 5, by converting the minor premiss into I; and the 6, by transposing the premises, and simply converting the conclusion. After the transposition, we consider A, X is Z, as I, X is Z, for only the particular is required for the conclusion. Indeed, these forms are quite unnecessary, since a particular affirmative conclusion requires only one universal premiss; and two universals, arranged as above, cannot form the premises of any thing more.

IV. *Particular negative conclusion.* We have seen that from two particular premises no inference can be drawn, not even where a particular negative, of which the middle term is the predicate, and consequently distributed, is one of the premises. Nor, again, can any inference be drawn from two negatives. One at least of the premises, therefore, must be a universal, and only one of them a negative. If there be two universal premises, the extreme contained in the universal positive must be a predicate, so that it be not distributed, for if both extremes were distributed, then the conditions of a universal negative would be fulfilled. From this it follows that we can draw a particular negative conclusion only in the three following ways:

1. The whole of one extreme must be excluded from the middle term, and some of the other extreme must be contained in it. There are six forms in this division:

* Darapti. † Bramantip.

(1.)	(2.)	(3.)	(4.)
E, Z is X,*	E, X is Z,†	E, Z is X,‡	E, Z is X,§
I, Y is Z,	I, Y is Z,	A, Z is Y,	I, Z is Y,
O, Y is X.	O, Y is X.	O, Y is X.	O, Y is X.

(5.)	(6.)
E, X is Z,‖	E, X is Z,¶
A, Z is Y,	I, Z is Y,
O, Y is X.	O, Y is X.

2. The whole of one extreme must be contained in the middle term, and only some of the other extreme excluded from it. In this the preceding is reversed. Here is only one form, viz.:

(7.)
A, X is Z,**
O, Y is Z,
O, Y is X.

3. Some of the middle term must be excluded from one extreme, and the whole of it contained in the other extreme. Here also is only one form, viz.:

(8.)
O, Z is X,††
A, Z is Y,
O, Y is X.

Every one must perceive, upon a little reflection, that these three divisions embrace all possible negative conclusions.

Here, again, all the forms can be shown to be identical in their principle, by reducing all the others to the first

* Ferio. † Festino. ‡ Felapton. § Feriso. ‖ Fesapo. ¶ Fresison. ** Baroko. †† Bokardo.

form. 2 is reduced by simply converting the major; 3, by converting the minor into I; 4, by simply converting the minor; 5, by simply converting the major, and converting the minor into I; and 6, by simply converting both the major and minor. In these the mode of reduction is obvious and easy. 7 and 8 are reduced in a manner more circuitous: In 7, the major term must be changed by contraposition, and the minor changed into I, by connecting the negative particle with the predicate,* thus:

A, X is Z, *by contraposition* † E, $\overline{\text{not Z}}$ is X,
O, Y is Z, *by connecting the particle* I, Y is $\overline{\text{not Z}}$,
O, Y is Z, " " O, Y is X.

In 8, the minor is changed into E, by double negation, and is not converted as before; the major is converted into I, as before; the premises are then transposed; and lastly, the conclusion, by a double negation and conversion, is made to correspond legitimately as well as in form with the premises, thus:

O, Z is X *converted into* I, $\overline{\text{not X}}$ is Z,
A, Z is Y *by double negation becomes* E, Z is $\overline{\text{not Y}}$.

Transposing these premises we have { E, Z is $\overline{\text{not Y}}$,
I, $\overline{\text{not X}}$ is Z.

Then O, Y is X, *by double negation and conversion gives the proper conclusion* } O, $\overline{\text{not X}}$ is $\overline{\text{not Y}}$.

* Vide Section IV.

† Contraposition supposes a previous double negation; it is a simple conversion, after a change has been made by this negation, *e. g.* E, X is $\overline{\text{not Z}}$ is the double negation, and then by conversion, E, $\overline{\text{not Z}}$ is X.

As this is somewhat complicated, I will give an illustration:

O, "Some oppressed men are not discontented;
A, All oppressed men are wronged;
Therefore
O, Some wronged men are not discontented."

This, when reduced as above, becomes

E, "No oppressed men are not wronged;
I, Some not discontented are oppressed men;
O, Some not discontented are not not wronged."

This may also be reduced to the first form of the particular positive, viz., to A, I, I, by converting the minor term and the conclusion into I, by connecting the negative particle as before, and then transposing the premises, thus:

O, Z is X converted and transposed to minor I, not X, is Z
A, Z is Y transposed to major A, Z is Y
O, Y is X converted I, not X is Y
A, All oppressed men are wronged;
I, Some not discontented are oppressed men;
I, Some not discontented are wronged! *

From the foregoing analysis, it appears, that there are but four original distinct syllogisms, comprising the four possible conclusions, viz., A, A, A; E, A, E; A, I, I; and E, I, O, as arranged under the first form of each kind; —all the other forms being capable of a legitimate reduction to these primary forms.

* Whately's Logic, Book II., Ch. iii., § 5.

At the beginning of this section we considered the two primary axioms of pure science which determine the general formula of Deduction. But in analysing this formula under the ideas of quantity and quality, we find another axiom developed. In every form of the syllogism one of the extremes is more comprehensive than either the other extreme, or the middle term; and the middle term comprehends this other extreme, whether it be the whole or a part of the class to which it belongs, thus:

All Z is X,
All, or, some Y is Z,

therefore we may infer

All, or, some Y is X.

Hence, it appears, that what is affirmed of Z, viz., that it is comprehended by X, must be affirmed of Y also to the extent that it is comprehended by Z. So far with respect to *Quantity.*

With respect to *Quality*, the middle term is always universally affirmed, either to be comprehended by, or to be excluded from, the first extreme; and the other extreme is in whole or part affirmed to be comprehended in the middle term, thus:

All, or, no Z is X,
All, or, some Y is Z,

therefore we may infer

All, or, some Y is, or is not, X.

Here, again, what is affirmed of Z, viz., that it universally does, or does not, agree with, or belong to X, must be affirmed of Y also, to the extent that it is comprehended by Z.

Now all this is evident; and the axiom which forms the basis of it, is the *Dictum de omni et nullo* of Aristotle, viz., *Whatever is affirmed or denied of any term distributed, (i. e. taken universally,) is affirmed or denied of every particular comprehended under it.*

SECTION VI.

OF MOODS AND FIGURES.

THE Mood of a Syllogism is determined by the quantity and quality of the three propositions which compose it, and is represented by the corresponding symbols; thus, A, A, A, expresses the mood of the syllogism which gives a universal positive conclusion; and so with respect to the others.

The Figure of a Syllogism refers to the situation of the extremes in the premises with respect to the middle term. Now, obviously, there are but four variations that can be made, viz., the middle term must be the subject in both premises; or the predicate in both; or the subject of the major, and the predicate of the minor; or the predicate of the major, and the subject of the minor. The following table presents their several relations:

(1.)	(2.)	(3.)	(4.)
Z is X,	X is Z,	Z is X,	X is Z,
Y is Z,	Y is Z,	Z is Y,	Z is Y,
Y is X.	Y is X.	Y is X.	Y is X.

Now as there are four kinds of propositions, A, E, I, O, and three are appropriated to each syllogism, all the possible ways of combining them must be *sixty-four*. For four different majors multiplied into four different minors, and these again into four different conclusions, is a combination of four, three times, $4 \times 4 \times 4 = 64$. Regarding it as a mere arithmetical problem, since the sixty-four Moods can be each stated in the four different Figures, we shall have in all $4 \times 64 = 256$ varieties of the syllogism. The arithmetical determination, however, although noticed by logicians, is of very little use. We find out in this way the utmost limit of the syllogisms, but we are not aided, in the least, in discriminating between the true and the false.

This discrimination can be made only on the principles laid down in the preceding section ; and which have there been applied to determining the legitimate and required syllogisms, independently of the apparatus of Moods and Figures. And yet, after having completed this analysis, there may perhaps be some convenience in employing Moods and Figures in distinguishing the different forms.

The legitimate forms, we have seen, are in all nineteen ; of which, one only is used for universal positive conclusions, four for universal negative, six for particular positive, and eight for particular negative conclusions. These are found in the different Figures. That figure which embraces the four cardinal forms, is called the first. All the other forms, we have seen, can be reduced to these cardinal forms.

The following lines have been contrived to aid in committing the Moods to memory ; and to present, at one view, the mode of reducing the secondary Moods to the primary :

Fig. 1. bArbArA, cElArEnt, dArII, fErIOque prioris.

Fig. 2. cEsArE, cAmEstrEs, fEstInO, bArOkO, secundæ.

Fig. 3. tertia, dArAptI, dIsAmIs, dAtIsI, fElAptOn, bOkArdO, ErIsO, habet : quarta insuper addit.

Fig. 4. brAmAntIp, cAmEnEs, dImArIs, fEsApo, frEsIsOn.

In the above, the initial letters b, c, d, f, denote the mood of the first figure to which the secondary mood must be reduced: *e. g.* In brAmAntIp the b indicates that it is to be reduced to bArbArA ;* and so of the others.

The capital letters denote the moods ; s, denotes the simple conversion of the proposition which precedes it ; p, the conversion *per accidens* of the proposition which precedes it, *i. e.*, the conversion of A into I, or of I into A †; m, (*mutandi*) that the premises must be transposed.

Baroko and Bokardo are names given in reference to *Reductio ad impossibile;* a method of reduction employed by some, particularly in respect to these moods. The B denotes that the new mood is to be formed in Barbara ; and the K, that for the proposition immediately preceding it, the contradictory of the conclusion must be substituted. These moods, however, have in the preceding sections been reduced in the ordinary way.‡

* If reduced to *Barbara*, it of course is true in *Darii.*

† This last occurs in *Bramantip* only, and here not because a *particular* can legitimately be converted into a *universal*, but because the new arrangement of the premises requires a universal conclusion. The transposition of the premises places the mood in the 1st Fig. and it becomes Barbara necessarily.

‡ The kind of arguments to which the different moods are in their nature best adapted, is an investigation of very high interest. I have not entered upon it in this treatise. Perhaps I shall undertake it hereafter. In the absence of any thing original to offer, I take the liberty of appending the following striking remarks from Dr. Whately's excellent work. They are given in a note at the foot of one of the pages of Book II., Ch. III., § 4:

"With respect to the use of the first three Figures (for the fourth is never employed but by an accidental awkwardness of expression,) it may be remarked, that the First is that into which an argument will be found to fall the most naturally, except in the following cases:—First, When we have to *disprove* something that has been maintained, or is likely to be believed, our arguments will usually be found to take most conveniently the form of the Second Figure, *viz.* we prove that the thing we are speaking of cannot belong to such a Class, either because it *wants* what belongs to the whole of that Class (Cesare), or because it *has* something of which that Class is destitute (Camestres); *e. g.* 'No impostor would have warned his followers, as Jesus did, of the persecutions they would have to submit to;' and again, 'An enthusiast would have expatiated, which Jesus and his followers did not, on the particulars of a future state.'

"The same observations will apply, *mutatis mutandis*, when a Particular conclusion is sought, as in Festino and Baroko.

"The arguments used in the process called the 'Abscissio Infiniti,' will in general be the most easily referred to this Figure.

"The Third Figure is, of course, the one employed when the Middle term is *Singular*, since a Singular term can only be a Subject. This is also the form into which most arguments will naturally fall that are used to establish an *objection* (Enstasis of Aristotle) to an opponent's Premiss, when his argument is such as to require that Premiss to be Universal. It might be called, therefore, the Enstatic Figure. *E. G.* If any one contends that 'this or that doctrine ought not to be admitted, because it cannot be explained or comprehended,' his suppressed major premiss may be refuted by the argument that 'the connection of the Body and Soul cannot be explained or comprehended,' *&c.*

"A great part of the reasoning of Butler's Analogy may be exhibited in this form."

SECTION VII.

OF THE REDUCTION OF SYLLOGISMS.

REDUCTION of Syllogisms is of two kinds, *Ostensive Reduction*, and *Reductio ad impossibile*. The aim in both kinds, in respect to Syllogisms, is to prove the validity of the secondary forms.

I. *Ostensive Reduction.*—Here the proof is made out by showing the identity of the secondary and primary forms ; and this is done by actually changing the secondary into the primary, without making them assert more, or, differently from what they did before.

This change is effected by *conversion of terms*, and *transposition of premises*. But it has been fully shown that these do not effect either the kind or the extent of the predication. When the secondary are reduced to the primary form, the proof is made out, because these forms are a direct expression of the *Dictum de omni et nullo*.

II. *Reductio ad impossibile.*—By this method we prove the validity of a secondary Syllogism as a *form* of reasoning, by showing that *if we grant the premises, the conclusion cannot be false*. For that in all cases must be a *valid form*, by which, from true premises, we cannot draw a false conclusion.

The method is simply this : Since by the opposition of propositions, every proposition must be true if its contradictory be false, and false if its contradictory be true, we take the contradictory of the conclusion of the Syllogism or form in question, and construct with it, as a premiss in connection with another unquestionable premiss, a new Syllogism in the first Figure. Now if the new conclusion thus deduced be false, then the assumed premiss must be false, for there is no question respecting the validity of the form in the first Figure; and if the assumed premiss be false, then the original conclusion of which it is the contradictory must be true: *e. g.* Let us take Baroko:

A, X is Z,
O, Y is Z,
O, Y is X.

If this conclusion be not true, its contradictory is true, viz., A, Y is X. Let us, then, construct a new Syllogism with this contradictory as a premiss, in the first Figure. This we can do by merely substituting it for the minor premiss in the above Syllogism; we shall then draw a conclusion in Barbara, thus:

A, X is Z,
A, Y is X;

therefore,

A, Y is Z.

Now it will be perceived that this new conclusion is the contradictory of the original minor premiss,—and the premises it will be recollected were granted; hence it must be false; and being false, the new premiss is false, and this being false, its contradictory, the original conclusion, must be true.

All the secondary forms may be tested in the same way, *e. g.* Feriso.

E, Z is X,
I, Z is Y,
O, Y is X.

Substituting the contradictory of the conclusion A, Y is X, for the major premiss, we form the following Syllogism in Darii:

A, Y is X,
I, Z is Y;

therefore,

I, Z is X.

But the new conclusion contradicts the original major E, Z is X; consequently it is false; and being false, the new premiss is false, and this being false, its contradictory, the original conclusion, must be true.

SECTION VIII.

OF MODAL, HYPOTHETICAL, AND DISJUNCTIVE PROPOSITIONS.

I. *Modals.*—These propositions do not differ in form from what are called pure categorical propositions. X is Y represents both. The modality is merely a peculiarity of the matter, and consequently does not pertain to the pure logical formula. Besides, in the matter itself, modal propositions can be so disposed as to become pure categoricals. This is effected by attaching the modal words to the subject or the predicate. *E. G.* "It is *probable* that all knowledge is useful," *i. e.*

Sub.		*Pred.*
"All knowledge	is	probably useful."

Again:

"It is possible that he may arrive to-morrow;" *i. e.*

Sub.		*Pred.*
"His arrival to-morrow	is	possible."

A subject and predicate may each be expressed by several words, but this cannot affect the form.

II. *Hypotheticals.*—These are propositions which contain a hypothesis in one of their terms, and are therefore like Modals capable of being reduced under the categorical form. Where the force of the reasoning lies in the hypothesis the case is widely different ; but it is evident that this is not the fact in Examples like the following :

Every Z is X or p,
Every Y is Z ;

therefore,

Every Y is X or p.

The aim here is not to conclude which of the two Y is, whether X or p : but only that Y is X or p.

III. *Disjunctives.*—These are a kind of compound propositions, consisting of several categoricals, one of which is affirmed to be true ; *e. g.* A is either B or C or D. Now if we can deny all but one, then that one is true ; or if we can affirm one to be true, then the others are false ; thus, But A is not B or C ; therefore A is D : or A is D, therefore it is neither B nor C.

A Disjunctive proposition, however, is capable of being reduced like a Modal to a pure categorical, thus :

$\overbrace{\text{All A not B or C}}^{\textit{Sub.}}$ is $\overbrace{\text{D}}^{\textit{Pred.}}$;

Or,

$\overbrace{\text{All A not B or D}}^{\textit{Sub.}}$ is $\overbrace{\text{C}}^{\textit{Pred.}}$.

A Syllogism with such propositions contains the usual forms ; *e. g.*

Every $\overline{\text{A not B or C}}$ is D.
All Z is $\overline{\text{A not B or C}}$.
Therefore, all Z is D.

"It is either Spring, Summer, Autumn, or Winter ; but it is neither Spring, Autumn, nor Winter ; therefore it is Summer," *i. e.*

Every $\overline{\text{season not Spring, Autumn, or Winter,}}$ is Summer.

The present season is a season not Spring, &c., therefore, the present season is Summer.

When we affirm one to be true, and infer the falsity of the others, the same reduction may be made ; thus :

No A being D is B or C,
Z is A being D,
Therefore, Z is not B or C.

No season being Summer, is Autumn or Winter, &c.

The present season is a season being Summer ; therefore, &c.

Or, again, a Syllogism of this kind may be put into the form of a conditional, thus:

If A is not B or C,
Then A is D, &c.

It is evident, therefore, that the preceding kinds of propositions require no new formula, but lie within the principles already established.

SECTION IX.

HYPOTHETICAL REASONING.

A CONDITIONAL proposition consists of an *Antecedent* and a *Consequent*, each of which is a distinct proposition,—*e. g.*,

Antecedent.
"If the Scriptures are not wholly false,
Consequent.
They are entitled to respect."

If Y is Z,
Then Y is X.

There are two rules generally applied in hypothetical reasoning.

1. If the Antecedent be granted, the Consequent is granted also; *e. g.*,

If Y is Z,
Then Y is X.
But Y is Z,
Therefore, Y is X.

2. The Consequent being denied, the Antecedent must be denied also.

If Y is Z,
Then Y is X.
But Y is not X,
Therefore, Y is not Z.

The first rule is founded upon the obvious principle, that a false Antecedent or Premiss cannot yield a true conclusion. The second rule is founded upon the no less obvious principle, that an Antecedent or Premiss must be false, which yields a false conclusion.

But, from the falsity of an antecedent, we cannot infer the falsity of the consequent, for the consequent may flow out of some other antecedent which is true : *e. g.*,

If Y is Z,
Then Y is X.

Now, suppose Y is Z to be false, still Y is X may be proved by some other antecedent, *e. g.*, Y is P.

Hypothetical reasoning really differs from categorical, only in that, one of the premises is a hypothesis. The formula and all the principles are the same. If Y is Z, then Y is X : this is an affirmation that if one proposition be granted, another must be granted also. But, one proposition *alone* cannot authorize an inference. We here then have only part of an argument, viz. : the conclusion and one of the premises. Which premiss have we, and can we supply the other? There is no difficulty. The conclusion always contains the minor and major terms, the other premiss contains the middle, together with either the major or minor. Now, if there be a term in the antecedent or premiss, the same as the *subject* of the consequent or conclusion, then the given premiss is the minor premiss ; but if the same as the *predicate* of the consequent, then the given premiss is the major. And in either case, in order to supply the wanting premiss, we have only to connect the middle term with that term of the conclusion which is not found in the given premiss or antecedent : *e. g.*,

If Y is Z,
Then Y is X.

Here the wanting premiss, obviously, according to the above, is the major, which supply, and we have the following syllogism:

Z is X,
If Y is Z,
Then Y is X.

Or we may state it thus: It is affirmed, that if Y is Z, then Y is X: but *why* does it follow, that, if Y is Z, Y is X also? The answer to be given is, Because Z is X —if Y is contained in Z, then Y must be contained in X also, because Z is contained in X.

"If the Scriptures are not wholly false, then the Scriptures are entitled to respect."

But, *why* does this follow? Because, "Whatever is not wholly false, is entitled to respect." Or, "Every book of pure morality and heavenly promises, &c., not wholly false, is entitled to respect:"

"If the Scriptures are such a book, not wholly false,"

"Then the Scriptures, &c."

Take another case * in which the minor premiss is wanting:

If Z is X,
Then Y is X.

The antecedent here must be the major premiss, because it compares the middle with the *predicate* of the

* The suppression of the minor premiss, and the construction of a conditional out of the major and the conclusion, gives that case in which the antecedent and consequent have a different subject, and which, by some, is supposed to involve peculiar difficulties. See Whately's Logic, Book II., Chap. iv., § 6, note at the foot of the page.

consequent or conclusion. We can easily supply the minor: The affirmation is that, If Z is X, then Y must be X also. But, *why* must this follow? Because Y is Z.

"If whatever exhibits marks of design is the work of an Intelligent Creator;

"Then the universe must be the work of an Intelligent Creator." But why?

Because, "The universe exhibits marks of design."

In ordinary language, all reasoning is usually in an *Enthymematic* form; *i. e.*, one premiss is suppressed; because, when one premiss and the conclusion are stated, the mind, generally, readily supplies the other. Thus the syllogism just above, usually appears, in ordinary language, with the major suppressed; since when it is affirmed that, "The universe must be the work of an Intelligent Creator, because it exhibits marks of design," every one assents on the ground that, "Whatever exhibits marks of design, must be the work of an Intelligent Creator."

What therefore is called by logicians, a Conditional Proposition, is nothing more than an enthymeme, with the given premiss hypothesised. And to grant the antecedent, is merely to remove the hypothesis. The hypothesis has nothing to do with the pure logical form, for, that we ever hypothesise is owing to considerations lying wholly in the matter or subjects of our reasoning. And to reduce a conditional, we have only to supply the suppressed premiss.

The validity of the Rules before given, now, also, appears clearly to arise out of the nature of the syllogism. To grant the antecedent, is to grant the consequent, because, since the suppressed premiss is of course granted, not being hypothesised, to grant the antecedent is to remove the hypothesis from the other premiss, and consequently to remove all doubtfulness from the argument. And to deny the consequent, must be the destruction of the argument, since it is equivalent to granting the contradictory of the conclusion, and consequently denying the premises.

SECTION X.

OF THE DILEMMA.

A DILEMMA is formed by bringing together several Conditional Propositions, so that *different antecedents shall have the same consequent;* or, *different antecedents shall have different consequents;* or, *the same antecedent shall have different consequents.*

I. Different Antecedents with the same Consequent.

If A is B,	And if A is C,	And if A is D,
Then A is X,	then A is X,	then A is X, &c.

Now, if the matter be such that we can disjunctively grant the antecedents, thus :

But, A is B, or C, or D ; then it must follow that A is X.

II. Different Antecedents with different Consequents.

If A is X,	If A is Y,	If A is Z,
Then A is B,	then A is C,	then A is D.

Now here again, if the matter is such that we cannot disjunctively grant the antecedents, then we must disjunctively grant the consequents likewise : thus :

But A is X, or Y, or Z.
Therefore A is B, or C, or D.

III. The same Antecedents with different Consequents.

If A is B,	If A is B,	If A is B,
Then A is X,	then A is Y,	then A is Z.

Now, if we perceive from the matter, that the common antecedent admits of all these consequents, then of course, by granting the common antecedent, we grant all the consequents.

Where we grant the antecedent, and establish the consequent, the dilemma is called *constructive.*

But where we deny the consequent, and destroy the antecedent, the dilemma is called *destructive.*

We have already remarked in the preceding section, that the hypothesis arises from the peculiar character of the matter of the proposition; for the logical form supposes the connection between the subject and predicate to be certain. And so here again the possibility of disjunctively affirming the antecedents, or of disjunctively denying the consequents, lies in the peculiar character of the matter. The force and keenness of the dilemma, as a weapon in debate, arises from the matter also, and from many relations and circumstances of which the forensic disputant knows how to avail himself: *e. g.*, An individual may be so situated that his words, or conduct, or both, justify two or more inferences unfortunate for himself, from one or the other of which he cannot escape. He must admit one fact or the other, and either is an antecedent involving a stinging consequent. We have here described the second kind of Dilemma, and of which the several antecedents are the "horns": *e. g.*, "If Æschines joined in the public rejoicings, he is inconsistent; if he did not, he is unpatriotic; but he either joined or not; therefore he is either inconsistent or unpatriotic."

From the denial of one or the other of the consequents, we necessitate the denial of one or the other of the antecedents; and this proves no less forcible than the other mode. Thus we may state the preceding example in the following manner: "If Æschines is consistent, he did not join in the public rejoicings; if he is patriotic, he did join in them: but he either joined or not; therefore he is either not consistent, or not patriotic."

The first kind is forcible taken in the constructive mode; for here the individual who is the subject of the dilemma is involved in several facts, so related, that some one must be admitted, and any one leads to the torturing inference.

The third kind is the weakest, and perhaps ought not to be considered a dilemma at all. Having only one antecedent, it wants the "horns." In the constructive mode, it is merely a conditional, in which the antecedent involves several consequents; and this is common to many conditionals, without yielding any peculiar advantage in debate. On the other hand, there is no point in disjunctively denying the consequents, since the denial of any one of them destroys the common antecedent, so that the whole force of the argument is found in one of the simple conditionals.

Where the dilemma has the subject of the consequents different from the subject of the antecedents, the antecedents are major premises. This is obvious from what was shown in the preceding section.

Since the dilemma is merely a combination of conditionals, it may be resolved into these again, and each conditional reduced to the complete syllogism, by supplying the suppressed premiss.

SECTION XI.

OF THE SORITES.

This is an abridged form of an argument consisting of several Syllogisms. It is either categorical or hypothetical.

I. *Categorical Sorites.*—This is so arranged that the predicate of the first proposition is the subject of the second, and the predicate of the second the subject of the third, and so on. In every new proposition a new predicate appears; and in the last proposition it is inferred that the first subject agrees with the last predicate; *e. g.* A is B, B is C, C is D, D is E; therefore A is E. It is evident that in the same manner the last predicate may be affirmed of all the intermediary subjects. The truth of the argument is evident. If all A is contained in B, and all B in C, and all C in D, and all D in E, then all A, B, and C must be contained in E likewise.

By carefully inspecting the Sorites, we shall perceive that the first proposition of the series is a minor premiss, and all the other propositions major premises, except the last, which is a conclusion; so that we have here parts of several Syllogisms, which are so related that the conclusion of the preceding becomes the minor premiss of the succeeding; and the Sorites is constructed by suppressing all the minor premises but the first, and all the conclusions but the last; thus:

A is B,
B is C,
C is D,
D is E,
Therefore A is E.

(1.)
B is C,
A is B,
Therefore A is C,

(2.)
C is D,
A is C,
Therefore A is D,

(3.)
D is E,
A is D,
Therefore A is E,

The Sorites is formed of the Primary Syllogisms, *i. e.* those of the first Figure, because in this, inasmuch as it is the natural form of the Syllogism, no change by conversion or otherwise has to be made in the propositions in transferring them from one Syllogism to another, which will be the case in the other figures, since the middle term is continually changing; *e. g.* In Darapti the 1st Syllogism would be,

B is C,
B is A, and then the next Syllogism is C is D,
Some A is C, Some A is C,
Some A is D,

Which is Darii; and this can be prevented only by converting A is C.

It will be perceived, also, that the first and last propositions of a Sorites alone can be *Particular;* for the major premiss in the first Figure is always universal, but the minor term and the conclusion may be particular.

Where a Sorites has a Negative Conclusion, only the last term of the series, before the Conclusion, can be negative. Thus, A is B, B is C, C is D, and No D is E, therefore No A is E. Otherwise we should have two Negative Premises in the Syllogisms.

II. *Hypothetical Sorites.*—This consists of a series of Conditionals, so related and arranged, that the Consequent of the first becomes the Antecedent of the second; and the Consequent of the second, the Antecedent of the third, and so on; and then, by granting the first Antecedent, we grant the last Consequent, and indeed all the Consequents, thus: If A is B, then A is C, and if A is C, then A is D, and if A is D, then A is E; but A is B, therefore A is E.

By denying the Consequents successively, we of course deny the Antecedents; and this forms the *destructive* Sorites. The Conditional can, as before shown, be reduced to complete Syllogisms; and then the Syllogisms will be found to be related in the same way with those of the Categorical Sorites, viz., the conclusions of each preceding Syllogism being the minor premiss of each succeeding one. The only difference, then, between the two kinds, lies in the hypothetical character of one of the premises in the last kind.

A Sorites may be constructed either by suppressing the major or minor, just as conditionals in general.

Scholium.—It appears from the preceding Analysis of Hypothetical reasoning under all its different modes, that it involves no new formulæ or principles. Every kind of Deduction therefore is comprehended by the *Dictum de omni et nullo*, and the axioms of agreement and disagreement. The fundamental Ideas are Evolution, Identity and Difference, Quantity and Quality.

SECTION XII.

APPLICATION OF THE DEDUCTIVE FORMULA.

THE greater part of human reasoning is of the Deductive kind. The number of first principles and general truths is comparatively few, but their application is infinite. Many of them, and especially in Religion, Morals and Politics, have been spontaneously developed in the human mind; and many others, the result of nice and laborious investigation, have become current, through the means which now exist for widely circulating knowledge. In the constant expansion of knowledge by scientific men; and the improvements of art by the ingenious and skilful; and in the multiform practical duties of the general human life, these first great principles and truths receive their continual and diversified application. Hence there is no department of knowledge, of art, or of duty, where Deductive Logic is not required.

But are Conclusions, in order to be legitimate, required to be drawn strictly according to the deductive formula? By no means, if we intend by this the formal expression of every step of the reasoning. This is not necessary, for many things are so plainly implied when not expressed, that their formal expression would only encumber the style. But still, in every case of legitimate inference no logical principle can be violated, and the language is capable of being reduced to the Syllogistic form. Hence, whenever it is required to test the validity of inferences, a resort to the Syllogism is decisive.

It would not be difficult to give here examples of the application of the formula in testing deduction in a variety of subjects. I at first intended this. Upon reflection, however, I have concluded to limit these examples to one subject, and this one eminently clear and beautiful. I mean Geometry. My first plan would have tended considerably to swell a work, already, perhaps, transcending the just bounds of an elementary treatise; besides, all the ends of illustration will, I think, be found to be answered by this one.

Demonstration is of two kinds, *direct* and *indirect.* Direct demonstration is the deduction of a conclusion from admitted truths and principles: indirect shows the truth of a proposition by proving that its contradictory violates admitted truths and principles. Geometry employs both. It is a science * of absolute certainty, for its fundamental Ideas are clearly developed; its Axioms are perfect; † its Definitions adequate and precise: its subject pure and exact quantity; and its deductions are made with the utmost rigour.

After laying down its axioms and definitions, Geometry proceeds to make its deductions. The first deduction must necessarily be made directly from the axioms and definitions. But the next may employ the deduction already made as a basis, in connection with the axioms and definitions, and so onward. Hence the field of deduction is continually enlarging.

In constructing this science, much depends upon the

* Pages 89, 90.

† Page 232

order of arrangement: for since propositions already demonstrated are employed in demonstrating others, it is evident that one arrangement may be superior to another in affording facilities for the progressive demonstration.*

After the science has been constructed, it is highly advantageous and beautiful, to reverse the order, and trace back remote propositions through the connected chain of demonstrations to the axioms and definitions.

In illustrating the application of the Deductive formula in this science, I shall first take an instance of direct demonstration. The proposition I have selected is the following:

"A line which bisects the vertical angle of a triangle, divides the base into two segments, which are proportioned to the adjacent sides."

We have in this proposition, deductions both from axioms, and from propositions previously deduced, so that it will serve to illustrate both.

A C B is the triangle, and the angle at C is bisected by the line C D.

Now to aid the deduction by bringing in other relations besides those simply presented in the triangle, we produce a line A C, and draw B E parallel to C D, so that the two lines thus added meet in E. We now have a case of alternate angles included between two parallel lines and an intersecting line, and this is our first syllogism, as follows:

* *Corollaries* are important links in the chain of demonstration. They are propositions which in all cases require demonstration. In the usual definition of a Corollary, it is said to be "An obvious consequence deduced from something going before." But because it is "obvious," the deduction is not given, but left to be supplied by the learner; and yet in some instances the deduction of the Corollary is more difficult than that of other propositions where it is formally given.

All alternate angles are equal ;
But the angles B C D and E B C are alternate angles ;
Therefore these angles are equal.

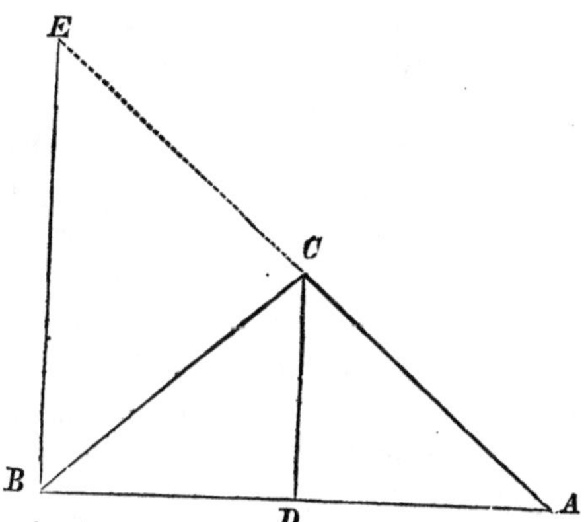

But B C D and A C D are equal by construction ; and this leads to another syllogism, viz. :

B C D is equal to A C D,
E B C is equal to B C D,

Therefore

E B C is equal to A C D :

i. e. All B C D, as an equal, is contained in A C D,
All E B C, as an equal, is contained in B C D,

Therefore

All E B C, as an equal, is contained in A C D.

In the second deduction, the conclusion of the first deduction is made the minor premiss : it will be remarked, that this is therefore a case of the Sorites ; but the Sorites comprehends all cases where one deduction flows out of another.

Or we may deduce it directly from the axiom, " Things equal to the same thing, are equal to each other : " thus,

All things equal to the same thing, are equal to each other;

E B C and A C D are things equal to the same thing, viz. B C D;

Therefore they are equal to each other.

This is a syllogism of which the axiom forms the major premiss. It is evident that in all cases of deduction from an axiom, the axiom must form the major premiss.

Inspecting the diagram still farther, we perceive that the angles A C D and C E B are an outward and inward angle, opposite to each other on the same side of a line A E, cutting the two parallel lines C D and E B; hence their equality is inferred as in the first deduction; the major premiss being here again a proposition before proved, viz., "All outward and inward opposite angles on the same side of a line intersecting two parallel lines, are equal."

But we have just before inferred the equality of A C D and E B C, therefore we infer again from the axiom already quoted, and, in the same way, the equality of C E B and E B C; thus,

All things equal to the same thing are equal to each other;

C E B and E B C are things equal to the same, viz. A C D;

Therefore, they are equal to each other.

We have now two angles of a triangle E B C, opposite two of its sides, equal; we therefore infer the equality of these sides from a proposition already proved, which here again becomes the major premiss of the syllogism, thus:

"Every triangle equal in respect to two of its angles, is equal also in respect to the two sides opposite these angles;"

The triangle E B C is a triangle equal in two of its angles, viz. C E B and E B C;

Therefore, it is equal in the two sides opposite these angles, viz. the sides E C and B C.

Inspecting next the whole triangle A B E, we perceive that it is a triangle having its two sides, A B and A E, divided by a line C D parallel to its base E B; we can therefore infer the proportionality of the segments of the sides from a proposition already demonstrated, thus:

"Every triangle having a line drawn parallel to its base dividing its other two sides, is a triangle whose sides are divided proportionally;"

The triangle A B E is such a triangle;

Therefore its sides are divided proportionally, viz.

A D : D B : : A C : C E.

But, if A C is proportional to C E, it must be proportional to C B, equal to C E; for

E C is a proportional of A C; and
C B is E C; therefore
C B is a proportional of A C.
Hence A D : D B : : A C : C B.

The above analysis shows conclusively that the formula of Deduction permeates geometrical demonstration.

Although, for the purposes of demonstration, it is not necessary, generally, to draw out the whole deduction in detail, still a better insight would be gained of Geometry, and striking illustrations afforded of this part of Logic if it were occasionally done. Indeed, by raising questions respecting the axioms and definitions in order to show their necessary and intuitive character, as well as by analysing the demonstrations, the study of Geometry may be connected with the highest parts of Logic, and be made to embrace the whole, with the exception of Induction; and this again may be happily connected with the whole range of natural science. The study of science would thus be placed on the most elevated grounds, and Science herself be clothed with light as with a garment.

In the course of the preceding analysis we have referred to several propositions previously proved. Now we might go back to these and analyse them in like manner, until we should repose amid the axioms and definitions and their governing Ideas. But this process has been so amply, and I hope so clearly indicated, that I do not deem it necessary. One of the propositions referred to, however, affords an illustration of the *indirect* mode of demonstration, otherwise called the *Reductio ad absurdum*, or the *Reductio ad impossibile*. I will therefore proceed to give an analysis of the demonstration of this one proposition more. The proposition is stated as follows :—

"Every triangle equal in respect to two of its angles, is equal also in respect to the two sides opposite these angles."

If this be not true, its contradictory is true, viz. :—

"Some triangles equal in respect to two of their angles, are *not* equal in respect to the two sides opposite these angles."

Let A B C be the triangle having its two angles A and B equal.

Now if the contradictory be true, and the two opposite sides B C and A C, are not equal, then of course one must be greater than the other. Let us therefore suppose A C to be the greater, and take A D, on A C, equal to B C. Next join B D. Now we have a triangle A D B within the triangle A B C; and, comparing them, we have, by the contradictory, in the first triangle, side A D equal to side B C, in the second ; also the side A B is common to both ; also, by the hypothesis contained both in the proposition and the contradictory, the angle A in the first, is equal to angle B, in the second. But it has previously been shown in the chain of geometrical deductions, that "Any two triangles having two sides and the included angle in the one, equal to two sides and the included angle in the other, are equal each to each." This we assume as a major premiss; and then add as a minor, "The two triangles A D B and A B C, by the contradictory, are, two triangles having two sides and the included angle in the one, equal to two sides and the included angle of the other." Hence the conclusion, "The two triangles A D B and A B C are equal."

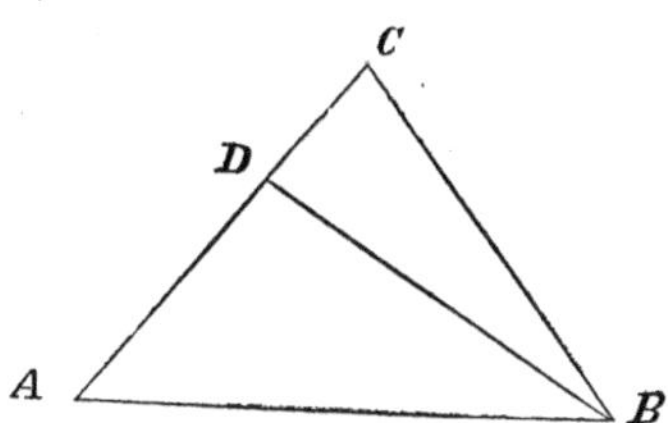

Here we assumed the contradictory as a minor premiss in connection with an unquestionable major. But what is the conclusion ? That one triangle, A D B, contained in another triangle, A B C, is equal to its container ; *i. e.* That a part is equal to a whole. The conclusion then, inasmuch as it violates the axiom, "A whole is greater than any of its parts," is false. But the falsity of the conclusion must be traced to the falsity of one or both of the premises, since the form is correct ; but the major was granted ; therefore the falsity is in the minor ; and the minor being false, its contradictory must be true ; but the contradictory is the original proposition.

Illustrations of the Syllogism can be drawn from Geometry and from the Mathematics generally, to an indefinite extent. The above, however, will answer the ends of a general and elementary work.

SECTION XIII.

OF FALLACIES.

A FALLACY is a false argument artfully constructed, with the intent to deceive; or, unwarily stumbled upon, from an ignorance of the Logical form, or of the subject under consideration.

The full examination of this subject would lead us into a wide field, and one in which all the principles of Logic would have to be brought under review. The limits we have judged fit to assign ourselves will prevent an examination in detail; but we hope, nevertheless, to present the important points with sufficient amplitude.

In giving a division of Fallacies we must follow the divisions of Logic itself. We shall not, however, pursue the same order: but as we have just now been engaged with the Deductive Formula, we shall first consider the Fallacies pertaining to this part, so as not to break the continuity of the investigation, and reserve what remarks we may have to make on Fallacies pertaining to the other parts of Logic for the close of this Section.

FALLACIES OF DEDUCTION.

These are divided into *Fallacies in the formula;* and *Fallacies in the matter.*

The latter are not strictly logical; but inasmuch as

they lie in the matter of propositions employed in deduction, and where also a rigid adherence to the formula is used to conceal the Fallacy in the matter, this appears to be the most appropriate division to which they can be assigned.

I. Fallacies in the Formula.—These have virtually been set forth already in the Analysis of the Formula in Section V. Nothing more is necessary here than a summary view of them :

1. *Undistributed Middle; e. g.*

I, Z is X,
A, Y is Z,
A, Y is X.

Here, although all Y is contained in Z, yet as only some Z is contained in Y, and only some Z in X, that part of Z which is contained in X may contain no part of Y, and thus there can be no ground for an inference.

2. *Illicit Process.*—This designates the fallacy of distributing a term in the conclusion which has not been previously distributed in the corresponding premiss, and thus drawing a conclusion beyond the *data; e. g.*

A, Z is X,
A, Z is Y,
A, Y is X.

3. *Two Negative Premises.*—Here, since both terms are excluded from the middle, no comparison of them can be made through it ; *e. g.*

E, Z is X,
E, Y is Z,

4. *Positive Conclusion,* where there is a Negative Prc miss ; or a *Negative Conclusion,* where both premises ar positive.

5. *Particular Premises.*—In all cases where both prc

mises are particular, we shall have an undistributed middle, or an illicit process of the major or the minor term, or both combined.

6. *More than three terms plainly expressed.*—This is an attempt to combine two Syllogisms into one.

7. Inferring the *falsity of the conclusion* from that of the *premiss;* or the *truth of the premiss* from that of the *conclusion.*

The first of these fallacies appears where, when an inadequate or false argument has been used to establish a conclusion, and the argument having been successfully refuted, it is inferred that the conclusion is false; *e. g.* If it be argued in favor of the immortality of the soul that all men entertain a belief of it; admitting that the argument might be refuted by adducing the instance of some nation who manifest no conception of immortality, still this is no ground for concluding against the doctrine. The *argument* must *go for nothing*, but the doctrine of immortality may still have a real and impregnable foundation. This fallacy, indeed, identifies itself with the illicit process; *e. g.*

A, Z is X,
I, Y is Z,
I, Y is X.

Now, if the minor be refuted, as is supposed in the example above, then the argument will stand

A, Z is X,
O, Y is not Z,
O, Y is not X.

In which there is an illicit process of the major.

The second of these fallacies, viz., inferring the truth of the premiss, from the truth of the conclusion, is a case of undistributed middle; *e. g.* If from the truth of the doctrine of immortality we infer its universal belief, thus,

"Whatever is universally believed is true. The doctrine of Immortality is true. Therefore it must be universally believed;" *i. e.*

A, Z is X,
I, Y is X,
I, Y is Z.

The above, therefore, is not really a distinct branch of fallacies in the formula, although at first view it might appear to be so.

II. Fallacies in the Matter.

In this class of Fallacies, the formula is supposed to be strictly observed.

1. *Ambiguous Middle.*—This fallacy consists in using a word, as a middle term, which admits of two significations. In the major premiss, the major term agrees with the middle, taken in one of its significations; and in the minor premiss, the minor term agrees with the middle, taken in another signification; and then in the conclusion, the minor and major are, according to the formula, inferred to agree with each other. The two extremes are, indeed, compared with the same word, but with two very different ideas; so that in reality we have two middle terms; *e. g.*

"A *pitiful* man is beneath respect.
Howard, the philanthropist, was a pitiful man.
Therefore he was beneath respect."

Many words, however, are so settled in their significa tion, that such fallacies cannot be successfully practised with them. Perhaps the word *pitiful* is one of these.

Logicians have distinguished several kinds of Ambigu ous Middle:

Fallacia Figuræ Dictionis, in which the middle term is not precisely the same word, in form, in both premises but so nearly akin that they may be assumed to have the same meaning; *e. g.*

"A *designing* man is unworthy of confidence.
This man has *formed a design.*
Therefore he is unworthy of confidence."

Many fallacies may be formed in this way; and the slighter the shades of difference in the meaning of the two kindred words, the more likely is the fallacy to pass undetected.

Fallacia Plurium Interrogationum.—This fallacy consists in asking several questions apparently the same, and yet in reality of several different meanings, and therefore admitting of several different answers. The question forms one of the premises of the argument; and then, when an answer is given, the sophist stands ready with another premiss to make out a conclusion, which, because unexpectedly opposite to what the one replying intended, serves to embarrass, if not to confound, him; *e. g.* There are cases in which we may strictly follow the statute law, and yet be guilty of great injustice and cruelty. Now let the question be asked, Is not a man justified when he does that which is lawful? Here a reply would not be likely to be given in the negative: and when given in the affirmative, another premiss might be formed embodying some act of oppression—as a landlord seizing the goods of a worthy, but sick and unfortunate tenant; and then the conclusion appended that the landlord is justified in doing so.

Fallacy of Division and Composition.—In this fallacy the middle term in one premiss is taken *collectively*, in the other, *distributively.* If in the major premiss it be taken collectively, and in the minor distributively, it is a Fallacy of Division; *e. g.*

"Five is one number;
Three and two are five; therefore,
Three and two are one number."

If in the major the middle term be taken distributively, and in the minor collectively, it is a fallacy of composition; *e. g.*

"Three and two are two numbers;
Five is three and two; therefore,
Five is two numbers."

"There is no fallacy more common, or more likely to deceive, than the one now before us; the form in which it is most usually employed, is, to establish some truth, *separately*, concerning *each single* member of a certain class, and thence infer the sense of the *whole collectively;* thus some infidels have labored to prove concerning *some one* of our Lord's miracles, that it might have been the result of an accidental conjunction of natural circumstances. Next, they endeavor to prove the same concerning *another;* and so on; and thence infer that *all* of them might have been so. They might argue in like manner, that because it is not very improbable one may throw sixes in any one out of a hundred throws, therefore, it is no more improbable that one may throw sixes a hundred times running." *

Fallacia accidentis.—In this form of the ambiguous middle, the middle term in one premiss is used to express merely the *essence* of a thing; and in the other premiss, to express the same thing, together with its *accidents; e. g.*

"What is bought in the market is eaten;
Raw meat is bought in the market;
Therefore raw meat is eaten."

In the major premiss we are considering edible sub

* Whately's Logic, Book III., § 11.

stances in general, without referring to their circumstances; in the minor, we bring into view one of these substances with its circumstances; and then infer of the latter what was true only of the former.

There are many ways in which words become ambiguous; but the discussion of this subject does not properly belong to Logic. To reason well, a thorough knowledge of some one language, at least, as the vehicle of thought, is evidently indispensable; but the language in which our ratiocinations are expressed, and the principles and formulæ which are to govern and direct the reasoning process itself, are two different branches of study.

2. *Fallacies relating to the connection between the matter of the premises and that of the conclusion.*

The preceding head related to the matter of the middle term as ambiguously expressed in the two premises. Now as the same matter is expressed in the two premises, and in the conclusion, inasmuch as the last compares together the two terms, which in the former had been compared with the middle term, it is obvious that Fallacies may arise also in respect to the correspondency between the representations of the premises and the conclusion, admitting the form to be correct and the middle term to be unambiguous.

Logicians have distinguished and given names to several forms of this Fallacy.

1. *Petitio Principii, or, arguing in a circle.*—In this form of the Fallacy in question, the connection between the premises and conclusion is such, that the premises themselves are dependent upon the conclusion; so that the conclusion must first be assumed to be true, before we can find premises to prove it. This Fallacy, in order to be successful, must of course be artfully constructed, for,

when exposed, it is too gross to delude any mind for a moment. Hence, much here depends upon obliquity and obscurity of the language. To attempt to prove the existence of a God from the Sacred Scriptures must be a *petitio principii*, since they profess to be a revelation from God, and therefore assume His existence.

This Fallacy, however, is not by any means always an intentional one. Acute reasoners have sometimes very honestly fallen into it.

Thus the famous argument used by many writers on Moral Agency, to prove that the "Will is always determined by the *strongest* motive," is a notable instance of this fallacy, where the reasoners were eminent both for logical skill and moral integrity.*

"The will is always determined by the strongest motive." How do you prove this? "The will is always determined to some volition or other, and it is always determined by motives, for they always are present." But how does this prove that it is determined by the *strongest* motive? "That must be the strongest which determines it." Why? "Because it could not otherwise be determined." How do you know that? "Because it must be determined by the strongest motive." It is evident that the very point to be proved is the point assumed.

2. *False or undue assumption of premises.* This embraces those instances in which the premises, although not dependent upon the conclusion, require to be proved before the reasoning can be admitted to have any force. In all cases of Deduction we have to begin with principles already established; or if assumed at the beginning of

* One of the roots, if not *the root*, of this error, is the not distinguishing between an order of sequence, and the principle of causality; between the *motives* as uniform antecedents to volitions, and Will as itself, the cause of volition

course of reasoning—as is sometimes convenient—they must, before the course is completed, be satisfactorily proved. It is, therefore, always an important enquiry, whether the principles with which we begin are sufficiently established to be made the premises of an argument. A judicious and honest reasoner will be cautious in this respect; but it is of the nature of sophistry boldly to assume, and to supply by a show of confidence, the want of a true or an adequate basis.

"Sometimes men are shamed into admitting an unfounded assertion, by being confidently told that it is so evident that it would argue great weakness to doubt it. In general, however, the more skilful sophist will avoid a *direct assertion* of what he means unduly to assume, because that might direct the reader's attention to the consideration of the question whether it be *true* or not; since that which is indisputable does not so often need to be asserted: it succeeds better, therefore, to allude to the proposition as something *curious* and remarkable; just as the Royal Society were imposed on by being asked to account for the fact that a vessel of water received no addition to its weight by a live fish put into it; while they were seeking for the *cause*, they forgot to ascertain the *fact*, and thus admitted, without suspicion, a mere fiction."

There are several species of false assumption mentioned by Logical writers, but as they all involve the same principle, we shall only give a brief summary of them.

Non causa, pro causa. A false assumption of causes.

Here the facts are given, and assuming a cause for them, we reason from it as a real and established connection.

A non vera, pro vera. This, if it differs from the

* Whateley's Logic, ibid. § 14.

preceding, is probably meant to designate a false assumption of facts, as in the anecdote of the Royal Society, quoted above.

When causes and facts both exist, the connection between the two may be assumed on insufficient grounds: it may be assumed either that the causes necessarily involve the facts, or that the facts cannot be referred to any other antecedents. The first relates to the inherent nature of causes; the last to the necessary conditions of the facts.

A non tali, pro tali. This is reasoning from a false assumption of parallelisms; or from false analogies.

False assumption of references. This appears chiefly in references made to the Holy Scriptures. Every passage is authoritative. Hence, although a writer may find few or none which in reality bear upon a favorite dogma, still a mere array of the references strikes the eye; and if the passages are not examined, which, through the indolence of human nature, is apt to be the case, the desired end of the sophist is obtained.

Assumption of probabilities. When the premises are each probable with a certain degree of probability, the combined probability is assumed to be an *addition of probabilities*, whereas it is only *a probability of a probability*.

If Z is only probably X, and Y is only probably Z, then Y is probably X, not with an *increasing*, but with a *decreasing* probability; *e. g.*

Z is probably (say $\frac{3}{4}$) X,
Y is probably (say $\frac{2}{3}$) Z; therefore
Y is probably ($\frac{3}{4} \times \frac{2}{3} = \frac{6}{12}$) X.

In a sorites the probability is still more weakened, and weakened the more the sorites is extended. A *cumulation* of arguments consists of arguments drawn from distinct sources; this differs widely from arguments depending one upon the other.

3. *Ignoratio elenchi, or irrelevant conclusion.*—This fallacy consists in connecting with given premises, not the legitimate conclusion, but one which, although widely different from it, shall, in the language, so resemble it, or be so covertly substituted for it, that the deception goes undetected by the reader or hearer. "Various kinds of propositions are, according to the occasion, substituted for the one of which proof is required. Sometimes the particular for the universal; sometimes a proposition with different terms; and various are the contrivances employed to effect and to conceal this substitution, and to make the conclusion which the sophist has drawn answer practically the same purpose as the one he ought to have established."

"A good instance of the employment and exposure of this fallacy occurs in Thucydides, in the speeches of Cleon and Diodotus, concerning the Mitylenæans: the former (over and above his appeal to the angry passions of his audience) urges the *justice* of putting the revolters to death; which, as the latter remarked, was nothing to the purpose, since the Athenians were not sitting in *judgment*, but in *deliberation*, of which the proper end is expediency."

Archbishop Whately, from whom the above extracts are taken, has so admirably exhibited the different forms of this fallacy, that I cannot resist the temptation of becoming still more largely his debtor. Indeed, on the whole subject of Deductive Fallacies, I freely confess my indebtedness to him.

Argumentum ad hominem, &c.—"There are certain

kinds of argument recounted and named by Logical writers, which we should by no means universally call Fallacies; but which *when unfairly* used, and *so far as they are* fallacious, may very well be referred to the present head; such as the '*argumentum ad hominem*,' or personal argument, '*argumentum ad verecundiam*,' '*argumentum ad populum*,' *&c.*, all of them regarded as contradistinguished from '*argumentum ad rem*,' or, according to others, (meaning probably the very same thing,) '*ad judicium*.' These have all been described in the lax and popular language before alluded to, but not scientifically: the '*argumentum ad hominem*,' they say, 'is addressed to the peculiar circumstances, character, avowed opinions, or past conduct of the individual, and therefore has a reference to him only, and does not bear directly and absolutely on the real question, as the '*argumentum ad rem*' does:' in like manner, the '*argumentum ad verecundiam*' is described as an appeal to our reverence for some respected authority, some venerable institution, &c., and the '*argumentum ad populum*,' as an appeal to the prejudices, passions, &c., of the multitude; and so of the rest. Along with these is usually enumerated '*argumentum ad ignorantiam*,' which is here omitted, as being evidently nothing more than the employment of *some* kind of Fallacy, in the widest sense of that word, towards such as are likely to be deceived by it. It appears then, (to speak rather more technically,) that in the '*argumentum ad hominem*' the conclusion which actually is established, is not the absolute and general one in question, but relative and particular; *viz.* not that 'such and such is the fact,' but that '*this man* is bound to admit it, in conformity to his principles of Reasoning, or in consistency with his own conduct, situation,' &c. Such a Conclusion it is often both allowable and necessary to establish, in order to silence those who will not yield to fair general argument; or to convince those whose weakness and prejudices would not allow them to assign to it its due weight: it is thus that our Lord on many occasions silences the cavils of the Jews; as in the vindication of healing on the Sabbath, which is paralleled by the authorised practice of drawing out a beast that has fallen into a pit. All this, as we have said, is perfectly fair, provided it be done plainly, and *avowedly;* but if you attempt to *substitute* this partial and relative Conclusion for a more general one—if you triumph as having established your proposition absolutely and universally, from having established it, in reality, only as far as it relates to your opponent, then you are guilty of a Fallacy of the kind which we are now treating of: your Conclusion is not in reality that which was, by your own account, proposed to be proved: the fallaciousness depends upon the *deceit* or attempt to deceive. The same observations will *apply* to '*argumentum ad verecundiam*,' and the rest."

Fallacious refutation. This is the refutation of a proposition assumed to belong to an opponent; and thus really an evasion of the point in dispute.

Nearly akin to this is the expedient of *shifting one's ground*, by covertly adopting and discussing some other question than the one taken up at the beginning.

"A practice of this nature is common in oral controversy especially; viz. that of combatting *both* of your opponent's premises *alternately*, and shifting the attack from the one to the other, without waiting to have either of them decided upon before you quit it."

We refer to the same head, "the very common case of proving something to be *possible* when it ought to have been proved highly *probable* ; or *probable*, when it ought to have been proved *necessary* ; or, which comes to the very same, proving it to be *not necessary*, when it should have been proved not probable ; or improbable, when it should have been proved *impossible*.

Fallacy of Objections. This consists in "showing that there are objections against some plan, theory, or system, and thence inferring that it should be rejected ; when that which ought to have been proved is, that there are *more* or *stronger* objections against the receiving than the rejecting of it. This is the principal engine employed by the adversaries of our Faith : they find numerous 'objections' against various parts of Scripture, to some of which no satisfactory answer can be given ; and the incautious hearer is apt, while his attention is fixed on these, to forget that there are infinitely more and stronger objections against the supposition that the Christian religion is of *human* origin ; and that when we cannot answer all objections, we are bound in reason, and in candor, to adopt the hypothesis which labors under the least. That the case is as I have stated, I am authorised to assume, from this circumstance : that *no complete and consistent account has ever been given of the manner in which the Christian religion, supposing it a human contrivance, could have arisen and prevailed as it did.*"

Fallacy of proving part of a Question. The skilful sophist having proved or disproved a part of the question, by enlarging upon this, often succeeds in removing out of view another part, perhaps the most important of all.

"This is the great art of the *answerer* of a book ; suppose the main positions in any work to be irrefragable, it will be strange if some illustration of them, or some subordinate part in short, will not admit of a plausible objection; the opponent then joins issue on one of these incidental questions, and comes forward with 'a Reply' to such and such a work.

"Hence the danger of ever advancing more than can be well maintained, since the refutation of *that* will often quash the whole: a guilty person may often escape by having too much laid to his charge; so he may also by having too much evidence against him, *i. e.* some that is not in itself satisfactory: thus, a prisoner may sometimes obtain acquittal by showing that one of the witnesses against him is an infamous informer and spy; though perhaps if that part of the evidence had been omitted, the rest would have been sufficient for conviction."

Suppressing the Conclusion. There are two ways of suppressing the true conclusion: First, by omitting to state the proposition you are to prove, at the beginning of the argument; and then, after a long spun and elaborate argument, drawing a conclusion remote from the true one, with a confident and plausible air. Secondly, by omitting to give the conclusion altogether, but framing an argument in such a way as to lead the hearer to draw the wrong conclusion, which the sophist aims at. We have a striking instance of this species of reasoning in Antony's speech over the dead body of Cæsar.

"*Jests.* Jests are Fallacies; *i. e.* Fallacies so palpable as not to be likely to deceive any one, but yet bearing just that resemblance of argument which is calculated to amuse by the contrast; in the same manner that a parody does, by the contrast of its levity with the serious production which it imitates. There is indeed something laughable even in Fallacies which are intended for serious conviction, when they are thoroughly exposed. There are several different kinds of joke and raillery, which will be found to correspond with the different kinds of Fallacy: the pun (to take the simplest and most obvious case) is evidently, in most instances, a mock argument founded on a palpable equivocation of the middle Term: and the rest in like manner will be found to correspond to the respective Fallacies, and to be *imitations* of serious argument."

Jests, however, are often very serious arguments, when their effects are considered; for that which is turned into ridicule, becomes, in some degree, an object of contempt, or, at least, ceases to command respect and careful attention. They are also *popular* arguments, for they require no thought, and afford a piquant amusement.

Fallacy of Epithets. This appears in the disputes of political parties and religious sects. The fallacy is of a twofold character: First, the odious name may be fastened upon an individual, or upon the party or sect to which he belongs, with the utmost injustice: there may be merely a seeming agreement arising from similar names and circumstances, without any real identity of principles; or there may be an agreement only in points unimportant, or even commendable; but, notwithstanding, when the *hue and cry* is once raised, the multitude are prone to rush to the chase, and join in the ferocious sport. Secondly, the name itself may have become odious unjustly: it may be a good name, darkened and marred by the prejudices and persecutions of a benighted and bigoted age; but its character has become fixed in the popular apprehension, and no one now stops to enquire into its origin or its principles: it is the symbol of enormous error, if not of crime, and he who is adjudged worthy to wear it, may fail to gain a second hearing. In this fallacy, the conclusion is not generally concealed until the close of an argument, and covertly applied; it is brought out at the beginning in the epithet itself, and frequently supersedes the necessity of even the show of an argument.

We close here our view of the Deductive Fallacies. It will be seen that those arising from the matter of the propositions are numerous. It requires both mental discipline and tact to guard against and to detect them. But one thing is evident, that a pure, benevolent, and truth-loving spirit is the most effectual protection against this species of false reasoning.

The fallacies which I next propose to consider, are those of Induction and Intuition: fallacies belonging to the two former parts of Logic, and therefore rather improperly introduced here. Notwithstanding this seeming impropriety, I have concluded to do so, for the purpose of making the whole subject of fallacies a unique portion of the work. Besides, I propose to handle what remains briefly, as it is not of a nature to require nor to admit of an exposition running much into details. The common human life is peculiarly the theatre of deduction, for it is here that principles are applied or violated most extensively; it is therefore the theatre which presents most abundantly both the opportunities and the temptations of sophistry.

FALLACIES OF INDUCTION.

These are of three kinds: Fallacies of Observation, Fallacies in determining General Facts, and Fallacies in inducting Laws.

I. Fallacies of Observation.—We note here three Fallacies:

First. Inadequate Observation. All the phenomena, if possible, in relation to a given subject should be observed: and the mind should not rest content while any phenomena probably remain which, by any labor and diligence in observation and experiment, may be brought to light. But human nature is prone to accept as sufficient a set of limited but familar observations lying within the immediate neighborhood of the individual. Men are, as it were, divided into tribes dwelling in deep valleys; and each tribe looketh upon its valley as the wide universe, and the high mountains around as the horizon of being and the impassable boundary of thought. This begetteth narrow-mindedness, bigotry, and imperfect and crude knowledges. The philosopher passes over the mountain tops, walks through valley after valley, converses with all the different tribes, sees the same things as they appear in different places; and thus prepares himself to learn the general laws which govern God's creatures, and to enjoy the harmony and beauty of all things. Again, human nature is impatient of the slow and persevering labor demanded in prosecuting observation and experiment. It is far more pleasant to our natural indolence to take such observations as force themselves upon us, and to leave the rest to conjecture, than to endure the toil and restraint, and wait for the results of thorough investigation.

Another form of this Fallacy appears where the observation, although extensive, is imperfect and hurried. Such are the busy collectors of facts, the ambitious founders of lyceums and cabinets, who bring us abundance of things and but little thought; who indeed *manipulate*, but do not nicely examine.

Facts show the state of the world. He, therefore, who does not look at all the facts, and examine their characteristics minutely, is not prepared to form sound judgments. He may express opinions, but he is not entitled to any authority.

Secondly. The Fallacy of making Observation and Experiments without a purpose, or a prophecy of the end in the form of a rational hypothesis.

We have already alluded to the catalogues of facts made by Bacon.* These are an example of the Fallacy under consideration. By the knowledge already attained of the constitution of the world, and the spontaneous inspiration of Ideas awakened in profound and patient meditation, the mind when it comes within a new field of investigation is prepared and impelled to form some hypothesis of the order of sequences, if not of the ultimate law. We call this a rational hypothesis, because it considers laws already ascertained, and thoughtfully watches the indications of the initiative phenomena. Such a hypothesis at the early stage of investigation is necessary, in order to arrange the facts already gained, and to know where to make further observations, and how to adjust experiments.

Without such a hypothesis, every thing is done at random. It is indeed sheer empiricism—a trying of experiments like a blind casting of dice, with a wondering and puerile curiosity to know what will turn up next. Philosophical investigation foresees its end with more or less clearness. Like Bunyan's pilgrim, it at least sees a little shining light a great way off, and by keeping that little light in its eye, it at length reaches the straight and narrow way of Truth. When Newton saw the apple fall, he formed his hypothesis; he thenceforward had a definite and great end before him.

Thirdly. The Fallacy of making facts bend to favorite theories.—When Theories are once formed, men are ever

* Page 284.

ready to become intoxicated with them. An ingenious Theory is a proud effort of the Intellect, and, therefore, not easy to be relinquished by its author; and the light and order which it gives to facts which before appeared complicated and inexplicable, soon brings it into general favour with enquiring minds. Hence there springs up a passion to apply it, and to make every thing accord with it. Men begin to forget that it is a mere hypothesis, which may or may not be true; and that, if not confirmed by general observation, it must yield to some more perfect conception. In this way they are often betrayed into great absurdities. We have an illustration of this, in the tenacity with which some chemists for a while adhered to the Phlogistic Theory.

Now Truth and Philosophy alike demand that a Theory shall be adopted, always with the tacit understanding, that it is to be held in abeyance to farther discoveries. And here the great Philosopher shows his greatness, in that he becomes wedded to nothing but truth; and holding theories only as a means of truth, he is ready to modify them according to the indications of new facts, or even to renounce them when they cannot be verified, or a better light is obtained. Thus Newton, for a time, laid aside the law of gravitation, while the calculations did not appear to sustain it. But in the end he had his rich reward.

II. Fallacies in determining General Facts.

First. The fallacy of affirming a uniform Sequence, from a mere observation of coincidences.—This Fallacy is very common. The superstition of dreams and omens, the empiricisms of medicine, and a thousand empty popular maxims, all belong here.

Because two phenomena are found to be conjoined in

time and place, therefore, by this Fallacy, one is assumed as the uniform antecedent of the other, and we are to expect the recurrence of the one wherever we find the other. Now, before we have a right to conclude that the two are in uniform sequence, we must prove by experiment that the given Consequent *never* takes place except where the Antecedent in question is present; *i. e.* We must prove by *Negative* instances as well as *Positive.* Upon further examination, we may find the same Consequent to coincide in time and place with a thousand other phenomena; but *that* alone can be its proper Antecedent, *without which it does not take place.* This indeed is the Fallacy condemned in the memorable language of Bacon: —"Inductio quæ procedit per enumerationem simplicem, res puerilis est, et precario concludit, et periculo exponitur ab instantia contradictoria, et plerumque secundum pauciora quam par est, et ex his tantum modo quæ præsto sunt pronunciat. At Inductio quæ ad inventionem et demonstrationem Scientarum et Artium erit utilis, Naturam separare debet, per rejectiones et exclusiones debitas; ac deinde post negativas tot quot sufficiunt, super affirmativas concludere."*

Secondly. The Fallacy of denying whatever has not been found hitherto in the common observation of men, or does not exist in generally received maxims.

This Fallacy is of the same nature with the preceding,

* "That induction which proceeds by a mere enumeration of instances, is a puerile affair, and concludes precariously, and is exposed to danger from contradictory instances, and for the most part it gives its decisions according to fewer instances than is proper, and from those only which are then present. But an induction that would be useful to the discovery and demonstration of the sciences and arts, ought to distinguish nature through proper rejections and exclusions, and then, after a sufficient number of negative instances have been adduced, to draw the conclusion upon the positive ones."

and equally condemned by the language of Bacon. The former affirms that those are proper Antecedents and Consequents which have been found together; the latter, that none can exist beyond those which have hitherto been found together. The one gives authority to untested empiricism; the other denies any truth to exist beyond it. The one consigns us to the despotism of bigotry and ignorance; the other cuts us off from all hope in the future. The one affirms the majesty of ancient authorities; the other denies all farther improvement.

In opposition to both, Philosophy affirms that she will receive nothing which she has not tested by the principles of human Reason; and that she will dare to receive every thing which she has thus tested.

The above are the chief Fallacies, given in brief, which belong to this division. They will be found upon reflection to comprise a violation of the Principles of Elimination laid down under Inductive Logic; for, the aim of those principles is to provide a test for sequences in general, so that we may determine amid the mass of phenomena, which are properly related as Antecedents and Consequents.

III. Fallacies in Inducting Laws.

We have seen that the tests of a Law are its sufficiency to account for the phenomena, its characteristics of universality and necessity, and its correspondence to an Idea. Now we note as a Fallacy under this head:

First. The confounding of a general fact with a law. —To establish a general Fact, is to establish a uniform order of sequence in relation to certain phenomena; *e. g.* the influence of the sun and moon upon the tides. The law under which this particular sequence is comprehended is the law of gravitation taken in connection with the peculiar interior constitution of fluids, which causes them to yield to an influence which does not affect the solid parts of the earth in the same manner. It is common to call the general facts laws; and thus the two lines of investigation are not clearly distinguished. This, perhaps, is not so strictly a Fallacy in Induction, as a confusion in the end aimed at, and which may lead to fallacious inductions. A general fact viewed in itself is contingent; it receives higher characteristics only when viewed as an exponent of Law, and then of course is distinguished from it. But a perfect method of philosophising demands that it keep its true place in every stage of the induction, and thus, instead of shutting up investigation, it becomes a means of leading it on to its last results.

Secondly. The great Fallacy, and one which has been alluded to more than once in this work, is, *the separation of Observation and Ideas.* This Fallacy has two modes, accordingly as it reposes upon Ideas independently of observation, or as it employs observation independently of Ideas.

The true logical development of Ideas takes place in connection with the reality of Nature; and the laws of Nature are discovered and expounded only in the light of Ideas. The first mode of the Fallacy, therefore, shows itself in splendid but obscure conceptions of the order of Nature; while the other presents us collections of sequences without system.

FALLACIES IN RESPECT TO INTUITION.

I have already remarked,* that in the sphere of Intuitive Truths falsehood cannot well find place, because

* Primordial Logic. Idea of Truth, pp. 207, 208.

the characteristics of these truths are so clear and decided; and because if there be falsehood here, there can be no absolute test of Truth. But, on the other hand, it cannot be denied that affirmations have been made, apparently with an intuitive positiveness, which afterwards have been totally set aside; *e. g.* The celebrated philosophical maxim, that, "A thing cannot act where it is not." Even Newton, in order to escape the force of this maxim in its bearing upon the law of gravitation, imagines a subtle ether diffused through the space between the sun and the planets, as a mediate cause; affirming that, "It is inconceivable that inanimate brute matter should, without the mediation of something else, which is not material, operate upon and affect other matter *without mutual contact.*" He even pronounces it "so great an absurdity," that he cannot believe that any man, "who in philosophical matters has a competent faculty of thinking, can ever fall into it." * And yet in our day the most philosophical minds do not perceive it to be at all incredible that the sun and planets can act upon each other through the intervening space without any medium whatever.

It would appear from this and similar instances that might be adduced, that there are Fallacies in respect to Intuition. I say *Fallacies in respect to Intuition*, for fallacious intuitions there cannot be. An Intuition carries with it its own truth, it is necessary and absolute; to deny it is to belie Reason itself, and to destroy the possibility of certainty. What was said, therefore, under the "Idea of Truth," as above referred to, I conceive to be impregnable.

* See Playfair's Dissertation on the Progress of Mathematical and Physical Science.

But the question still remains, How are we to account for Fallacies in respect to Intuition? If it be granted that an intuitive truth cannot be disputed, how can a false maxim put on, to appearance, the characteristics of such a truth?

In the first place, there is to be remarked an ambiguity in the word "inconceivable;" it may be taken either absolutely or relatively: the *absolutely inconceivable* is the contradictory of all rational conception, and therefore equivalent to the *impossible;* the *relatively inconceivable,* on the other hand, is only the opposite of the particular conceptions of an individual, of a class, or of an age. Now nothing is more common than men adhering to even wild and puerile maxims, and denying whatever lies beyond the range of their immediate experience with the utmost positiveness and pertinacity; this undoubtedly is owing to the undeveloped state of their minds, and the tyranny of prejudice.

This fallacy is one which we have already noticed under a preceding head.* Philosophers, it must be confessed, have given us similar examples: having embraced certain dogmas, and committed themselves to maintain them, they manifest the utmost certainty of conviction, and that too with great sincerity. It follows, therefore, that in maintaining false maxims, men may assert with great earnestness, and apparent strength of belief, and may use the epithets "absurd" and "inconceivable," only because of their education, prejudices, and point of view. Now suppose these same men to be relieved from all these hindrances, and to occupy the same relative ground that we do, with whom their fondly cherished maxims are ex-

* Page 398.

ploded, would it not be possible for them to believe as we do? And would they not see that they had before occupied a fallacious position, but that, now, they had attained to the right one? While in error, we are often very confident, and may be even so much so, as to think that our judgments are intuitive; but when we really attain the truth, then we see plainly enough that those confident errors had not the strength and clearness of intuition. We are now in a condition to make a comparison; before, we were not. Notwithstanding all the mistakes we may make, there is such a thing as perceiving absolute truth, and knowing that we are right.

In the second place, we can account for these pretented intuitions by a want of development in the Ideas which govern the sphere in which they appear. The maxim above mentioned was founded upon an erroneous conception of Causes; showing that the Idea of Cause was not clearly developed in the minds of those who advocated it. Now it is the clearer development of this Idea which enables us to conceive of the mutual attractions of the sun and the planets without any medium in the intervening space; nor can we ever again conceive such a medium to be necessary.*

All the Fallacies which arise in respect to intuition have their origin unquestionably in a want of philosophical development; for Philosophy is not merely a system of truths and a law of method, but a state of the Reason in man. Just as this development advances, does the vision of Truth become brighter and brighter unto the perfect day. But that perfect day is still to us an object of hope, and ever shall be, until we reach that Uncreated Light, in which we shall see Light itself.

* Primordial Logic, Sect. VII., and particularly p. 239.

BOOK IV.

THE DOCTRINE OF EVIDENCE.

SECTION I.

NATURE OF PROOF.

WHEN we have arrived at judgments, we may state them in the form of Propositions or Theorems, and then subjoin to them the Logical Process by which they have been determined. This is called the order of *Proof.*

Opposed to the order of *Proof* is the order of *Investigation.* When we are searching after Truth we pursue the order of Investigation; we employ our Intuitions, or the knowledge we may have already gained; we make observations and experiments; we compare; we generalize; we meditate; we employ Induction and Deduction; and when Truth appears, it appears as a Conclusion. The truths at which we thus arrive are entirely new, or were before but dimly seen as conjectures or theories.

When we undertake to prove a proposition, we either know it to be true or false, or we are uncertain of its character.

1. *If we know* it to be true, then we must be acquainted with the investigation upon which it rests; and

to prove it, will be only to subjoin that process of investigation, according to Logical formulæ, or, at least, in strict accordance with logical principles.

2. *If we know* it to be false, then we must see that it is either deduced from false premises or is a false deduction. To prove it false, therefore, will require either an exposition of its premises, or a statement of the fallacious syllogism.

3. *If we are uncertain* of its character, we proceed to *test it.* The method of testing it will depend upon the nature of the proposition.

1. If the proposition affirm an *Antecedent,* we test it by searching whether it stands as a necessary or probable condition to the existence of any known *Consequents.* 2. If the proposition affirm a consequent, we test it by searching whether any known antecedents involve it. In doing this we have to apply the principles of elimination laid down in Inductive Logic.

We have here, then, two kinds of proof developed which are defined according to the *nature* of the connection which they hold to propositions to be proved.

1. When the proof holds to the proposition to be proved, the relation of Antecedent to Consequent, or of Principle or Law to phenomena, as in its nature enveloping them,—it is called *à priori; i. e.* I prove that such consequents, or such phenomena as the proposition affirms to exist, must exist, because an antecedent or principle exists which involves them.

In this case, when the argument is reduced to the form of a syllogism, the antecedents or principles from which we prove the phenomena or consequents, form the premises: and the physical and logical sequences are said to correspond.

2. When the proof holds to the proposition to be proved, the relation of phenomena to law, or to necessary condition; in other words, the relation of consequent to a necessary principle or antecedent, it is called *à posteriori; i. e.* I prove that the antecedent or principle which the proposition affirms to exist, must exist, because phenomena exist, which demand the former as the necessary condition of their existence; in some cases as explaining the very fact of their existence,—in others, the mode of their existence.

When the *à posteriori* argument is reduced to the form of a syllogism, the phenomena or consequents constitute the premises, and the physical and logical sequences are opposed.

These two methods of proving, although introduced above in immediate connection with uncertain propositions, or those whose character remains to be tested, embrace likewise the preceding cases. When I am myself certain of the character of a proposition, in representing that character to another, that is, in proving it to him, I must necessarily adopt one or the other of these methods, according to the nature of the proposition, as above stated.

This is manifest from a comparison of these methods with the two great forms of reasoning, the Deductive and Inductive.

To prove *à priori* is to prove a consequent from an antecedent, a phenomenon from a law, by showing that the antecedent and law involve the consequent and the phenomenon. This corresponds to Deduction in its principle, for it is the containing whole determining the particular or particulars contained.

Again: To prove *à posteriori* is to prove an antecedent from a consequent, a law from phenomena, by showing that the existence of the consequent or of the phenomena can be accounted for only by the admission of the antecedent, or the law which the proposition affirms. This corresponds to Induction in its principle; for it is the particular or particulars determining the whole, as that which comprehends them and contains the cause and law of their being.

To prove, therefore, is to reverse the order of Investigation.

In the latter, we are searching after unknown truths; in the former, we are seeking to establish known truths. Both processes comprehend the same principles, and essentially the same materials; only, that in the order of investigation, many steps are merely tentative, and give no positive results; while in the order of proof, where the whole of the preceding investigation is before the mind, nothing but what is essentially constitutive of the argument is selected and appropriated. Where we test an uncertain proposition, there are tentative steps, and investigation and proof are in some degree commingled.

The *à priori method of proving* must not be confounded with *à priori principles.* The former assumes antecedents, which involve the consequents to be proved by them, without any reference to the logical property of the antecedents. But when principles are designated as *à priori*, we have direct reference to their logical property. By an *à priori* principle, we mean a principle which has not its origin in the *sense*, but in the *pure Reason.* Sense or experience is a *necessary condition* of its development, *i. e.* the reason would not go into action to develope the principle, were not an experience given as a *datum;* but when the principle is developed, we then clearly see that the experience itself would not have been possible had not the principle had a prior existence ; *e. g.* body and space, phenomena and cause—space and cause being *à priori* revealed, upon condition of body and phenomena ; but when revealed, we see there could have been no experience of body and phenomena, had not space and cause had a *prior* existence. Ideas, and all first truths and axioms, are, therefore, *à priori* principles.

SECTION II.

THE DIFFERENT KINDS OF À PRIORI AND À POSTERIORI PROOF.

ALL the other forms of Evidence or Proof may be reduced to the *à priori* and the *à posteriori.*

I. *Testimony.*—This belongs to the *à posteriori.* The testimony given is a fact which demands as the condition of its existence the truth of what it affirms, unless other conditions can be shown satisfactorily to account for it.

II. *Concurrent Testimony.*—The concurrence is a fact which can be accounted for, only by admitting the truth of the testimony.

III. *Argument from progressive approach. e. g.* the law of *vis inertiæ* may be proved in this way. This is likewise *à posteriori* proof. The facts of the progressive approach are supposed to be accounted for, only by admitting the existence of the law.

IV. *Proving by example or fact* is *à posteriori,* because it is establishing some point as the condition or necessary antecedent of the example or fact. Sometimes the *à priori* is united with the *à posteriori;* when, from inducted examples, we establish a principle, and then again apply this principle to a particular instance.

The whole process is not usually put down, but we go elliptically from the inducted examples to the particular conclusion, suppressing the formal statement of the general principle which intervenes in the mental process.

Simple reasoning from example is nothing more than inductive reasoning.

V. *Reasoning from experience.*—This is reasoning either from the past and present to the future, or from the present to the past. *When we reason from the past and present to the future,* we show *à priori* what the *future* must be from the causes which have been, and now are, at work. *When we reason from the present to the past,* we show *à posteriori* what the *past* must have been from the facts now existing.

VI. *Reasoning from resemblance and analogy.*

1. *Resemblance.*—Resemblance is distinguished from identity by admitted differences; identity excludes differences. Now, reasoning from resemblance is reasoning either from the differences or the agreements of the two parallel cases; *i. e.* the actually existing agreements are shown to involve other points of agreement, or the actually existing differences are shown to involve other points of difference. This is done *à priori,* or *à posteriori,* according to the nature of the case; *à priori,* when the existing facts of resemblance or difference are antecedents to those which are to be proved from them; and *à posteriori,* when the existing facts of resemblance or difference are sequences of those to be proved from them.

2. *Analogy.*—This is not direct or simple resemblance, but a resemblance of relations, or a resemblance of circumstances in a common relation. In simple resemblance there are only two terms; in analogy, there are three and four.

1. Where there are *three terms,* there is a relation of two to a common third. This is a resemblance of circum-

stances in a common relation. In this case, our object is either—the analogy being granted—to prove circumstances in one relation by resembling circumstances in the other relation, or to prove the common relation or analogy itself, by the resembling circumstances. Where we wish to prove circumstances in one relation by resembling circumstances in the others, the reasoning is *à priori* or *à posteriori*, according to the nature of the relation between the existing particulars and those to be proved;—*e. g.* an *analogy* is granted to exist between mind and body, as respects education;—their development has a common relation to exercise. Now, there are many resembling circumstances in this common relation, and these circumstances may be made a basis of reasoning to the existence of other circumstances of resemblance after the *à priori* or *à posteriori* method, as the nature of the connection shall determine.

Where we wish to prove the common relation, or the analogy itself, from the resembling circumstances, we proceed according to the *à posteriori* method. The resembling circumstances are shown to require the analogy as the condition of their existence;—*e. g.* Butler's Analogy: here the common relation of Revelation and the Universe to God is shown, from the resembling circumstances; and objections to the first answered, by showing that similar objections must lie against the second.

2. Where there are *four terms*, there is a resemblance of relations. If this resemblance is granted, then we proceed *à priori* to prove results;—*e. g.* it being granted that an analogy exists between the relation of a king to his subjects, and of a father to his children, we may prove *à priori* that a king must guard and guide his people, and yield his personal interests to their wants.

If we wish to prove an analogy of relations from facts, we proceed *à posteriori.* The establishment of such an analogy is like the establishment of a general principle by induction ; and the analogy thus established is employed like a principle in reaching new conclusions.

Indeed, the analogy always contains a principle. In the first case, that of a common relation of two terms to a third, this third, on the *à priori* method, is the principle enveloping the circumstances of the other two ; and, on the *à posteriori* method, is the principle evolved from the circumstances of the other two. In the second case, that of the resembling relations of four terms, when we proceed *à priori,* we assume a principle which envelopes and accounts for these relations ; and when we proceed *à posteriori,* although we stop short, usually, when we have established so many circumstances of resemblance as, to common and general apprehension, demand an analogy to account for them, still the analogy itself is but the exponent of a principle. The same holds true with respect to all reasoning from resemblance : the resemblance is taken as the exponent of a law. In order to make this plain, let it be remarked that in reasoning from simple resemblance,—*i. e.* of two terms, or from analogy of three or four terms—there is always a comparison of certain circumstances in one term or relation to resembling circumstances in the other term or relation. Now, in the first term, or relation,—that is, the one from which we reason,—we find these certain circumstances to be connected *à priori* or *à posteriori* with other circumstances ; and then passing over to the second term or relation to the resembling circumstances there found, we infer that these must likewise be *à priori* or *à posteriori,* as the case may be, connected with other circumstances, like those other circumstances referred to in the first. But why do we infer this? The answer is obvious. Nature is uniform in her operations, and therefore the resembling circumstances in the second term or relation form an exponent of the same law operating here, which is known to have produced those other circumstances in the first term or relation :—*i. e.* on the *à priori principle* of the uniformity of nature, as the ultimate basis of the reasoning, we assume the same law to envelope both terms, or both relations.

The same is true, when, from resembling circumstances, we aim to establish an analogy, or a strict resemblance. We then say, inasmuch as nature is uniform in her operations, these resembling circumstances can be accounted for only by referring them to the same law as governing the two terms, or relations.

VII. *Reasoning from axioms and definitions.*—This is usually called *Demonstrative Reasoning,* or simply *Demonstration.* This reasoning is, plainly *à priori ;* for all the conclusions are wrapped up in the axioms and definitions, and are, therefore, determined by them in a necessary and absolute relation of consequents to antecedents. The principles here, are necessary and *à priori* principles, and all the conclusions exhibit but their manifold unfoldings.

SECTION III.

OF THE NATURE OF THE RELATION BETWEEN ANTECEDENTS AND CONSEQUENTS.

WE have seen that all the different modes of proof are comprehended under those two,—the *à priori* and the *à posteriori*. The *à priori* is the proof of a consequent by an antecedent, which involves it. The *à posteriori* is the proof of an antecedent by a consequent, which demands it as the condition of its own existence. But the question must here arise, What is the nature of that connection which exists between the two terms of antecedent and consequent? It cannot be a mere juxtaposition in time or space, because this juxtaposition may be arbitrary or accidental, and therefore form no basis of certainty, or even of probability. It is obvious that the connection must be of a nature to demand the existence of the one when the existence of the other is granted. Hence, let it be observed, that in our explication of the *à priori* and the *à posteriori*, we were careful to point out this connection as a connection of antecedent and consequent, or of a principle in necessary relation to comprehended particulars, or of a condition without which the consequent *could not* have existed. But all these different forms of expression do really refer to relations of the same nature, viz., either the relation of cause and effect, or of law and phenomena, or of first truths and their necessary consequences.

When we attain to merely uniform sequences, as general facts, the uniformity we assume to be comprehended by some law and necessitated by it. Cause of course is all-pervading, and therefore always implied; but is not the great object of investigation, as has been before shown.* The *consequent*, then, whether regarded as an effect, or a particular comprehended under law, or an inference arising from an axiom, is really contained in its *antecedent;* so that the affirmation of the *latter* comprehends the affirmation of the *former;* and the existence of the former proves the latter, when, by applying the principles of elimination,† or by tracing upwards the necessary sequence, it is shown that the *former* depends upon the *latter*.

A *condition*, without which a *consequent could not have existed*, is not always an immediate antecedent; as when we say of a tender plant, that it was destroyed, because the servant carelessly left it out of doors during a frosty night. Here we do not assign the carelessness of the servant as the immediate antecedent of the destruction of the plant; but still, it was the immediate antecedent of the exposure of the plant; and, had it not been left out of doors, it would not have been destroyed. In this case, there is a series of antecedents and consequents, all of which are necessary to account for the effect; but, instead of stating the whole series, we put down a remote antecedent as the condition of the last effect, and form thus an abbreviated form of expression for the whole. But the reasoning depends upon the relations we have given above.

The cardinal principles involved in the foregoing, axiomatically expressed, are,

1. "Every phenomenon must have its cause and its law."

* Supra, p. 254. † Page 288.

2. "Nature is uniform in her operations."

This uniformity is the uniformity of the action of causes, as regulated by wise laws: and the uniformity of nature, therefore, may be expressed as follows:

"Like antecedents involve like consequents;" and

"Like consequents imply like antecedents;" *

Or, to give it a more general expression,

"Cause is immutably regulated in time and space;" *e. g.* fire—gravitation—magnetism.

3. "Whatever is predicated of the Whole is predicated of all the parts contained under it."

Upon these three principles all the different kinds of proof above explained are based.

In all the different forms of the *à posteriori*, we prove antecedents from consequents or phenomena. But, obviously, we cannot proceed in this proof, unless we assume that "Every phenomenon must have its cause and its law;" and "That law governs uniformly."

In the *à priori*, likewise, where we prove consequents or phenomena by antecedents, we cannot proceed without assuming that "Every cause is governed by law uniformly."

* Page 301.

SECTION IV.

OF DEGREES OF EVIDENCE.

THE terms *necessary, possible, contingent,* and *impossible,* refer to the nature of the connection between a given antecedent and consequent. The terms *certain, probable,* and *presumptive,* refer to our *knowledge* of this connection.

A *necessary* connection between the two is one determined by absolute law ; *e. g.* the connection between an Idea and an Axiom, as the Idea of space and the axiom of the three dimensions in space ; the connection between an axiom and consequences deduced from it ; the connection between the law of gravitation and the phenomena of nature ; the connection between the premises and conclusion of a syllogism ; and so on.

A *possible connection* is one which no law absolutely prevents ; and which might take place by an adequate power which we know to exist, but which, at the same time, may not appear *probable.* It is therefore a *contingent* connection.

A *contingent* connection implies a law in relation to a cause which may or may not be governed by it. It is the opposite of a necessary connection. There is no contingency in the connection between natural causes and laws, and their phenomena. Contingency is found only in the connection between a Free Will, and motives consisting of Moral Laws, Reasons, and Inducements.*

An *impossible* connection, is one prevented by law;—*e. g.* that a stone thrown into the air should remain suspended there, or that a mass of solid iron should float in water, or that a part should be greater than a whole, or that 2+2=5.

Impossibility is of two kinds, *logical* and *physical.* The first is a connection which would contravene Ideas and Axioms, and laws founded in them. Such a connection is an impossibility in itself,—*e. g.* that a part is greater than a whole, that there are four dimensions in space, or that 2+2=5. A *physical* impossibility is the impossibility of any phenomena in contravention of physical laws. While these laws exist, or remain unsuspended, their proper phenomena must take place. But Omnipotence may suspend or modify these laws. This of course is a *miracle* or *wonder.*

The other set of terms, we have said, refers to our *knowledge* of any supposed connection between an antecedent and consequent.

To an Omniscient Being there are no degrees of knowledge. Such a Being sees, with the utmost clearness, the necessary and the contingent, the actual and the possible. To such a Being, all knowledge is certain. It is only to the knowledges which belong to beings like ourselves that the terms *presumptive* and *probable* can be applied; it is only of such knowledges that *degrees* of certainty can be affirmed.

There are then to us three kinds of certainty, according

* Doctrine of the Will, p. 62.

to the nature of the connection between the terms which are the object of proof.

First. *Absolute certainty.* This is based upon the necessary connection between the two terms. Our knowledge of Ideas and Axioms is absolutely certain,—*e. g.* time and space; that every body is in space. So also our knowledge of deductions from axioms is absolutely certain, as in geometry, for example. Our knowledge of the connection between the premises and conclusion of a syllogism is of the same nature: this is sometimes called *logical certainty.*

Secondly. *Physical certainty.* This is the certainty which lies in the connection between established physical antecedents and sequents, as exhibited in the phenomena of gravitation, heat, chemical affinities, mechanical forces, and so on.

Now, the reason does not conceive of this connection as necessarily fixed with an absolute necessity, because it ultimately depends upon the Will of God; and the same Will which ordained it, can change, suspend, or even annihilate it.

When, therefore, we affirm any thing to be physically certain, we mean that our knowledge of it is based upon *physical,* and *not* upon *necessary* relations.

Thirdly. *Moral certainty.* This is the certainty which lies between the connection of Motive and Will. By Will, we mean a self-conscious, intelligent and sensitive cause, or a cause in a triunity with Reason and Sensitivity. It is in the fullest sense a cause *per se;* that is, it contains within itself proper efficiency, and determines its own direction. By *Motives,* we mean the *reasons* and *inducements,* in view of which the Will acts.* In general, all

* Doctrine of the Will, p. 138.

activity proceeds according to rules, or laws, or reasons, for they have essentially the same meaning: but in mere material masses, the law is not contemplated by the acting force; it is contemplated only by the Intelligence which ordained and conditioned the force. In spirit, on the contrary, the activity which we call Will, is self-conscious, and is connected with a perception and sense of the reasons and inducements, or ends, or motives of actions. These motives are of two kinds:

First. Those found in the ideas of the practical reason, which decides what is fit and right. These are reasons of supreme authority.

Secondly. Those found in the understanding and sensitivity; *i. e.*, the immediately useful and expedient, and the gratification of the passions. These are right only when subordinate to the first.

Now, these reasons and inducements are a light to the Will, and serve to guide its activities. The human conscience, which is but the Reason, under its practical function, in relation to the moral, has drawn up for the Will explicit rules, suited to all circumstances and relations, which are called *ethics*, or *the rules*. And so, on the other hand, the understanding, by which we mean the Reason, under its practical function, in relation to mere utility, has formed rules of prudence or expediency. The law of the sensitivity, taken in itself, is unique; it is simply "To do whatever is most agreeable or pleasing to itself."

These various rules the Will is not compelled or necessitated to obey. In every volition it is conscious of a power to do, or not to do.

In the moral harmony and purity of the soul, the three kinds above named do not conflict with each other. The right has utility as an ultimate and certain result. The soul loves the right, in this state, *because* it is right, and reposes quietly in hope of the consequences. And all the passions find their highest gratification in obeying the law of the right. Hence moral certainty, as to the actions of moral beings, can exist only where the harmony of the spiritual being is preserved in a perfect, or at least paramount degree : *e. g.* God, and good angels, and good men. In God, moral certainty is perfect. His dispositions are infinitely pure, and his Will freely determines to do right; it is not compelled or necessitated, for then His infinite meritoriousness would cease. Moral certainty is not *absolute*, because Will being a power to do, or not to do, there is always a possibility, although it may be an infinite improbability, that the Will may disobey the laws of the Reason.

In the case of good angels, and good men, the moral certainty is such, as to be attended with no apprehension of a dereliction.

With respect to such men as Joseph, Daniel, Paul, Howard, and Washington, we can calculate, with a very high and satisfactory moral certainty, of the manner in which they will act in any given circumstances involving the influence of motives. We know they will obey truth, justice, and mercy,—that is, the *first* class of motives; and the *second*, only so far as they are authorised by the first.

If the first class of motives is forsaken, then human conduct must be calculated according to the influence of the second class.

Human character, however, is mixed and variously compounded. We might make a scale of an indefinite number of degrees, from the highest point of moral excellence to the lowest point of moral degradation, and then our predictions of human conduct would vary with every degree.

In any particular case, where we are called upon to reason from the connection of motives with the will, it is evident we must determine the character of the individual as accurately as possible, in order to know the probable *resultant* of the opposite moral forces which we are likely to find.

We have remarked that moral certainty exists only where the harmony of the moral constitution is preserved. Here we know the Right will be obeyed. It may, however, be remarked in addition to this, that moral certainty may be said to exist in the case of the lowest moral degradation, where the Right is forsaken. Here the rule is, "To do whatever is most agreeable," and "Whatever is useful in the immediate or temporal consequences." The volition, indeed, in such instances seems merged into a mere sense of present gratification. But, in the intermediate state, lies the wide field of probability. What is commonly called the *knowledge of human nature*, and esteemed of most importance in the affairs of human life, is not the knowledge of human nature as it *ought to be*, but as *it is*, in its vast variety of good and evil. We gain this knowledge from consciousness, from observation, and from history. What human nature ought to be, we learn from Reason and Revelation.

Will has already been represented as forming a triunity with the Reason and the Sensitivity, and in the constitution of our being is designed to derive its rules and inducements of action from these. Acts, which are in the direction of neither reason nor sensitivity, must be very trifling acts; and therefore, although possible, we may conclude they are very rare. In calculating, then, future acts of will, we may, like the Mathematicians, drop infinitesimal differences, and assume that all acts of the will are in the direction of the reason, or of the sensitivity, or of both in their harmony. Although the will is conscious of power to do, out of the direction of both the reason and the sensitivity, still in the triunity in which it exists, it submits itself to the general interests of the being, and consults the authority of conscience, or the enjoyments of passion. Now every individual has formed for himself habits and a character, more or less fixed. He is known to have submitted himself from day to day, and in a great variety of transactions, to the laws of conscience; and hence we conclude, that he has formed a fixed purpose of doing right. He has exhibited, too, on many occasions, noble, generous, and pure feelings; and hence we conclude that his sensitivity, in a predominant degree, harmonises with conscience. Or, he is known to have violated the laws of the conscience from day to day, and in a great variety of transactions; and hence we conclude that he has formed a fixed purpose of doing wrong; and that his sensitivity is in conflict with the reason.

In both cases supposed, and, in like manner, in all supposable cases, there is plainly a basis, on which, in any given circumstances, we may foresee and predict the volitions, and consequently the actions of men.

There is something "that is evident, and now existent, with which the future existence of the contingent event is connected." On the one hand, these predictions exert no necessitating influence over the events, for they are entirely disconnected with the causation of the events; and, on the other hand, the events need not be assumed as necessary, in order to become the objects of probable calculations. If they were necessary, in any sense, the calculations could no longer be merely probable; they would, on the contrary, take the precision and certainty of the calculation of eclipses and other phenomena based upon necessary laws.

But these calculations can aim only at *moral* certainty, because they are made according to the generally known and received determinations of will in a triunity with the reason and the sensitivity; but still, a will which is known, also, to have the power to depart at any moment from the line of determination which it has established for itself. Thus the calculations which we make respecting the conduct of one man in given circumstances, based upon his known integrity, and the calculations which we make respecting another, based upon his known dishonesty, may alike disappoint us, through the unexpected, though possible dereliction of the first, and the unexpected, though possible reformation of the latter.

When we reason from moral effects to moral causes, or from moral causes to moral effects; as, for example, in testimony, where we reason from the fact of the testimony to the motive which led to the testimony,—we cannot regard the operation of causes as positive and uniform under the same law of necessity which appertains to physical causes; because, in moral causality, the free will is the efficient and last determiner. It is indeed true, that we reason here with a high degree of probability,—with a probability sufficient to regulate wisely and harmoniously the affairs of society; but we cannot reason respecting human conduct as we reason respecting the phenomena of the physical world, since it is possible for the human will to disappoint calculations based upon the ordinary influence of motives; *e. g.* The motive does not hold the same relation to will which fire holds to a combustible substance. The fire *must* burn; the will *may or may not* determine in view of the motive.

Hence, the reason why in common parlance *probable* evidence has received the name of *moral* evidence; moral evidence being always probable—all probable evidence is called moral.*

Next after *certainty*, we must consider *probability*.

By the *probable*, we mean that which has not attained to certainty, but which, nevertheless, has grounds on which it claims to be believed. We call it *probable* or *provable*, because it both has proof, and is still under conditions of proof, that is, admits of still farther proof.

That which is *certain*, has all the proof of which the case admits. A mathematical proposition is certain on the ground of necessity, and admits of no higher proof than that which really demonstrates its truth. The Divine volitions are certain on the ground of the Divine perfections, and admit of no higher proof than what is found in these perfections. The volitions of a good created being are certain on the ground of the purity of such a being, and admit of no higher proof than what is found in this purity.

But when we come to a *mixed* being, that is, a being of Reason, and of a Sensitivity corrupted totally, or in different degrees, then we have place not for certainty, but for probability. As our knowledge of the future or the past volitions of such a being can only be gathered from something now existent, this knowledge will depend upon our knowledge of the present relative state of his reason and sensitivity. But a perfect knowledge of this state is in no case supposable, so that, although our actual

* Review of Edwards on the Will, pp. 261–269.

knowledge of this being may be such as to afford us proof of what his volitions *may* be, yet, inasmuch as our knowledge of him may be increased indefinitely by close observation and study, so likewise will the proof be increased. According to the definition of probability above given, therefore, our knowledge of the future or past volitions of an imperfect being can only amount to probable knowledge.

The direction of the probabilities will be determined by the preponderance of the good or the bad in the mixed being supposed. But the state of the Reason itself must be considered. If the Reason or Conscience be in a highly developed state, and the convictions of the right consequently clear and strong, there may be probabilities of volitions in opposition to passion, which cannot exist where the Reason is undeveloped, and subject to the errors and prejudices of custom and superstition. The difference is that which is commonly known under the terms "Enlightened and unenlightened conscience."

With a given state of the Reason and the Sensitivity, the direction of the probabilities will depend also very much upon the correlated, or upon the opposing objects and circumstances.*

We have spoken of Probability thus far only in reference to human volition and actions, since here is the great field of probability. It evidently applies to other subjects also: it applies wherever the connection between an antecedent and consequent is *contingent*, or appears to us to be so.

We have pointed out several terms which refer to the nature of the connection between antecedents and conse-

* Review ut supra, pp. 291–3.

quents, viz., *necessary*, *consequent*, *possible*, and *impossible;* and several others, which refer to our knowledge of that connection, viz., *certain*, *probable*, and *presumptive.*

Now these terms answer to each other. A *necessary* connection of antecedents and consequents, or of any two terms, is the ground of absolute *certainty* of knowledge. In the connection of physical antecedents and consequents there is a relative necessity, *i. e.*, this connection is necessary while the system of nature remains unchanged; but as such a change is possible by the Divine Will, the certainty of knowledge here is called *physical*, and not absolute.

An *impossible* connection involves the Idea of necessity. Hence, when a connection is seen to be impossible, our knowledge that it will not take place is absolutely or physically certain, according to the nature of the antecedents and consequents connected.

Answering to a *contingent connection* between antecedent and consequent, we have a *probable knowledge.* We have indeed spoken of a moral certainty in respect to the volitions of pure beings. But the *nature* of the evidence in these cases is not changed. Moral certainty still admits a possibility in the opposing scale; but the grounds of belief are so stable and conclusive as to leave no room for doubt. Generically considered, moral certainty is probable knowledge.

Again, answering to a *possible* connection between antecedents and consequents, our knowledge is *presumptive.* A possible connection is a contingent one, also; it may or it may not be. The difference between this case and the preceding, *i e.*, where a *contingent* connection of antecedents and consequents has a *probable* knowledge answering to it, is as follows: In the preceding there is always a certain amount of proof for or against the connection, with at least a possibility in the opposing scale. Frequently the probabilities on either side are so rife, that a nice judgment is required in determining the preponderance.

But where the connection is said to be merely *possible*, there is no proof for or against, as yet, adduced ; and then, according to the point of view at which we stand in relation to it, we are said to have a *presumptive* knowledge that the connection does or does not exist. As soon as proof is adduced, a probability arises on one side or the other.

But, while there is no *probability*, to which side does the *presumption* belong? This, I have said, depends upon the point of view at which we stand. And this point of view must itself be determined on some fit principle ; for it is, by no means, a matter of indifference. Where a question arises between two parties, it must necessarily be so put as to involve an affirmative and a negative ; and the presumption will then be said to lie in favour of the affirmative or the negative. Now the point of view is determined :

1. By the previous state of the question. If it has by old opinions or established usage been settled in the affirmative or negative, then from this point must it be viewed. Independently of all argument, and of all inherent probability, there is a *presumption in favour* of the old opinion, and the established usage. He who attacks the question is said to *assume the burden of proof;* and, unless he can bring proof to the contrary, the old decision must stand.

2. The point of view is determined by any natural right which may chance to be involved in the question,

such as the right of life, liberty, property, character, and freedom of opinion; *e. g.* A man arraigned as a criminal is *presumed* to be innocent, until he is proved guilty. A man in possession of an estate is *presumed* to be the owner, until his title is invalidated by sufficient proof. Any ancient institution is *presumed* to be well founded, until its principles can be shown to be false and mischievous; or it can be shown, by fraud or violence, to have supplanted a more ancient institution. In the latter case the burden of proof falls upon the more modern, and the presumption lies in favor of the more ancient institution. It happens, sometimes, that those are called *innovators,* who are, in reality, the advocates of what is truly ancient and venerable. If they prove this to be the fact, they, of course, tranfer the burden of proof to where it justly belongs.

Presumptive evidence must be distinguished from *à priori* or *antecedent* probability. This last is strictly *inherent* probability, arising from *à priori* or established principle. Any fact or proposition possesses this kind of probability, when it is a *probable consequence* of such a principle; *e. g.* From the known character of an individual, there is an antecedent probability how he will act under certain circumstances. There may be a moral certainty that he will do right; but the circumstances may be such as not simply to involve a question of rectitude. From the knowledge which we have of the circumstances, in connection with the character of the individual, we judge that an antecedent probability exists as to the manner in which he will act.

There is antecedent probability in favor of a Divine revelation, arising from the character of the Deity and the moral condition of man.

In making experiments in Natural Science, there is

often an antecedent probability of the results arising from known antecedents.

In conclusion, we remark, that the evidence by which we gain *certain* knowledge of the connection of antecedents and consequents, or of any fact or proposition, is in general called *demonstrative evidence.* The terms *demonstrative* and *demonstration* are technically and particularly applied to mathematical reasoning. Moral reasoning may be demonstrative in respect to *moral truth;* but not in respect to *moral action.* The evidence by which we gain *probable* knowledge is called *probable evidence;* the highest degree of probability is called *moral certainty.* And the evidence by which we gain *presumptive* knowledge is called *presumptive evidence.*

We shall next proceed to apply the foregoing principles to the different kinds of evidence contained under the two general divisions of the *à priori* and the *à posteriori.*

SECTION V

TESTIMONY.

THIS is moral evidence, because it depends upon the human will. The highest certainty, therefore, to which testimony can attain is moral certainty.

Testimony, as a species of evidence, must embrace very extensive considerations of human nature, and of the influence of motives. Testimony, in any given case, is a fact which must *à posteriori* be accounted for. It is accounted for by referring it to the motives which led to it. If it can be shown that the truth of the fact testified to, is the morally certain ground of the testimony, then the testimony proves the truth of that fact with a moral certainty. If the truth is the only probable ground, then the testimony proves the probability of the fact to a degree determined by the character of the witness and the circumstances in which he is placed.

But to proceed to a more particular exposition of this subject—

I. *What circumstances determine the truth of testimony with a moral certainty?*

1. The character of the witness: if he have all the qualities of a perfect moral being, then his veracity, under any circumstances, may be deemed morally certain.

Only one degree, at least, below moral certainty is the

veracity of such men as we have already referred to, viz., Paul, Joseph, Daniel, Washington, &c. We can hardly conceive of a trial so severe as to lead such men to sacrifice their integrity.

2. Sufficient opportunities for observing the fact testified to, *i. e.* The fact must have been the direct and unquestionable object of sense or experience: "That which we have heard—which we have seen with our eyes—which we have looked upon (*i. e.* have steadily contemplated) and our hands have handled—declare we unto you."

3. The witness must be a man of sane mind.

The first, however, may be regarded as including the two last. A man of high and perfect moral character will not testify to facts which he has not carefully and fully observed: nor will he testify, if he is not conscious of having been in a proper state of mind at the time they were presented.

II. *What circumstances determine the truth of testimony on grounds of mere probability?*

1. The last particular mentioned under the preceding head is essential to all testimony; and the probability will always be directly in proportion to the first two.

2. The probability established by testimony will vary with the number and character of the motives under which the witness testifies.

First. If the witness has an interest in the facts to which he testifies, arising from pride, ambition, or the gratification of any desire, or the fulfilment of any selfish purpose which he is known to entertain, then will his testimony in proportion be invalidated. Still, however, the known character of the witness must be taken into the account. The same motives relatively to one man will invalidate testimony to a greater degree than relatively to another ; *i. e.* the motive and the character must be taken together, and the probability be accordingly deduced.

Secondly. If the motives be such as on principles of self-gratification would lead the witness to testify contrary to his actual testimony, then is the testimony strong in proportion to the motives ; *e. g.* A man testifying to facts at the expense of reputation—or worldly possessions and honours—or of life.

III. *Testimony in relation to opinion and in relation to fact.*

By opinion we mean a judgment of the mind, respecting a proposition as true or false. Opinion is to be distinguished from absolute knowledge, as implying that the proposition which is its object, is still debatable.

Testimony cannot establish the truth of opinions or judgments. Their truth can be established only on some necessary principle of the Intelligence.

Testimony, as evidence, relates merely to matters of fact. All, therefore, that a witness can testify to, in relation to opinions, is the fact that he or some other person entertains such and such opinions. But the truth or falsity of the opinions must be determined on other grounds, and wholly independently of testimony.

A man may be of the highest integrity, and of sane mind, and may sacrifice reputation and possessions, and life itself, in maintaining his opinions, without affording any evidence of their truth. His testimony only goes to establish the fact that he believes the proposition in question, and that he believes it ardently and firmly.

Divine testimony is adequate to establish a truth as well as a fact, because God is Infinite Reason, and the very substance of truth. We believe, therefore, what God affirms, although we may be incapable of determining the truth, independently, on the principles of our reason.

The testimony of good and wise men is entitled to high consideration. But we do not ultimately and securely settle a point which they profess to believe, until we have ascertained the grounds on which they believe. The same principles of evidence are common to them and to ourselves; if, therefore, they have believed on just principles, we must be capable of perceiving them.

IV. *Truth and Fact.*—By fact, we mean phenomena,—something which we know by observation merely. Facts are of two kinds: 1. Facts of the Senses, or external observation. 2. Facts of the Consciousness, or internal observation.

By truth, we mean that which is arrived at by the pure Reason. We always assume observation as conditional to the exercise of Reason. But while observation supplies facts, Reason supplies the principles under which the facts are to be reduced. Now, whatever the Reason supplies, whether in intuition or in deduction, we call truth. From this comparison of truth and fact, it must still more clearly appear that testimony cannot prove truths or doctrines. Testimony is only an attestation of what has been observed. Truths or doctrines can be proved by reasoning alone.

V. *Historical Evidence.*—The leading feature of this species of evidence, is testimony.

1. Where the historian relates what he has himself seen. This is pure testimony, and must be judged of accordingly.

2. Where the historian relates cotemporaneous events, upon the testimony of others. Here, in addition to what has been laid down under testimony, we must take into account: First. The prejudices and antipathies of

country, party, and sect. Secondly. The philosophical ability of the historian to investigate, compare, and deduce. Thirdly. The time and attention bestowed on the work.

3. Where the historian depends for his information upon the writings of others, and upon national monuments, records, and antiquities. Here the most various and lofty qualifications are requisite. First. All the qualities of a true witness. Secondly. Varied and profound erudition : viz. a knowledge of languages—of science —of arts—of government ;—great skill in antiquarian researches ; and above all, original, all-comprehensive, and penetrative genius, as a philosopher. Thirdly. Adequate materials. A history is entitled to belief in proportion as these particulars appear in its compilation.

VI. *Concurrent Testimony.*—This must be distinguished from *accumulated testimony*, which is a mere multiplication of witnesses. In concurrent testimony, on the contrary, although the evidence be stronger, according to the number of the witnesses, yet the evidence itself does not lie in the qualifications of the witnesses ; but only in *their concurrence.*

Their concurrence, on supposition, cannot be accounted for, without granting the fact testified to ; *i. e.* If the fact did occur, then the concurrence was possible ; if the fact did not occur, then the concurrence was not probable, or possible, as the case may be.

In the *first place.* It is plain that this evidence will be strong, in proportion to the *improbability of previous concert.* If previous concert can be shown to be impossible, then the evidence occupies one of its highest grounds.

But, in the *second place,* although the probability, or

even possibility, of previous concert may be disproved, it will still remain to be shown that the concurrence can be accounted for only by the admission of the fact in question.

Now, if the concurrence can be accounted for in any other way, it must be by showing, in the case of each witness, separately, that there were motives which were adequate to lead to the given testimony, without supposing the reality of the fact testified to. This would of course invalidate the concurrence. If the existence of such motives in the case of each witness should be shown to have existed, there would of course be an utter annihilation of the evidence: or, if the above be shown in the cases of only a part of the witnesses, it must tend to destroy the evidence. In all these cases the concurrence turns out a singular fortuity. Now, if in any given concurrence no such invalidating or destructive circumstances can be detected, then it must remain as valid evidence.

VII. *Concurrent Testimony in relation to fact and opinion.*—The principles above stated refer to concurrent testimony, as evidence of facts merely.

Concurrent testimony, in relation to opinion, is mere concurrence of opinion. Where this concurrence exists without previous concert, it affords evidence of sincerity. Where an opinion is thus concurred in by men of high integrity and wisdom, it is entitled to great consideration; but ultimately it must rest upon *principles*, as forming its only decisive evidence. This has been above shown in discussing opinion in its relation to simple testimony.

SECTION VI.

CIRCUMSTANTIAL EVIDENCE.

By *circumstances*, we mean, as the etymology denotes, whatever stands around a principal.

Thus the circumstances of an individual comprise all the particulars which make up his external condition. Thus the circumstances of an event comprise all the particulars of time, place, action, modes, degrees, causes, and effects; *i. e.* every thing attending upon it—accessory to it—or every thing making up a description of it.

Now, circumstantial evidence in general takes place where we adduce the circumstances which belong to a principal, to prove the existence of that principal. But what is the connection between circumstances and a principal which enables us to reason from the one to the other? It must be something more than mere juxtaposition. An arbitrary and accidental connection cannot be the foundation of reasoning. The connection then must be that of necessary, or at least probable consequent to a stated antecedent, or the connection of phenomenon with cause and law: *i. e.* The principal being necessary to account for the existence of circumstances, its existence is *à posteriori* proved from the circumstances.

In calling this circumstantial evidence, however, we only give another name to the ordinary *à posteriori* reasoning.

Circumstantial evidence, as a really distinct kind of evidence, is constituted by a *concurrence* of circumstances.

The circumstantial evidence above described is a mere accumulation of *à posteriori* proof,—a bringing together of many effects, or consequents, to prove a common cause, or antecedent. But the *concurrence* of circumstances or facts is, in itself, a new and peculiar fact, independently of the nature of the facts taken separately. Concurrent testimony and concurrent circumstances are analogous. In both kinds, the proof lies in the necessity of accounting for the concurrence. It is a phenomenon,—it must have a cause.

That which as condition or cause accounts for the concurrence is proved by it, either with certainty, or with more or less probability, as the case may be.

Circumstantial evidence possesses the highest degree of *certainty* when there is absolutely no other way of accounting for the circumstances, except by the admission of the principal in question.

It possesses the highest degree of *probability* when although it be possible to conceive other ways of accounting for the concurrence than the one adopted, still every one of these is far-fetched, altogether hypothetical, and having no known connection with any existent fact.

Where there are several ways of accounting for the concurrence, and all have claims to probability, we must of course weigh the opposite probabilities, and determine accordingly.

Any given concurrence of facts cannot be set aside, as of no weight, except by accounting for each fact separately, in its time, place, and relations, so as to make the concurrence appear altogether fortuitous.

Reasoning from facts, merely, and reasoning from a

concurrence of facts, since they may both appear in the same case, and in relation to the same facts, are apt to be confounded. It need hardly be remarked that it is of the utmost importance to discriminate between them, and to present them each on its own independent basis.

The evidence admitted in a court of justice to prove the guilt of a prisoner, must be positive, or at least morally certain. Circumstantial evidence, therefore, regarded either as a collection of facts, or as a concurrence of facts, can be admitted as decisive, only where the guilt of the prisoner can be taken as the only way of accounting for the facts, or the concurrence of facts: *i. e.* It is not enough that it is the *most* probable way of accounting for them,—it must be the *only* probable way.

Where the rights of two parties are opposed, so that a determination necessarily involves loss to one or the other, as in a question respecting the title of an estate, the determination must, of course, be made according to the result of a comparison of probabilities, if no positive evidence can be obtained.

In concurrent testimony, we have a number of witnesses coming together, without previous concert, and supporting each other's evidence. In concurrent circumstances, we have a number of circumstances coming together without any previous contrivance, and supporting each other in relation to a principal.

If the testimony be true, then this concurrence is what we might have expected. If this principal exist, then the concurrence of circumstances is what we might have expected.

In addition to this, we have assumed that unless the concurrence of facts can be proved to be fortuitous, by showing how each fact came to happen in that precise time, place, and relation, without requiring any connection between the several facts; and that unless the concurrent testimony be accounted for in the motives of each witness separately, so as not to require the truth of their common statement; and, we may add, unless it can be shown to be fortuitous, as in the case of concurrent circumstances, we are compelled to admit *that* antecedent or cause which most clearly accounts for the concurrence. But there is an objection made to this which requires attention, and may compel us to prove our assumption.

It is as follows:

"Any given phenomena brought into juxtaposition must of necessity assume some order of arrangement. But against any particular order there are chances indefinitely great in number; and as the phenomena must come into some order, it is plain they may come into one order as well as into another; and hence they may as well come into that regular and connected order which we call concurrence, as into one of utter confusion and want of connection." Says the objector, therefore, "What right have you to assume this concurrence as proof of the principal to which the facts seem to relate? I have an equal right to assume the fortuity of the concurrence."

We have here, then, two assumptions directly opposed; but one or the other must fall; both cannot be true. Which shall stand? The objector may say, "Please support your assumption." We may rejoin, Please to support yours. Now, we may both make the attempt, and may both fail in positively settling the question. After all our discussions, there may appear something plausible on both sides. In this case, he who can adduce the greatest number of probabilities for his assumption, must win the argument. In supporting our assumption, we urge the fact, that at least in the great majority of cases where there is concurrence, there is some cause directly and clearly producing it; *e. g.* Of all the books ever made, we do not find that any were made by a fortuitous concurrence of the letters; of all the instruments and machines that have ever been constructed, we do not find any that were constructed by the fortuitous occurrence of the materials; and as to the phenomena of nature, we find, as our knowledge of natural philosophy and chemistry is extended, that laws are brought to light which explain them in all their multifariousness, and leave us little or no place of appealing to fortuitous combination? As, then, we produce the greater number of instances of this kind, we claim the greater number of probabilities for our assumption. Indeed, tne candid objector must be constrained to admit that he finds it very difficult to bring a single instance where fortuitous combination explains concurrence and regularity.

This reasoning goes to show that a concurrence must always have the balance of probabilities in its favor, as connected with some principal which unites the facts in the concurrence in opposition to the assumption of a fortuitous concurrence.

But here another question may arise: Whether reasoning from concurrence can ever possess the highest degree of certainty of any kind, as we have appeared in the preceding pages to take for granted, where we say, "this evidence possesses the highest degree of certainty when there is absolutely no other way of accounting for the concurrence except by the admission of the principal in question," inasmuch as in every case there is a possibility of fortuitous concurrence? This is a serious question, and involves the possibility, although not the probability, of every concurrence whatever,—even the creation of the world being fortuitous. We may indeed comfort ourselves with the overwhelming probability that the world is the work of design; but still are we prepared to grant the possibility, however remote, of a fortuitous creation?

We are not prepared to grant this. We think we can prove the impossibility of fortuitous concurrence, as well as explain those cases which appear to be such.

In the *first place*, the axioms "Every phenomenon must have a cause," and "Every phenomenon must have a law," cannot be set aside. These are necessary principles of the reason. But concurrence is a phenomenon, and, therefore, must have a cause and a law. Now if by fortuity we mean to negate cause and law, then fortuity is impossible in concurrence: and thus the question is settled at once. In the *second place*, those concurrences which appear fortuitous are not really so; *e. g.* a cast of dice: The dice have a certain position before they are cast; a certain degree of projectile force is given them, and the result is a certain concurrence of sides. Now in this case there are causes definite and regular; but because we are unable to determine them with precision, we call the result fortuitous. All cases of apparent fortuity may be resolved in the same way. There are causes, and they work regularly according to their nature, but we cannot penetrate their action. In any case of concurrence, therefore, the question is not, as we have above allowed, out of courtesy, to the objector, between the assumption of cause and no cause; but whether a certain antecedent accounts for the concurrence, or whether it is to be accounted for by some other.

Now, from our knowledge of antecedents and concurrences, there are some concurrences which we do generally attribute to certain antecedents, because generally connected with them ; *e. g.* The print of a man's foot in the sand. This we should naturally attribute to the pressure of an actual foot ; but still, it is possible that it might have been produced by the action of the waves. If produced by the action of the waves, it has its definite cause, and is not fortuitous ; but it has in this case an *unusual* antecedent. On an inhabited coast, we should affirm at once that the probabilities greatly preponderate in favor of a man's foot as the cause ; but a man in the situation of Robinson Crusoe, finding such a print upon the sea-shore, might be in doubt.

Now the only case where concurrence would afford the highest certainty, is, as we have above affirmed, one in which there is but one way of accounting for the fact—not in opposition to fortuity, but in negation of the possibility of other causes.

SECTION VII.

ARGUMENT FROM PROGRESSIVE APPROACH.

THIS belongs to the *à posteriori* form of proof, because we ascend from facts to a law. If, however, the facts of the progressive approach, introduced on the principle of causality, are the only elements of the proof, then we have an ordinary case of induction ; *e. g.* We put a ball in motion on a rough surface, and its motion soon ceases ; we put it in motion on a smoother surface, and the motion is proportionally prolonged ; and we find generally, that the time of the motion is inversely as the resistance. Hence we infer that if all resistance were removed, there would be no change in the motion ; *i. e.* From the uniformity of a given number of facts, we infer an universal uniformity of facts.

But are we certain, on the mere induction, that we may not in actual experiment arrive at a point where the phenomena shall be reversed? where the resistance, after having been reduced to a degree lower than has ever yet been attained, shall suddenly be greatly augmented? Recollect we are merely deducing from known facts ; and the uniformity of nature on which we base our conclusion respecting the unknown, is a uniformity which relates to law in general, and not merely to the particular law which we assume. There may, therefore, be a change in the facts in the extended experiment, which shall require them all to be reduced under another law in view of higher points of uniformity. The suns which we before deemed uniform, as fixed centres, may be found uniform as revolving about some higher and common centre.

The argument from progressive approach, therefore, would not in itself absolutely establish the *vis inertiæ* of bodies; although it might afford a high degree of probability.*

An argument has been drawn in favor of Christianity, from the fact that in proportion as nations are enlightened, their religious views approximate towards Christianity. The argument in this case differs widely from the preceding, in respect to its subject, and is conclusive. The cause or principle here is the human Reason. Now, we conceive of this as uniform and continuous in its action; *i. e.* as having fixed laws of action, and as inherently active. Let it go into action, therefore, and it will act in the direction of these laws, and continue to act, unless counteracting and modifying causes are brought in. Hence, as the Reason is the faculty of perceiving truth, if we remove all obstructions, and give it its full play and development, its perceptions must be taken as truth. That religion, therefore, which the Reason adopts, when thus developed and unobstructed, must be the true religion. And so also we must conclude that those perceptions which follow the progressive development of Reason, must be perceptions approximating proportionally towards truth. Now, if it can be shown from the history of human opinions—the history of philosophy, that these opinions have approximated regularly towards Christianity with the progressive development of the Reason, then we

* Supra, p. 231.

have in this progressive approach the highest internal evidence of the truth of Christianity. And the evidence in this case is not a mere induction of facts, whose uniformity enables us, on probable grounds, to proclaim a general fact; but that of a principle regularly developing itself, and hastening on to its certain issue. In this argument for Christianity, we first lay down the necessary criterion of a true religion, viz. its correspondence with the Reason truly and fully developed; and, as resulting from this, the progressive concentration of the human mind upon certain opinions, in proportion to its development. This forms our major premiss. Then, by historical evidence, and the evidence derived from philosophical criticism, we establish the fact that Christianity is the point upon which the human mind, in its progressive development, thus concentrates. This forms our minor premiss. The conclusion is then inevitable.

SECTION VIII.

PROVING BY EXAMPLE.

The point to be proved is either a principle or a particular fact. If a principle, then the facts which go to establish it, are inducted, and this is nothing more than induction, employed in the order of proof.

If a particular fact, then the establishment of a principle, although not appearing in the statement, really intervenes in the mental process, and forms the ground of the conclusion, in reference to the particular fact. In both cases, the establishment of the general principle is the cardinal part of the proof. It may therefore be termed more appropriately,—proving by Induction. This differs from Inductive Investigation only in the order. In Inductive Investigation, we begin with the facts, and advance to the principle. In Proof by Induction, we first lay down the principle, or a fact which reposes upon and presumes the principle, and then we induct the facts, or examples, to prove it.

It is necessary, however, to recall in this connection an important distinction, which applies both to inductive investigation and to inductive proof. In Induction, we do not bring together facts promiscuously. We make a selection—we bring together only such facts as have some connection with each other. They are alike either in form, time, and place, or in their relations. But, why do we bring only such facts together as are alike? I will answer, by asking another question. Why do we bring facts together at all? Obviously, to understand or to comprehend them.

But, if we wish merely to understand them by generalizing them under a common name, then we must, of necessity, observe likeness, and, of course, difference. And, if we wish to comprehend them by reducing them under a law, then also must we observe likeness and difference, because our idea of a law, or cause, comprehends uniformity,—and the uniformity of the effects must be regarded as an exponent of the law.

When, therefore, we are seeking for a law by Induction, in the order of investigation, or when we are proving by induction a law already laid down, we follow those connections of the facts which presume a law.

Now, in inductive investigation, we do not always succeed in finding the law. We are often compelled, at least for a time, to stop short with a mere generalization under a common name, and the announcement of a theory. The generalization and the theory aid our farther investigations, and may enable us, eventually, to find the law; but in them we have not arrived at certainty.

So also in the order of proof. The point to be proved may not be a law, at the conception of which we may not yet have arrived, but merely a general uniformity, or a theory. The facts which we bring together are of course limited, since induction, from its very nature, is never complete. We are compelled, therefore, to infer the universal from the limited. This is illogical. The inference must therefore be contingent. It may or may not be. We apply, next, to the inference, the laws of probability.

What reason have we, in any given case, to infer an

universal uniformity from a limited observation,—*e. g.* from the fact that the sun has risen, at regular intervals, for five thousand years, what reason have we to infer that he will always rise at the same intervals, supposing, of course, that we have as yet ascertained no law of the planetary movements? It is because we feel assured that the uniformity of the facts is the exponent of some law, although the law be concealed; and upon the authority of law, uniform and continuous, do we infer the universal from the limited. The particular and limited facts are a condition on which a law is conceived of, and then the inference is imbued with the whole energy, and stretched to the whole compass of law. But, if the inference thus rests upon the conception of some law, why is it not always characterized by certainty?

When the conception is not merely of *some* law, but arrives at a *particular* and *certain* law, then the inference is certain,—*e. g.* when the law of the planetary movements is ascertained, then we are physically certain that the sun will continue to rise at the same intervals. But, until we have ascertained the particular law, although we know from the uniformity there must be a law, and although we may form a shrewd theory, we cannot be certain but that the uniformity observed is only a part of some other and higher uniformity, where the law really resides, and that this higher uniformity, in its wider cycle, presents the particular uniformity which we have observed as only one of a long succession where the facts are uniform under one characteristic for a certain period, and then change and become uniform under another characteristic, and so on, throughout the whole succession; all the different uniformities being held together by the law which penetrates and concentrates all.—*e. g.* Let an Intelligence, whose existence numbers only a few days, like the butterfly of the opening summer, have the term of his being in those beautiful months: from the regular succession of sunshine and soft showers which he observes, he concludes there must be some law; and taking the observed uniformity as the exponent of that law, he concludes that the whole succession of climate is made up of sunshine and soft showers. While as yet he knows no particular and certain law of the planetary movements, he knows not that the uniformity which he observes is only one of a series of uniformities, under different characteristics, making up the cycle of the seasons: but let him ascertain the law, and then he at once passes beyond the narrow sphere of his inductions, and comprehends the whole succession.

So also, had we not ascertained the law of the planetary movements, our own observation, as well as the observation of five thousand years, could not enable us certainly to conclude respecting the future movements, inasmuch as the whole five thousand years might be only one of a succession of uniformities, under different characteristics, and attached to a higher system.

You now clearly perceive the distinction at which we aim. The distinction between reasoning upon the basis of a law, or upon the basis of a mere uniformity.

In the first, we infer, or we prove, with certainty. In the second, our basis is also some law, but a law unknown, and only theorised, and therefore our conclusions are only probable.

This is a general statement. There are apparent exceptions; where a limited observation of uniformity seems to enable us to conclude with certainty to the future and universal uniformity. Indeed, there are cases where, upon a single observation, we thus conclude: *e. g.* the fusibility of a substance; the combination of substances by elective affinity.

Upon such cases we remark:

1. The observation, although limited in the particular case, is supported by more extended observations in similar or analogous cases.

2. The cases are of such a character that all the possible circumstances and relations that can be of any weight, are embraced in the observation, though limited both as to time and space.

3. The cases in which a succession of uniformities is conceivable, and in which therefore certainty is attainable only by the discovery of a law, are cases where we take into consideration not the specific natures or powers, and susceptibilities of substances, but general and extended relations in time and space; whereas, in these other cases, the specific natures or powers, and susceptibilities of substances, are what we particularly take into consideration. Take the elective affinity of two substances, and apply to it these principles as an illustration. 1. This is supported by observations in numerous analogous cases. 2. All the circumstances of the case, of any weight, are embraced in our observation. No change of time or place can add to or take from the completeness. 3. We are considering only the specific natures of these substances, in no general relation, but simply in relation to each other.

SECTION IX.

REASONING FROM EXPERIENCE.

I. *From the present to the past.*—This, in the general statement, is called *à posteriori*. We wish to ascertain the past. We take the facts of the present, and, in accounting for them, call up the past. This presumes that the past is the cause of the present. Regarded, however, more closely, this form of proof presents itself as follows:

1. The facts of the present are accounted for by referring them to causes—causes which are also present, and now acting. But, causes are inherently energetic, and are uniform; hence, since they existed in the past, they must have produced effects like those which we now witness. We thus draw the facts of the past from the facts of the present, not by assigning the former as the causes of the latter, but by referring both to common causes, and then analogically concluding the past from the present.

Thus we may prove the physical condition of the ancient world; and, taking human nature as a cause, we may prove its moral condition.

2. The distinction between moral and physical causes, and between moral and physical certainty, must be borne in mind. The former brings in the consideration of free will, in connection with a vast variety of moral character,

and therefore gives birth to a vast variety of results, while the latter is fixed and precise.

The physical condition of the ancient world, it is not difficult to determine on well known and uniform general principles. But, in order to determine the moral condition with any precision, we need data from history. There is indeed a reciprocal action between history and general moral principles, in reasoning: the latter often serving to determine points of history otherwise doubtful; the former supplying, leading, and determining facts to the latter.

3. Laws have often a gradual, instead of an immediate development. Thus a law, in order to complete its cycle, may require ages. This appears in Geology and Astronomy, and in Politics and Philosophy.

Now, if we can ascertain that given and present facts are a part of such a development, gradual and progressive, then we have at once a chain by which we can *à posteriori* ascend to the past as well as *à priori* descend to the future.

II. *From the present to the future.*—Our present experience is connected with causes. If these causes are known, on the uniformity of law, we predict the future.

The distinction between moral and physical causes, and between moral and physical certainty above referred to, is of equal importance here. On laws gradually developing, no additional remarks are necessary.

The above proceeds on the supposition that we have ascertained Laws. In many instances, however, we may proceed merely on an uniformity more or less extensive. The distinction given under *Reasoning from Example* will apply here also, viz. That when we reason upon the basis of mere uniformity, generally, our conclusions are only probable: but when we reason upon the basis of a law clearly ascertained, our conclusions are certain, morally or physically, as the case may be.

Those instances where we reason to a past and a future, uniformity upon a single experiment, or a very limited experience,—*e. g.* the fusibility of a substance—have already been considered.

SECTION X.

REASONING FROM RESEMBLANCE AND ANALOGY.

RESEMBLANCE is defined as agreement in certain points, and is thus distinguished from identity, which is universal agreement, and excludes difference. Other things being equal, the more numerous the points of agreement, the closer the resemblance. Some points, however, are more important than others. Agreement in a few important points constitutes a closer likeness than agreement in a multitude of unimportant or trifling points.

Resemblance is of two general kinds: First, Resemblance in properties. Secondly, Resemblance in relations.

Now, in reasoning from resemblance, we must of course reason either from the resemblance of properties or of relations. The *first* is called reasoning from direct or simple resemblance. The *second*, reasoning from analogy.

In reasoning from resemblance, there are two terms. In reasoning from analogy, there are three or four terms, and two relations.

I. *Direct Resemblance.*—The object in this case is to determine particulars of resemblance unknown to exist, from known particulars; *i. e.* From known corresponding properties, to reason to others which are unknown. One property in a subject is seen to involve another, either on the ground of uniform sequence or of law. Hence we infer the agreement of two terms in properties, which are involved in those which are known to exist. The reasoning is *à priori*, when the unknown property holds to the known, the relation of consequent to antecedent; and, *vice versa*, the reasoning is *à posteriori*.

The probability of the reasoning obviously must be determined by the nature of the connection between the known and unknown; if it be a connection of mere stated uniformity, the reasoning is generally only probable; if it be a connection of law, the reasoning is certain. Cæsar and Buonaparte resemble each other in certain properties —ambition, &c. But ambition can be shown to involve the love of supreme power, and the love of supreme power involves attempts to gain the supremacy, if the time and opportunity be auspicious: hence, Cæsar and Buonaparte may have the consequential points of resemblance, inasmuch as they have the quality which involves them. *This is à priori;* and the conclusion morally certain.

In arguing that the planets are inhabited, from their resemblance to this world, we proceed *à posteriori*. From like provisions for social existence, we infer social existence. We argue here to the motive or design. This likewise is morally certain.

II. *Indirect Resemblance or Analogy.*

1. Where there are two terms related to a common third, we may call the two relations a common relation, inasmuch as the common third is a cause of both, or at least a uniform antecedent of both. In this case, when the analogy is granted, and we reason from particulars of one relation, or of one member of the common relation to particulars of the other, our reasoning is probable or certain; *In the first place*, according to the nature of the connection between the common third and the two related terms: if it be only a connection of uniform

sequents, the reasoning is generally only probable; if of Law, the reasoning is certain.

The reasoning is probable or certain in the *second place*, according to the nature of the particulars from which we reason: if they are particulars necessarily comprehended in the third term, the reasoning is certain: if they be merely circumstantial, the reasoning will be probable, according to the degree of uniformity. When the third term is merely a uniform antecedent, and the particulars of the relation likewise only circumstantial, with more or less of uniformity, we shall have the case of a probability of a probability.

When the analogy is to be proved from the resembling particulars, we have substantially a case of simple *à posteriori* reasoning. Each set of particulars is shown to demand the common third as an antecedent. The principles, therefore, which apply to *à posteriori* reasoning in general will apply to this case.

2. Where there are four terms and two distinct, but resembling relations.

What constitutes the analogy? The resembling relations? But this resemblance may be accidental. It must be at least a uniform resemblance, therefore, that constitutes the analogy. The particulars in one relation must uniformly resemble the particulars in the other relation. But this uniformity is an exponent of some law. Whatever conclusion is drawn, therefore, must rest upon this law as certainly ascertained, or as existing only in theory, and accordingly will be a conclusion certain or probable.

Now, this law must comprehend both relations, because it explains the uniformity of the resemblance between the two relations. But are not these relations themselves relations of antecedent and consequent, as respects the two terms respectively, comprehended by some higher and common term? It is even so. The two terms on either side of the analogy are related as antecedent and consequent; and then their relations exhibit resemblances which must be referred to a higher law comprehending and penetrating both; *e. g.* The seed of a plant, and the egg of a fowl. The plant is in some sense the cause of the seed—and the fowl in some sense the cause of the egg. The two terms on either side have very slight direct resemblances. And the two relations do not resemble each other merely in being relations of cause and effect, for they resemble a multitude of relations in the same way. But the point to be nicely and strictly observed is, that these two relations have particulars of resemblance beyond their general agreement with each other, and with all other relations of cause and effect. What is this agreement? It is this. The egg and the seed, besides being effects the one of the fowl, the other of the plant, contain alike the *principle of generative life.* Now, when we reason from one to the other, we reason on the basis of this common principle. Whatever particulars are necessarily comprehended in the action of this principle, and developed as such on one side of the analogy, may be concluded as likewise existing on the other side.

If the principle be only in theory, then the reasoning cannot advance beyond probability. If the particulars have only a uniform, and not a necessary connection, to our perception, with the principle, the reasoning here likewise is only probable. If both the preceding concur in a given case, we have only a probability of a probability.

Not unfrequently in this kind of analogy the great

object of the reasoning is to establish the analogy itself; *i e.*, Four terms being given, and two terms respectively being related each to each, constituting two relations, the object of the reasoning is to bring these relations under a common principle. This may be done *à priori*, by showing that a principle exists which necessarily or probably comprehends these relations; or, *à posteriori*, by showing that there are particulars of resemblance in these relations which probably or certainly require the principle to account for them.

This analogy thus established, as we have before shown, becomes a general principle to these relations and forms the basis of deductions. We have an illustration of this in an argument adduced by phrenologists.

There is an obvious connection between the governing and specific propensities of animals and their physical structure: thus carnivorous animals may be distinguished from graminivorous—the lion from the ox.

There is a connection likewise between the intellect of man and his physical structure. His senses and his brain are unquestionably connected with the development of his intellect.

Now the object of the reasoning is to establish an analogy; *i. e.*, That the relations on either side are comprehended by the same principle or law. This, if established at all, must be established either *à priori* or *à posteriori*. If *à priori*, then we must find some principle or law actually existing which comprehends these relations necessarily, or at least probably. Is there any such principle? They are bound to show it. I cannot perceive any. If *à posteriori*, then we must find such particulars of resemblance in the two relations as demand necessarily, or at least probably, a common principle to account for them. Are there such particulars of resemblance? Let us see. In the first relation; *i. e.*, between the animal propensities and physical structure, we perceive that the propensities have reference to ends which can be accomplished only by a physical structure directly adapted to them. The thirst for blood demands the teeth and paws of the lion and tiger; palpably the nature cannot be complete without these instruments. But are there any like particulars in the relation between the intellect of man and his senses, brain and skull, &c.? The senses and brain are indeed conditional to the exercise of thought; but are they the *instruments* of thought? Can it be shown that the senses and brain are to the intellect, what the teeth and paws are to the propensity for prey? Can it be shown from any particulars in this relation, that any power of the mind requires a portion of the brain as its instrument for accomplishing its end, just as the beast palpably requires the strong jaws with all their furniture, and the muscular legs and paws!

The relation between the intellect and the brain and senses, contains no such particulars as the relation between the animal propensities and the instruments which are necessary to accomplish their ends. Hence we cannot infer that they come under the same law—hence we cannot reason from one to the other.

A beautiful and familiar analogy, and one which aptly illustrates analogy consisting of four terms, is that between the human being at death and insect metamorphoses. Here are the two relations, of the human being to death, and of the caterpillar to its chrysalis. In the latter case we see the whole process, a dissolution of the caterpillar, and the infolded germ of a higher being reposing for a time within the chrysalis and there preparing for its new form of life, and, when the hour arrives, bursting from its shell a winged and gorgeous *psyche*, dwelling in the sunbeams and feeding upon the aroma of flowers. In like manner the human being lies down to die; but in this last case we do not see the whole process,—we cannot by the microscope discover the wings of the immortal form infolded in the "mortal coil;" nor do we see the struggling *psyche* after it has burst its shell. The analogy, therefore, does not present us many resembling circumstances in the two relations compared. But, nevertheless, there are some points very striking. The death of the caterpillar is not the extinction of the organific Life within—*that* survives. And yet he who first witnessed this metamorphosis, when he saw the worm die, and the chrysalis formed, must have concluded that Nature in her sportive and beautiful fancy had only given the frail and insignificant creature a golden tomb. But when he looked again, he saw a bright and spirit-like creature struggling into a nobler life. We see thus, in Nature, an *apparent death* only the *precursor of another and a higher form of life.* Now take the human being, with all his sublime capacities—capacities admitting of indefinite improvement—and with his actual conceptions of, and longings after immortality, and does it not seem *à priori*, a fit and reasonable thing that he should live again when he appears to die? And if any should object to the conclusion, that all the circumstances of dissolution ought to lead to a contrary induction, then we may reason from the analogy of the butterfly, that in Nature an apparent death is but the process through which a new and more perfect form of life is produced.

The use of the analogy here is not to prove the doctrine of immortality, but to answer an objection to it.

The principle which comprehends both relations is that of LIFE, not as the product of organization, but as itself the organific power. To this we may add the fitness and harmony of the Divine design.

The above exposition of reasoning from Resemblance and Analogy, suggests the following rules for conducting this reasoning:

First. Be careful to distinguish between direct resemblance and the resemblance of relations, and between the analogy of three and that of four terms.

Secondly. Distinguish between important and unimportant resemblances. Those are unimportant which are merely accidental. Every degree of uniformity claims a corresponding degree of attention, because uniformity is an exponent of law. Those resemblances which stand directly and unquestionably connected with law, are the most important.

Thirdly. Another rule commonly given is, not to carry out our comparison of the terms or relations to too many resemblances.

The resemblances evidently cannot be too numerous if they all be important. This rule contemplates substantially the same point as the preceding. A comparison is always carried out too far when it is carried out to unimportant points of resemblance.

SECTION XI.

DEMONSTRATIVE PROOF.

In noticing the application of the *Deductive Formula,** I drew illustrations from Geometry. Geometry then is Deduction. But it is Demonstrative Proof also. The principles are the same—the process of reasoning the same. The only distinction lies in the order of proof and the order of investigation already noticed.† He who first constructed Geometry proceeded of necessity according to the latter order. Now, that it is constructed, the learner proceeds according to the former.

Indeed, where we lay down a proposition, and then give the demonstration, we evidently only announce beforehand the conclusion at which we are to arrive ; and this we are enabled to do, because in a previous investigation, this proposition was found to be the conclusion of the very *chain of premises,* or the *sorites,* which we now call *the demonstration.*

Demonstrative proof applies to all subjects where our deductions can be made from absolute principles.

* Supra, p. 370. † Supra, p. 403.

SECTION XII.

CALCULATION OF PROBABILITIES AND CHANCES

THE calculation of probabilities, is generally called the calculation of chances, but improperly. Let us try to distinguish them. I have already defined *the probable* as implying, both, that a certain amount of proof has already been obtained for a given proposition, and that still more is required for complete certainty. The *possible,* in distinction from this, exists where no proof has actually been obtained, but where the proposition is of such a nature as to *admit of proof.**

Now, a proposition, while in the state of progressive proof, shows probabilities on either hand. It is here that a calculation is required, viz. : a calculation of the opposing probabilities, so as to determine the ratio of probability for the proposition in question.

Now, on the other hand, the calculation of chances would be the calculation of *possibilities,* or rather of *presumptions* founded upon possibility. We have shown above,† that where a presumption is said to lie in favor of any proposition, there is always some principle which, in reality, determines it. Some natural right claims to be respected until positive reasons be given why it should be set aside ; or the sanctions of time and usage surround

* Supra, Section IV. † Ibid.

the disputed point, and claim to hold it, until a higher authority be adduced. Now, here is something of the nature of probability. The fact that I am in possession of an estate, is proof that I am the owner, until my right is invalidated : and the fact of the existence of any institution, is proof in its favor, until it be proved to have had its origin in fraud or violence. Presumption may therefore be called the *lowest* degree of probability, as moral certainty is sometimes called the *highest* degree.

A calculation of pure possibilities, or chances, is impracticable, because there are no data. In pure possibilities, all the terms are equally improbable, or without proof, and hence there is no calculation by which one result may be shown to be more likely than another. For example, in the cast of a die there are six possibilities, and yet any one side is improbable, for no reason can be assigned why it, in particular, should come up : there indeed is a reason lying in the position of the die,—the manner in which it is thrown—giving it just such a direction, and such a degree of force ; but it is unascertainable. It may indeed be said that the probability in favor of a particular side is one-sixth, because there are six sides to the die ; but this is not true, since it is possible that the same side might come up successively many times.

What is called the *calculation of chances*, therefore, is really the *calculation of probabilities*, either as probabilities simply, or under that form which we have termed *presumptions*. There are always data—something given upon which we may base our calculations. This is amply illustrated in insurance upon life and property. The term of human life, under different climates, in different employments, and, taking as a point of departure, different ages, has been made the subject of very extensive observations, by which data have been accumulated sufficient to enable us to calculate the probable number of years still remaining to any individual, so as to affix to it a definite commerçial value. The rates of insurance on houses and ships are determined upon data acquired in the same way. Here there is no chance or mere possibility, but tangible proof. It is true, indeed, that the results calculated, may, in particular instances, fail of being attained ; but this obviously arises from the fact, that our data are necessarily limited, embracing only the more general and striking circumstances of the risks of human life, by disease and accident, and of houses and ships, by fire and tempests. We have not, in respect to these, determined any absolute law, nor even any stated and fixed sequences, for then we should have certainty ; we have only arrived at certain aggregate sequences and a complexity of influences and laws, where we are liable to the introduction of some new influence or law which may change the whole state of things. And this is the reason why the process is called a calculation of chances, since men are accustomed, in common parlance, to call that chance which happens unexpectedly ; and we are here calculating particular results in opposition to possible fortuities. Or, perhaps, a juster representation is, that *presuming* an end, we calculate the *risks*—in other words, the probabilities, that it will not take place.

Indeed, there are just two orders in which the proof may proceed : First. We may consider what antecedents may exist in relation to a particular consequent, and which of them is *most likely* to produce it. Secondly. The consequent may be one in whose favor the presumption lies, so that the burden of proof rests with him who would dispute it. In this case, probabilities are to be arrayed against the consequent.

Under the first order there are obviously three possible cases:

1. The several possible antecedents may not differ as to the probability of their existence, but they may differ as to the probability with which each one claims to be the actual antecedent. In this case, the ratio to be determined respects the immediate connection of antecedent and consequent.

2. The antecedents may not differ as to the probability of their actual antecedence, but, as to the probability of their existence. Here the ratio to be determined respects the antecedents themselves, and not their connection with the consequent.

3. The antecedents may differ in both respects. In this case, the ratio of the probabilities will be as the product of the probabilities of the existence, and of the actual antecedence of the one, to the products of the same probabilities of the other; *i. e.* the ratio of a probability of a probability to a probability of a probability : *e. g.* suppose the probabilities of existence be as 5 : 6, and the probabilities of actual antecedence as 3 : 4, then the resultant probability will be as 5 : 8.

Under the second order, the same cases must occur. This is the order of proof in insurances. The presumption is always in favor of life and property; for the propagation and sustentation of human beings, and the accumulation and preservation of property, is the fixed and predominant order of things. He who insures them, can lose only by their being lost. He therefore, under the given circumstances, must calculate the probabilities, that antecedents exist which may occasion this loss; and if this be granted, or rendered probable, then he must calculate the ratio of the probabilities of the several antecedents.

There are cases which appear at first entirely fortuitous, but which afterwards are invested with probability, through data acquired by sheer empiricism : *e. g.* nothing appears more fortuitous than the casting of a particular side of a die ; and yet, by casting the die a great many times, it has been found that a particular side returns with a considerable degree of exactness, according to a certain ratio.

We have not attempted, in this place, any thing like a full explanation of the calculation of probabilities ; for this would lead us into the domain of Mathematics. We have only aimed to state the leading principles as they stand connected with the Doctrine of Evidence.

THE END.

FIRST LESSONS IN ENGLISH COMPOSITION.

BY G. P. QUACKENBOS, A. M.

12mo. Price 45 Cents

These "First Lessons" are intended for beginners in Grammar and Composition, and should be placed in their hands at whatever age it may be deemed best for them to commence these branches—say from nine to twelve years. In the first fifty pages, by means of lessons on the inductive system, and copious exercises under each, the pupil is made familiar with the nature and *use* of the different parts of speech, so as to be able to recognize them at once. He is then led to consider the different kinds of clauses and sentences, and is thus prepared for Punctuation, on which subject he is furnished with well considered rules, arranged on a new and simple plan. Directions for the use of capital letters follow. Next come rules, explanations and examples, for the purpose of enabling the pupil to form and spell correctly such derivative words as *having, debarring, pinning*, and the like, which are not to be found in ordinary dictionaries, and regarding which the pupil is apt to be led astray by the fact that a change is made in the primitive word before the addition of the suffix. This done, the scholar is prepared to express thoughts in his own language, and is now required to write sentences of every kind, a word being given to suggest an idea for each; he is taught to vary them by means of different arrangements and modes of expression; to analyze compound sentences into simple ones, and to combine simple ones into compound. Several lessons are then devoted to Style. The essential properties, purity, propriety, precision, clearness, strength, harmony, and unity, are next treated, examples for correction being presented under each. The different kinds of composition follow; and, specimens having been first given, the pupil is required to compose successively letters, descriptions, narrations, biographical sketches, essays, and argumentative discourses. After this, the principal figures receive attention; and the work closes with a list of subjects carefully selected, arranged under their proper heads, and in such a way that the increase in difficulty is very gradual. The work has received the universal approval of Teachers and the Press throughout the Union.

QUACKENBOS'

ADVANCED LESSONS IN COMPOSITION AND RHETORIC.

(NEARLY READY.)

A DIGEST OF ENGLISH GRAMMAR.

BY L. T. COVELL.

12mo. Price 50 Cents.

This work, which is just published, is designed as a Text-Book for the use of Schools and Academies; it is the result of long experience, of an eminently successful Teacher, and will be found to possess many peculiar merits.

At a regular meeting of the Board of Education of Rochester, held June 13, 1853, the following resolution was unanimously adopted:

"*Resolved*, That Covell's Digest of English Grammar be substituted for Wells' Grammar, as a Text-Book in the public schools of this city, to take effect at the commencement of the next school year."

Extract from the Minutes of a Regular Meeting of the Board of Education of Troy, May 31st, 1853.

"Mr. Jones, from Committee on text-books, and school librarias, moved, that Bullion's English Grammar be stricken from the list of text-books, and Covell's be substituted.—Passed."

From forty-four Teachers of Public Schools, Pittsburg, Pa.

"The undersigned have examined 'Covell's Digest of English Grammar,' and are of opinion that in the justness of its general views, the excellence of its style, the brevity, accuracy, and perspicuity of its definitions and rules, the numerous examples and illustrations, the adaption of its synthetical exercises, the simplicity of its method of analysis, and in the plan of its arrangement, this work surpasses any other grammar now before the public; and that in all respects it is most admirably adapted to the use of schools and academies."

From all the Teachers of Public Schools of the City of Alleghany, Pa.

"We, the undersigned, Teachers of Alleghany city, having carefully examined Mr. Covell's Digest of English Grammar,' and impartially compared it with other grammars now in use, are fully satisfied that, while it is in no respect inferior to others, it is in very many respects much superior. While it possesses all that is necessary for the advanced student, and much that is not found in other grammars, it is so simplified as to adapt it to the capacity of the youngest learner. We are confident that much time and labor will be saved, and greater improvement secured to our pupils in the study of this science, by its introduction into our schools; hence we earnestly recommend to the Boards of Directors of this city, its adoption as a uniform text-book upon this science in the schools under their direction."

From John J. Wolcott, A. M., *Pr. and Supt. 9th Ward School, Pittsburg, Pa.*

"'Covell's Digest of English Grammar' not only evinces the most unceasing labor, the most extensive research, the most unrelaxing effort, and the most devoted self-sacrificing study of its author, but it is the most complete, the most perfect, and, to me, the most satisfactory exposition of English Grammar that has come to my notice. It appears to me that every youth aspiring to become master of the English language, from the rudimental principles to the full, round, beautiful, faultless, perfect period. will make this volume his 'vade mecum.'"

EXPOSITION OF THE GRAMMATICAL STRUCTURE OF THE ENGLISH LANGUAGE.

BY JOHN MULLIGAN, A M.

Large 12mo. 574 pages. $1 50

This work is a comprehensive and complete system o English Grammar, embracing not only all that has been developed by the later philologists, but also the results of years of study and research on the part of its author. One great advantage of this book is its admirable arrangement. Instead of proceeding at once to the dry details which are distasteful and discouraging to the pupil, Mr. M. commences by viewing the sentence as a whole, analyzing it into its proper parts, and exhibiting their connection; and, after having thus parsed the sentence logically, proceeds to consider the individual words that compose it, in all their grammatical relations. This is the natural order; and experience proves that the arrangement here followed not only imparts additional interest to the subject, but gives the pupil a much clearer insight into it, and greatly facilitates his progress.

From Dr. James W. Alexander.

"I thank you for the opportunity of perusing your work on the structure of the English language. It strikes me as being one of the most valuable contributions to this important branch of literature. The mode of investigation is so unlike what appears in our ordinary compilations, the reasoning is so sound, and the results are so satisfactory and so conformable to the genius and great authorities of our mother tongue, that I propose to recur to it again and again."

Extract from a letter from E. C. Benedict, Esq., *President of the Board of Education of the City of New York.*

"I have often thought our language needed some work in which the principles of grammatical science and of the structure of the language, philosophically considered, were developed and applied to influence and control the *usus* and *consuedo* of Horace and Quintilian, which seem to me to have been too often the principal source of solecisms, irregularity and corruption. In this point of view, I consider your work a valuable and appropriate addition to the works on the language."

From Wm. Horace Webster, *President of the Free Academy, New York.*

"The exposition of the grammatical structure of the English language by Professor Mulligan, of this city, is a work, in my opinion, of great merit, and well calculated to impart a thorough and critical knowledge of the grammar of the English language.

"No earnest English student can fail to profit by the study of this treatise, yet it is designed more particulary for minds somewhat maturer, and for pupils who are capable and have a desire, to comprehend the principles and learn the philosophy of their own tongue."

DICTIONARY OF THE ENGLISH LANGUAGE

BY ALEXANDER REID, A. M.

12mo. 572 pages. Price $1 00.

This work, which is designed for schools, contains the PRONUNCIATION and Explanation of all English words authorized by eminent writers.

A Vocabulary of the roots of English words.

An Accented List of GREEK, LATIN, and SCRIPTURE proper names.

An Appendix, showing the pronunciation of nearly 3,000 of the most important GEOGRAPHICAL names.

It is printed on fine paper, in clear type, strongly bound.

And is unquestionably one of the best dictionaries for the school-room extant.

From C. S. HENRY, *Professor of Philosophy, History, and Belles-Lettres, in the University of the City of New York.*

"Reid's Dictionary of the English Language is an admirable book for the use of schools. Its plan combines a greater number of desirable conditions for such a work, than any with which I am acquainted; and it seems to me to be executed in general with great judgment, fidelity, and accuracy."

From HENRY REED, *Professor of English Literature in the University of Pennsylvania.*

"Reid's Dictionary of the English Language appears to have been compiled upon sound principles, and with judgment and accuracy. It has the merit, too, of combining much more than is usually looked for in dictionaries of small size, and will, I believe, be found excellent as a convenient manual for general reference, and also for various purposes of education."

GRAHAM'S ENGLISH SYNONYMS,

CLASSIFIED AND EXPLAINED;

WITH PRACTICAL EXERCISES. DESIGNED FOR SCHOOLS AND PRIVATE TUITION WITH AN INTRODUCTION AND ILLUSTRATIVE AUTHORITIES.

BY HENRY REED, LL. D.

1 Vol. 12mo. Price $1 00.

This is one of the best books published in the department of language, and will do much to arrest the evil of making too common use of inappropriate words. The work is well arranged for classes, and can be made a branch of common school study.

It is admirably arranged. The Synonyms are treated with reference to their character, as generic and specific; as active and passive; as positive and negative; and as miscellaneous synonyms.

HAND-BOOK OF THE ENGLISH LANGUAGE.

BY G. R. LATHAM, M. D., F. R. S.

12mo. 400 pages. Price $1 25.

This work is designed for the use of students in the University and High Schools.

"His work is rigidly scientific, and hence possesses a rare value. With the wide-spreading growth of the Anglo-Saxon dialect, the immense present and prospective power of those with whom this is their 'mother tongue,' such a treatise must be counted alike interesting and useful."—*Watchman and Reflector.*

"A work of great research, much learning, and to every thinking scholar it will be a book of study. The Germanic origin of the English language, the affinities of the English with other languages, a sketch of the alphabet, a minute investigation of the etymology of the language, &c., of great value to every philologist."—*Observer.*

HISTORY OF ENGLISH LITERATURE.

BY WILLIAM SPALDING, A. M.

PROFESSOR OF LOGIC, RHETORIC, AND METAPHYSICS, IN THE UNIVERSITY OF ST. ANDREWS

12mo. 413 pages. Price $1 00.

The above work, which is just published, is offered as a Text-book for the use of advanced Schools and Academies. It traces the literary progress of the nation from its dawn in Anglo-Saxon times, down to the present day. Commencing at this early period, it is so constructed as to introduce the reader gradually and easily to studies of this kind. Comparatively little speculation is presented, and those literary monuments of the earlier dates, which were thought most worthy of attention, are described with considerable fulness and in an attractive manner. In the subsequent pages, more frequent and sustained efforts are made to arouse reflection, both by occasional remarks on the relations between intellectual culture and the other elements of society, and by hints as to the theoretical laws on which criticism should be founded. The characteristics of the most celebrated modern works are analyzed at considerable length.

The manner of the author is remarkably plain and interesting, almost compelling the reader to linger over his pages with unwearied attention.

THE WORLD IN THE MIDDLE AGES.

AN HISTORICAL GEOGRAPHY, with accounts of the origin and development, the institutions and literature, the manners and customs of the nations in Europe, Western Asia, and Northern Africa, from the close of the Fourth to the middle of the Fifteenth Century; accompanied by complete Historical and Geographical indexes. By ADOLPHUS KŒPPEN, Professor of History, Greek, and German Literature in Franklin and Marshall College. 2 volumes, 12mo. 850 pages. Price $2.

ACCOMPANIED BY

AN HISTORICO-GEOGRAPHICAL ATLAS OF THE MIDDLE AGES.

Containing a Series of six General Maps, delineating the migration of the Northern and Eastern nations, together with the States arising from their fusion with the ancient Roman Empire in Europe, Western Asia, and Northern Africa, from the close of the Fourth to the middle of the Fifteenth century. Published from the great HISTORICO-GEOGRAPHICAL HAND-ATLAS of CHARLES SPRUNER, LL.D., Major of Engineers in the Kingdom of Bavaria. With a CONCISE EXPLANATORY DESCRIPTION. Folio. Price, $2 50.

THE SAME WORK. 1 volume, folio, 232 pp., containing the Historical Geography and the Atlas complete. Price $4 50.

"This truly excellent work supplies, in a very satisfactory manner, a want which has long been felt by every student of history."—*Evening Post.*

"One of the most valuable contributions of the day to American literature. It reflects great honor upon the author."—*Springfield Republican.*

"This work is one of a very high character, and is replete with valuable information."—*Phila. Inquirer.*

"The arrangement of this valuable work is at once ingenious and tasteful, and we are sure it will find great favor with students and readers generally."—*City Item.*

"A more valuable or important aid to historical reading and study has never appeared."—*N. Y. Churchman.*

"The volumes are indispensable to every reader who wishes for accurate information respecting the period in question."—*Boston Courier.*

"A work of elaborate learning and industry—a monument of the patient and laborious investigation of the Teutonic intellect."—*N. O. Bee.*

"A more comprehensive and reliable view of the world in the Middle Ages has never been given to the public."—*Prot. Churchman.*

"The importance of this work is evident at a glance, and the extensive attainments and ripe scholarship of the author are a guarantee for the accuracy of its execution."—*N. Y. Tribune.*

"It is distinguished by great method, faithful research, and concise style. We have seldom met so much historical information so ably condensed."—*Hartford Courant.*

"It is evidently prepared with great care, and by one thoroughly conversant with the subject. Its arrangement is excellent, and its lucid descriptions and the ease with which it can be consulted, must make it an indispensable book of reference."—*Traveller.*

"A faithful, scholarly, and valuable work."—*Christian Mirror.*

"This book is a wonder of learning, and justly reflects great credit on American literature."—*Life Illustrated.*

"This work evinces great and laborious researches on the part of the author, as well as a judicious, succinct, and careful arrangement of his materials, and supplies a great desideratum in the study of history."—*Boston Atlas.*

"This work will be found exceedingly valuable, not only for general reading, but as a text-book in all our higher institutions."—*N. Y. Observer.*

ADVANCED COURSE

OF

COMPOSITION AND RHETORIC

A Series of Practical Lessons on the Origin, History, and Peculiarities of the English Language, Punctuation, Taste, the Pleasures of the Imagination, Figures, Style and its Essential Properties, Criticism, and the various departments of Prose and Poetical Composition; illustrated with Copious Exercises. By G. P. QUACKENBOS A. M. 1 vol. 12mo. 450 pages. Price $1 00.

The title of this work fully sets forth its scope and character. It is an eminetly clear and practical text-book, and embraces a variety of important subjects, which have a common connection, and mutually illustrate each other; but which the pupil has heretofore been obliged to leave unlearned, or to search for among a number of different volumes. Claiming to give a comprehensive and practical view of our language in all its relations, this "Advanced Course" views it as a whole, no less than with reference to the individual words composing it; shows how it compares with other tongues, modern and ancient; points out its beauties; indicates how they may best be made available; and, in a word, teaches the student the most philosophical method of digesting and arranging his thoughts, as well as the most correct and effective mode of expressing them.

Few works have received such unqualified commendations from the press and the public.

"We think this an excellent treatise; excellent both for self-instruction and for the use of schools. *We are not familiar with any work of a similar character that is equally accurate and comprehensive.*"—*N. Y. Com. Adv.*

"It is admirably adapted to self-instruction as well as for the use of schools and colleges."—*N Y. Daily Times.*

"A carefully prepared and thorough educational text-book by an accomplished teacher"—*N. Y. Tribune.*

"A skilfully prepared manual, clear and practical throughout."—*Churchman.*

"Prof. Quackenbos is well known as the author of numerous works of high standing in the department to which the "Course of Composition" belongs. The present work is thorough in its treatment, and excellently arranged."—*Southern Lit. Messenger.*

"The pupil who studies this book, under the tutoring of a capable instructor, cannot fail to become an efficient English scholar."—*Ledger, Lancaster, S. C.*

GRAHAM'S ENGLISH SYNONYMES,

Classified and explained with Practical Exercises, designed for schools and private tuition; with an introduction and illustrative authorities. By HENRY REED, LL.D. 1 vol. 12mo. Price $1 00.

This is one of the best books published in the department of language, and will do much to arrest the evil of making too common use of inappropriate words. The work is well arranged for classes, and can be made a branch of common school study.

The Synonymes are treated with reference to their character, as generic and specific; as active and passive; as positive and negative; and as miscellaneous synonymes.

GILLESPIE'S LAND-SURVEYING;

THEORETICAL AND PRACTICAL.

By W. M. GILLESPIE, A. M., C. E., Professor of Civil Engineering in Union College; Author of "Manual of Roads and Railways," &c. 1 vol. 8vo. 400 pages. With four hundred engravings, and a MAP showing the *Variation of the Needle* in the United States. (Nearly ready.)

This is the most complete, and, at the same time, fundamental work on his subject ever published in any country. Among its leading peculiarities e these:—

1. ALL the operations of surveying are developed from only *five simple principles.*
2. A complete system of surveying with only a chain, a rope, or any substitute, is fully explained.
3. Means of measuring inaccessible distances, in all possible cases, with the chain alone, are given in great variety, so as to constitute a *Land Geometry.* It occupies 26 pages, with 58 figures.
4. The Rectangular method of Compass-surveying is greatly simplified.
5. The Traverse Tables gives increased accuracy in one fifteenth of the space of the usual tables.
6. The effect of the changes in the variation of the needle, on the re-survey of old lines, is minutely illustrated.
7. *Correct* tables of the times of elongation of the North Star are given; those in common use being in some cases nearly half-an-hour out of the way.
8. The adjustment of the engineer's Transit and Theodolite are here, for the first time, fully developed.
9. Methods of avoiding obstacles in angular surveying. Occupy 24 pages, with 35 figures.
10. Topographical Mapping is fully described with illustrations.
11. Laying out, Parting off, and Dividing up Land, are very fully explained, and illustrated by fifty figures.
12. The most recent improvements in the methods of Surveying the Public Lands of the United States, with the methods used for making "corners," are minutely described from official authorities.

A double object has been kept in view in the preparation of the volume; viz., to make an introductory treatise easy to be mastered by the young scholar or the practical man of little previous acquirements, the only pre-requisites being Arithmetic and a little Geometry; and, at the same time, to make the instruction of such a character as to lay a foundation broad enough and deep enough for the most complete superstructure which the professional student may subsequently wish to raise upon it.

The volume is divided as follows:—

PART I. General Principles and Fundamental Operations.—II. Chain Surveying.—III. Compass Surveying.—IV. Transit and Theodolite Surveying.—V. Trigonometrical Surveying.—VI. Tri-linear Surveying.—VII. Obstacles in Angular Surveying.—VIII. Plane Table Surveying.—IX. Surveying without Instruments.—X. Mapping.—XI. Laying out, Parting off, and Dividing up Lands.—XII. United States' Public Lands.

APPENDIX.—A. Synopsis of Plane Trigonometry.—B. Demonstrations of Problems.—C. Levelling.

TABLES.—Chords for Platting.—Latitudes and Departures.

FIELD-BOOK FOR RAIL ROAD ENGINEERS

By JOHN B. HENCK. Civil Engineer. One volume, with fifty eight Diagrams pocket-book form, $1 75.

Containing Formulæ for laying out Simple, Reversed, and Compound Curves, Parabolic Curves, Vertical Curves, Determining Frog Angles and Radii of Turnouts and Crossings, Levelling, Setting Slope Stakes, Elevating Outer Rail on Curves, Curving Rails, &c., &c.; together with many Miscellaneous Problems, and a New System of Earth-work. Also, Tables of Radii Ordinates, Chord and Tangent Deflections, Ordinates for Curving Rails, Long Chords, Elevation of Outer Rail, Frog Angles, Properties of Materials, Magnetic Variations, Squares, Cubes, Square Roots and Cube Roots, Logarithms of Number, Logarithmic Sines, Cosines, Tangents and Cotangents, Natural Sines and Cosines, Natural Tangents and Cotangents, Rise per mile of Grades, &c.

ANALYTICAL CLASS-BOOK OF BOTANY.

BY FRANCIS H. GREENE.

PART I.—ELEMENTS OF VEGETABLE STRUCTURE AND PHYSIOLOGY. PART II.—SYSTEMATIC BOTANY. To which is added a Compendious Flora of the Northern States; with descriptions of more than 1000 different species. Beautifully illustrated quarto. 1 vol. Price $1 50.

PRIMARY CLASS-BOOK OF BOTANY. Composed from First Part of the Analytical Class-Book, and designed for the use of common schools and families. Illustrated quarto. Price 75 cents.

Extract from the Author's Preface.

"Having been for several years a Teacher of Botany, I have had considerable opportunity of experimenting on the happiest means of imparting this delightful science. The importance of Pictorial Illustrations, systematically combined for regular exercises, early suggested itself. A new system of teaching was thence wrought out, consisting of a set of diagrams made to illustrate Oral Lessons; and the plan was eminently successful. Those Lessons and Diagrams are reproduced in the present work, with such extension and improvements as the written form, and the superior light and progress of the times, admit and demand. The illustrations are presented to the eye in large groups, and are either immediately, or very nearly, associated with the corresponding portions of the Text. They are designed to be used as regular exercises for study and recitation, the same as maps in Geography. They are, in fact, but a recapitulation of the text in another form; and thus, while they repeat the idea, they also give a pleasing variety to the lessons; and appealing from the eye to the mind, and the reverse, they awaken the most lively associations, tending to fix the impressions in the memory."

THE ELEMENTS OF AGRICULTURE.

A book for young farmers, with questions prepared for the use of schools. By GEORGE E. WARING, JR., Consulting Agriculturist. 12mo. 288 pages. Price 75 cents.

This is the latest publication on this subject, and all who have seen it concede that for simplicity, terseness, and practical usefulness, it is the best work on agriculture which has yet been written. No farmer or horticulturist should be without it. The Legislature of Vermont, at its recent session, authorized the purchase by the State of a sufficient number of copies to secure a full attention toward it, and made provision for its general introduction into every town and district school under its supervision.

Opinions of the Press.

"This is the work of a young student and farmer in the neighborhood of our city. And we defy any man or boy who can read the plainest English to run through this little volume without gaining from it a clearer, more consistent, more exalted idea of agriculture as a pursuit, as well as a science, than he previously entertained. We fervently wish that it could speedily find a place, not only in every school library but in every cottage in the land; for we are sure its perusal would make farmers of many who are now sweltering and starving in cities, and *good* farmers who are now afflicting the soil only because they must do so or famish."—*N. Y. Tribune.*

"It is just what is needed in every town where a ten-acre lot is cultivated."—*N. Y. Times*

NEW AND COMPLETE SYSTEMATIC SERIES

OF

SCHOOL GEOGRAPHIES

By S. S. CORNELL. IN THREE PARTS.

Each book being arranged on the same plan, and with special reference to the wants and capacities of the class, or grade of scholarship for which it is designed, the series is progressive and philosophical in its nature, and practical in its operation.

CORNELL'S PRIMARY GEOGRAPHY.

SMALL QUARTO. PRICE 50 CENTS.

One of the leading objects in the preparation of this work, was to make it in every sense of the word what its title indicates, a "Primary Geography;" consequently only those branches of Geographical Science that admit of being brought fully within the comprehension of the youthful beginner, have been introduced into the present number of the series.

The youthful student is put in possession of a simple and easy method of memorizing the contents of a map, by means of a carefully systematized set of questions.

The MAPS AND ILLUSTRATIONS ACCORD STRICTLY WITH THE CHARACTER OF THE LESSONS, each map containing all that is taught in its accompanying lessons—and nothing more.

The work is illustrated by upwards of seventy suggestive designs, exquisitely drawn and engraved FOR THIS BOOK.

The maps, twelve in number, are large, clear, and pleasing to the eye.

At desirable intervals, there is a systematic arrangement of promiscuous questions, designed as a review of preceding lessons, by which teachers, parents, trustees, and others, may satisfactorily ascertain, at any stage of the pupil's advancement, what he knows of the science.

A PRONOUNCING VOCABULARY, containing the names of all the natural and political divisions used throughout the work, is appended.

The mechanical execution of the work is equal or superior to that of any other school-book extant.

CORNELL'S INTERMEDIATE GEOGRAPHY

IS IN PRESS, AND WILL APPEAR AT AN EARLY DAY.

This book clearly explains the terms used in the Physical, Political, and Mathematical branches of the science, and contains a judiciously selected and carefully systematized amount of Descriptive Geography.

It is also supplied with numerous appropriate and beautiful maps, and illustrated by a large number of well-executed wood-cuts, comprising views of places, etc., never before presented in any school work on the subject.

CORNELL'S HIGH SCHOOL GEOGRAPHY AND COMPANION ATLAS

ARE IN PRESS AND WILL SHORTLY APPEAR.

The Geography is arranged for the pupils of advanced classes in Public and Private Schools. It has been prepared with much care to meet the requirements of the present age. Countries to which political change, or the progress of civilization, or the march of enterprise, has given new or increased interest, have been brought prominently forward, and their social and political condition described from the most recent information and the most reliable sources. This book is also ornamented with numerous useful and interesting wood-cuts, executed in the highest style of the engraver's art.

The Atlas contains numerous large and elegant Maps, which combine, in a high degree, accuracy with beauty of execution.

HAND-BOOK OF THE ENGLISH LANGUAGE.

A HAND-BOOK OF ANGLO-SAXON ROOT-WORDS. 12mo. Price 50 cts.

A HAND-BOOK OF ANGLO-SAXON DERIVATIVES. 12mo. Price 75 cents

A HAND-BOOK OF THE ENGRAFTED WORDS OF THE ENGLISH LANGUAGE. 12mo. Price $1 00.

BY A LITERARY ASSOCIATION.

The following statement will enable the reader to see at once the merits and peculiarities of the Hand-Book.

The English language consists of some *eighty thousand words*, drawn from the five principal sources, viz.: from the Anglo-Saxon, Celtic, Gothic, French, and Latin and Greek, or Classic languages. *Twenty-three thousand* of these words are from the Anglo-Saxon. The whole twenty-three thousand words may be traced back to *one thousand root-words.* The twenty-two thousand have been formed by adding one or more root-words, or parts of them, together. There are now of these twenty-three thousand Anglo-Saxon words, only some six or seven thousand in good use. The remaining fifty-seven thousand words of the language, may also be traced back to a few thousand root-words in the languages from which they have been borrowed.

Every child should be early taught the whole six or seven thousand choice Anglo-Saxon words, because they are those continually used in the various occupations of life. Few scholars can use more than six thousand of the words drawn from Celtic, Gothic, French, and Classic sources. But there is no reason why every pupil in our public schools should not be able also to use them. Indeed, the three Hand-Books are so arranged that the six thousand choice Anglo-Saxon words, and the six thousand choice words from other sources, may be acquired easily in one year.

But to teach the English language successfully, the teacher should have clearly before his own mind, *its origin, growth, elements,* or sources of formation, *grammatical structure, general history, and literature.* The following synopsis throws light upon the English language.

I. *Its origin.* In 450 after Christ, the Angles and Saxons introduced into Great Britain the Anglo-Saxon language, which is the mother tongue of the present English.

II. *Its growth.* The root-words of the Anglo-Saxon, which are few, have grown into twenty-three thousand by the use of some eighteen prefixes, and twenty-five suffixes. Six or seven thousand only of these are now in good use. Again some fifty-seven thousand words have been introduced into it from several sources, but chiefly from the Celtic, Gothic, French, and Classic tongues. It embraces, in all, some eighty thousand words.

III. *Its periods of growth.* About 450 B. C., the Anglo-Saxon words were introduced into Britain; prior to 600, many Celtic words; before the end of the ninth century, many Gothic words; and at 1066, French words were intermixed; and since the revival of letters, in the fifteenth century, a large number of Greek and Latin words have been incorporated with it.

IV. *Its grammatical laws and history.* The Anglo-Saxon or *root* element, not only *modified* the words from the other languages, but gave them *its own laws.* Hence the grammar of the English language should be built on the Anglo-Saxon basis, and not on the basis of the Celtic, Gothic, French, or Latin and Greek.

V. *Its literature.* English Literature does not date back more than some six centuries. Nay, all that is really valuable has been produced during the last three hundred years.

The Hand-Book of Anglo-Saxon Words gives 1000 Anglo-Saxon root-words, with their primary and secondary meaning, and teaches the use of them.

The Hand-Book of Anglo-Saxon Derivative Words. It explains the meaning of the prefixes, suffixes, and terminations which change the 1000 root-words into derivatives. It gives some 7000 of the choicest 23,000 words of Anglo-Saxon origin, with their meanings and use.

The Hand-Book of the Engrafted Words of the English Language gives 7000 of the best words from the Celtic, Gothic, French and Classic tongues, with their meanings and use.

Every thing valuable in the Thesaurus, Latham MacElligot, Lynn, and the Scholar's Companion, will be found in these books, and arranged according to the growth of language and the laws of mind. The plan is simple and natural.

CHEMICAL ATLAS;

OR, THE CHEMISTRY OF FAMILIAR OBJECTS:

Exhibiting the general principles of the science in a series of beautifully colored diagrams, and accompanied by explanatory essays, embracing the latest views of the subjects illustrated. Designed for the use of students in all schools where chemistry is taught. By EDWARD L. YOUMANS. Large quarto. 105 pages. Price $2.

The Atlas is intended to accompany the author's Class-Book; but it may be employed with equal convenience and advantage in connection with any of the school text-books. It is to be used in exactly the same manner as a geographical atlas. As the pupil proceeds with the work in hand, whatever it may be, reference should be made to the diagrams as often as the subject may require. For example; when combining proportions, salts, combustion, or compound-radicals are reached, the plates which illustrate these subjects will be resorted to for assistance by those who possess the work. The text contains not only full explanations of the diagrams, but it consists of a series of essays or chapters upon the subjects illustrated.

The following expressions of opinion concerning the plan of illustrating Chemistry adopted in the present volume, are from the most eminent teachers and scientific men in the country. It will be seen that the testimonials refer to the Author's "Chemical Chart;" but as the "Atlas" is a reproduction and improvement of that mode of exhibiting chemical facts and phenomena, the commendations apply to this work with much greater force.

From the HON. HORACE MANN, *President of Antioch College.*

"I think Mr. Youmans is entitled to great credit for the preparation of his Chart, because its use will not only facilitate acquisition, but, what is of far greater importance, will increase the exactness and precision of the student's elementary ideas."

From DR. JOHN W. DRAPER, *Prof of Chemistry in the University of New York.*

"It seems well adapted to communicate to beginners a knowledge of the definite combinations of chemical substances, and deserves to be introduced into the schools."

"We cordially concur in the above opinion."

JOHN TORREY, *Prof. of Chemistry in the College of Physicians & Surgeons, N. Y*
WM. H. ELLET, *Late Professor of Chemistry in Columbia College, S. C.*

From JAMES R. CHILTON, M. D., *Chemist.*

"It is a valuable means of readily imparting a correct knowledge of the nature of chemical combinations."

From DR. THOMAS ANTISELL, *Prof. of Chemistry in the Vermont Medical College.*

"It will be found an invaluable assistant to both teacher and pupil."

From PROF. GRAY, *Author of Text-books in Natural Philosophy and Chemistry.*

"The best means of illustration that I have seen; it would be especially useful to institutions not furnished with chemical apparatus."

From DR. ROBERT HARE, *Emeritus Prof. of Chemistry in the University of Pa.*

"The design is excellent, and I entertain the impression that it is well done."

From PROF. W. F. HOPKINS, *of the U. S. Naval Academy, Annapolis.*

"The plan is admirably adapted to assist the teacher in communicating, and the learner in receiving correct notions of the laws of chemical combinations. I commend it to the patronage of schools and academies."

From RT. REV. ALONZO POTTER, LL.D., *Philadelphia.*

"The conception embodied in Mr. Youmans' Chemical Chart is a very happy and useful one, and the execution is evidently the fruit of much care and skill. I should think its introduction into schools in connection with the study of the first principles of chemistry was much to be desired."

From BENJAMIN SILLIMAN, LL.D., *Prof. of Chemistry in Yale College.*

"The plan appears to be an excellent one."

www.ingramcontent.com/pod-product-compliance
Lightning Source LLC
LaVergne TN
LVHW020926110826
845150LV00004B/777

* 9 7 8 1 4 2 5 5 5 3 2 4 1 *